The Chinese Face in Australia

Lucille Lok-Sun Ngan · Chan Kwok-bun

The Chinese Face
in Australia

Multi-generational Ethnicity
among Australian-born Chinese

 Springer

Lucille Lok-Sun Ngan
Hong Kong Institute of Education
Tai Po, Hong Kong

Chan Kwok-bun
Chan Institute of Social Studies
Tuen Mun, Hong Kong

ISBN 978-1-4614-2130-6   e-ISBN 978-1-4614-2131-3
DOI 10.1007/978-1-4614-2131-3
Springer New York Heidelberg Dordrecht London

Library of Congress Control Number: 2012931359

Printed on acid-free paper

Springer is part of Springer Science+Business Media (www.springer.com)

Two Prologues

Lucille Lok-Sun Ngan

> *When I was just a little girl*
> *I asked my mother, what will I be*
> *Will I be pretty, will I be rich*
> *Here's what she said to me.*
>
> *Que Sera, Sera,*
> *Whatever will be, will be*
> *The future's not ours, to see*
>
> *Que Sera, Sera*
> *What will be, will be.*
>
> Lyrics from 'Que Sera Sera'—first sung by Doris Day (1956)

In the song *Que Sera Sera* (*Whatever Will Be, Will be*), the little girl wondered about her future and turned to her mother for answers. In a similar way, when I was growing up, I used to take my big question to my mother. My question so often was: "Am I Chinese or Australian?" I was born in Hong Kong and migrated with my family to Sydney, Australia, in 1988 when I was a young child. My father would fly back and forth between two homes in Hong Kong and Australia, while my mother, older sister, and I—the rest of the family—remained in Australia. Our family sustained a transnational existence and this phenomenon has been described in various guises in the migration literature: as astronaut fathers and parachute children, lone mothers in transnational families. Unlike my mother and other adult immigrants—those known as first-generation migrants—I was the 1.5 generation: born in Hong Kong and raised outside my country of origin, in Australia, and having a foot in the East and the West.

Until the mid-1990s and prior to the handover of Hong Kong to the People's Republic of China (PRC) in 1997, there were not many "real" Chinese kids in my school. Most of those who were around were Australian-born Chinese or what we commonly call ABCs—the ones who can't speak, or perhaps, write Chinese.

I remember my first day at school in the second year of primary school: everything seemed so strange to me, from the diversity of hair colors and amazing marble-colored eyes in contrast to the homogenous black; the vast green space where children could exhaust themselves in a world of fantasy and imagination in place of the small concrete playground at my school in Hong Kong; and the bland cold sandwiches Aussie kids had for lunch compared with the hot meals that I was accustomed to.

My first attempt at socializing at school was with a little Chinese girl in my class who I consciously picked as I felt a sense of commonality with her because of our similar physical appearances. We were both smaller than most other kids in my class and we were the only two with black hair. I recall myself uttering the words "Do you speak Chinese?" in my Chinese-accented English. She quietly said "a little" in Cantonese. I had gone to an English school in Hong Kong but since English was my second language it still required hard work to become fully competent. For the first few years after we arrived in Australia, my mother used to drive my sister and me to school every morning. Since my classes started later than my sister's as she was in a higher year than me, my mother would park the car at the school entrance and we would recite spelling and learn vocabulary before I went to class. My mother encouraged me to go in earlier so I could have more time to play and socialize with other children and get to know them better, but I much preferred doing spelling tests with her in the car. I was always reluctant to leave until the last minute as going to a new school and making new friends in an Anglo-dominated environment was very daunting to a little Chinese girl, and teachers discouraged Chinese children from speaking in languages other than English at school as it was important that we integrated with Australian kids and mastered the local language. Like most children, naturally wanting to fit in, I spoke English at school (but I conversed in Chinese at home with my family) and insisted my mother make me sandwiches (although I actually enjoyed having delicious hot Chinese dishes for lunch).

Eventually, I got over my fear and integrated well with Australians as well as kids from all other ethnic backgrounds, and issues of race and ethnicity never seriously crossed my mind despite the occasional teasing and name-calling by western and also ABC kids. My best friend in primary school, an Australian of Greek heritage, used to call me "Ching Chong" but at that time, to me, it was just fun and games and we always enjoyed spending time together. I would laugh at her long and funny surname. I was always her really good "Chinese" friend. She was my "Aussie" friend. However, I recall being rather disturbed when the teasing was directed at me by some ABC kids who looked Chinese but who were Australian in all other ways, particularly in their Australian-accented English. They actually acted even more Australian than other children at school by choosing only western people as friends and only bullying new Chinese students.

There seems to be more tolerance toward people who are perceived as different, rather than those of their own kind. Abuse by the former is to a certain level expected and accepted but ill-treatment by the later is felt as an act of betrayal, disloyalty. As I look back now, though I was not conscious at the time, the way some ABCs disassociated themselves from other overseas-born Chinese kids was a deliberate undoing of their Chineseness. There is often a pressure for immigrants to integrate into the mainstream society, but for children who are going through critical stages of individual identity development, the desire to conform to the dominant ways of life to affirm their belongingness to mainstream society is particularly intense. To a certain degree, while I was also trying to hide, disguise, and suppress my ethnic background in the public domain, the everyday small racial encounters reminded me that I was different from other western kids. I could never look the same as them. I was living in two cultures, maintaining a presence in both.

As I moved on to junior and high school, I somehow gravitated toward Asians who were mainly from Hong Kong and Taiwan as well as the locally born Chinese. There were a lot more Chinese kids at school by the mid 1990s, many more families leaving Hong Kong as the 1997 handover of the city back to China came closer. In the case of Taiwan, many families also emigrated around this period due to tense cross-strait relations with China. As a result the Hong Kong-born population in Australia grew from 27,793 in 1986 to 68,430 in 1986, a 41% increase in a decade, with New South Wales being the state with the highest Hong Kong-born settlement (Australian Bureau of Statistics, 2008). In my school, the growth was similar. I recall there were less than 10 Chinese children in primary 2 in 1989. By 1999 when I was in year 12, there were around 50 Chinese out of about 200 students.

Initially, I disassociated myself from new arrivals from Hong Kong as their behavior was different yet peculiarly familiar to me as I was culturally accustomed to a hybrid way of life. At home we ate Chinese food as well as Western food, and we celebrated Chinese New Year to the same extent as we would for Christmas. My family always called me "the little sister" in Cantonese. Anywhere else outside the home I was Lucille. I enjoyed Chinese movies as much as western ones. I could speak Chinese but can only read and write in English. My friends were made up of Chinese, ABCs, and Anglo-Australians.

These new arrivals from Hong Kong stood out oddly to me as they were "performing Chineseness" in a different way from what I was used to. They spoke Cantonese at school, brought thermo lunch boxes which had three compartments filled with hot steaming rice, soup and Chinese dish, and their topics of conversation at school were often about Hong Kong pop media which I was unfamiliar with and disinterested in. I was not used to people displaying their Chineseness in the playground, in the classroom, in public. Since my early childhood in Australia, an important stage of identity development, I had been practicing Chineseness only within the domestic sphere. As a child, it was necessary to conceal my Chineseness at school to successfully blend in with the mainstream and to find a sense of belonging and acceptance.

What drew me toward these new Chinese immigrant children might possibly have been our common migration experiences combined with a similar cultural background in terms of family values, family social networks, and academic aspirations. My parents had a few western friends but their closest social networks were maintained with other Chinese immigrants, mainly from Hong Kong, and whose family setups, like ours, were also divided between two places. Like other Chinese immigrant children at school, my attachment with Hong Kong was strong yet I always felt and thought my home was in Australia.

Like most Hong Kong students in my school, we were privileged to return to Hong Kong every year during the summer holidays. Although these visits became a routine, it was a yearly event that was never short of anticipation. My sister and I enjoyed looking forward to going to Hong Kong as we could spend valuable time with our father but there was something more—these holidays were always very exciting. Unlike Australia, Hong Kong had a unique cosmopolitan environment—in just one place you could meet overseas Chinese from all over the world. Hong Kong was about excitement, holidays, the festive season, shopping, whereas Australia was home, school, and the routines of daily life. At the same time I always felt I was different from the locals: I was an overseas Chinese who was westernized in my values, beliefs, and lifestyle.

When the number of Hong Kong immigrants began to increase in my school and in the community my initial feeling was that I didn't really feel I blended in very well with them, largely because I was unfamiliar with the way they displayed their Chineseness and feared being marginalized. However, our common migration experience, the everyday cultural practices, and the ambivalent emotional attachments associated with split Chinese families—all feelings that were not shared with my "white" Australian friends—made me feel at ease with the Hong Kong immigrants. They became and continue to be my closest friends. In Australia, I came to know myself as a Chinese inside and outside.

In 2008, I moved back to Hong Kong—my home town. And most of the Hong Kong immigrants' children that I grew up with have also returned there. Yet contrary to the general assumption of a smooth and easy resettlement of returnees and in a way that is similar to my early childhood experience in Australia, I am still trying hard to reconstruct and refigure my identity. I presumed that, with my established social network and understanding of local culture, upon my return I would easily fit in. In reality, differences stemming from all aspects of life—from the pace of walking, living space, mannerisms, topics of conversation, work culture, to social values—all at times lead to feelings of discommunity. While returnees in Hong Kong are similar in terms of their physical appearances to local Hong Kongers, they are nevertheless seen as outsiders due to their ineptness when it comes to behaving like a local who is trained to work in a high-power distance culture characterized by authoritarian hierarchy and conformity. Returnees have internalized characteristics of western cultures that thrive on creativity, innovation, equality and outspokenness. Local Hongkongers often see returnees as aloof, snobbish, candid, nonconformist, lazy, even crazy. Contrary to the myth of taking the best of both worlds, they are neither highly valued as western expatriates in terms of remuneration and social status, bestowed as they are with the status of "returnee," nor do they have the "Chinese characteristics" of language competencies and local knowledge of local workers, this lack putting them at a disadvantage. As a returnee, my awkward position is intensified due to my inability to read and write Chinese when I look and speak Chinese. By definition I cannot be a "real" Chinese because I do not possess the essential and essentialized quality of language competence. Overseas Chinese and returnees often see themselves as different from local Hongkongers whom they call "Hongkies"—a term which has connotations of money-mindedness, class consciousness, materialism, rudeness, unworldliness, and submissiveness.

Within the workplace, there is a cultural expectation and demand that I, a Chinese person, should be, or become, literate in the Chinese language, despite the value placed upon my competency in English. Similar expectations would not be made about the non-Chinese and they would not be judged in the same way as is the hybrid returnee. The link between language, physicality, and race is a deeply internalized essentialist ideology that defines "being Chinese." Thus if one is identified as racially Chinese because of one's physicality, the expectations that come are that one must speak, write Chinese, and have internalized general or generalized Chinese values as well as the particular norms of the Chinese society in which one inhabits. Returnees, particularly immigrants' children who grew up overseas and thus are not fluent in the Chinese language, are jeopardized by a double demand that is only made of Chinese-looking people. The intersecting factors of gender and age along with race can result in a triple jeopardy for the returnees.

There is also a constant question about origin—where are you from? When living in Australia, I was often asked about my origin by locals. Hong Kong or China seemed the only acceptable answer for someone who looked Chinese, despite having spent most of my life in Australia and having only lived in Hong Kong for a number of years during the early part of my childhood. Even those with long-term residence—like the Australian-born long-settled informants in this book whose families have, for three, four, five and even six generations, lived in Australia—would be interrogated in the same way because of their physicality. The face is an inescapable reality that acts as a centering device for segregation and marginalization of ethnic Chinese.

Such questions stem not only from white people—Chinese people, too, have preconceived ideas about origins. Once, a colleague in Australia who came from Shanghai asked me where I was from. Not really thinking about governance, politics, or geographical boundaries, I simply uttered two words "Hong Kong." She corrected me, saying "China. Hong Kong is now part of China."

After my return to Hong Kong I am still being asked similar questions about my background by local Hongkongers as there is a kind of strangeness that marks my difference from them. Recently I was browsing around an up-market department store in Central Hong Kong and a saleslady at a counter tried to sell me a luxury bathing product. Her strategy to entice me was to chat casually while promoting the product. She started by asking me where I was from, and I replied "Hong Kong." In Australia, I was used to giving this reply, as that was usually the acceptable and expected answer. However, my reply did not prevent her from insisting that I must have come back from somewhere; that I was either educated overseas or was an expatriate in Hong Kong. Not until I said, "Australia," was she satisfied with my answer. To be fair, I noticed that most of the shoppers at this particular department store were English-speaking Chinese women and Mandarin-speaking mainlanders, so her question about my origin was based on her preconceived ideas about the cultural background of her customers. Nevertheless, this incident is one among many other similar situations that I have encountered and indicates the process of in-group hierarchy of Chinese in Hong Kong including group stratifications based on categories such as overseas returnees, overseas-born Chinese, local-born Hongkongers who never migrate, mainlanders, etc. Returnees, like me, who are treated as outsiders are expected to negotiate a hybrid identity that combines the east and the west. Ironically, in Hong Kong, I could be an Australian.

When abroad, others see me as a Chinese. Two types of responses can result from encounters with strangers in a foreign country. For those who are less familiar with China, they often try, with kind intentions, to make a connection by saying "*ni hau*" (equivalent to "hello" in Mandarin), and some may even put their hands together and bow to demonstrate their knowledge of Chinese culture. This clearly reflects the racial discourse that unifies all Chinese-looking people as one homogenous, unchanging group. A second type of encounter would involve questions about Hong Kong. In answering the "Where are you from?" question—a common inquiry posed to tourists, travelers, and outsiders—"Australia" never seems to be an acceptable answer and people would either show a confused expression or persist with their inquiry about where I originally came from. The subsequent conversation would usually be about Hong Kong and only rarely about Australia where I spent nearly 20 years of my life. In the context of simultaneous displacement and relocation, both the inherent ambivalence and ambiguity of migrants have become part of my everyday life—now internalized.

On several trips to London from Australia or Hong Kong, I have been confronted with encounters that point to the adverse implications of prescribed notions of race and gender. I particularly remember being held back by a white, British officer at the UK immigration desk with a series of racially provoked questions while a long queue was behind me. He asked, "who will you be staying with?" I answered I was meeting my boyfriend and will be staying with him. The next series of questions he asked was "Where does he work, how much money does he make, and is he British (meaning white, Anglo-Saxon)?" If I were a white man, I am quite certain that I would not be interrogated in the same way. It is clear that being perceived as a young single Chinese woman, I was in a doubly oppressed position—marginalized by both race and gender constructions.

The continual subtle changes in my name perhaps illustrate my own unconscious negotiation of my ethnic and cultural identity through the course of my life. From the time I immigrated to Australia hardly anyone called me by my Chinese name, "Lok Sun," except my close relatives on my father's side who were living in Hong Kong. My parents and grandfather named me "Lok Sun" because it represents happiness, energy, vitality, and liveliness, and so my Chinese name was certainly not given lightly as it was carefully crafted with much thought and with the feelings of my parents. My English name, which was given to me by Auntie Milan, my father's sister-in-law was a derivative of my Chinese name. In contrast to the careful way in which my Chinese name was chosen, "Lucille" was picked because it sounded similar to "Lok Sun." So "Lucille," in a sense, came from "Lok Sun." Similarly, I gave my half brother the name "Charlton" as it sounded similar to his Chinese name, "Chiu Yung." Having an English name in addition to a Chinese name was common in Hong Kong as a British colony—western influences cause people to adopt western names. However, for most Hongkongers the given birth name is typically Chinese and the English name would be taken up later on at school or at work. Unlike most people, I was given both names at birth, although my English was born from my Chinese name. Prior to my time in Australia, I was known as "Ngan Lok Sun, Lucille."

After arriving in Australia, my Chinese name became my middle name: "Lucille Lok Sun Ngan." To conform to the Australian society, my parents adopted the western naming convention with the family name placed last, but kept my Chinese name to preserve my Chinese heritage. But as I mentioned earlier, my Chinese name was hardly used in Australia. As an author, I dropped my "middle name," "Lok Sun," in my earlier publications as I wanted to simplify and shorten my name. In consequence I was simply known as "Lucille Ngan."

After my return to Hong Kong my Chinese name "came back to life" as I have been constantly reminded of it. People would insist on finding out my name in Chinese even when I told them my name is Lucille. Yet all through the years I was in Australia my Chinese name was hardly used, except within my home, and so I feel rather awkward hearing myself being addressed as "Ngan Lok Sun." At the same time, and having lived in a more informal Australian social setting, I feel awkward calling others by their Chinese names as I am often unsure about the socially accepted way of addressing people. Do I call them by their full name (i.e., with their surname) or just the second and/or third characters of their names? To me, Chinese names have represented familiarity, closeness, intimacy, and domesticity so it has felt rather strange to address and be addressed by others in Chinese. The awkwardness is escalated by my Chinese illiteracy. Because I cannot read Chinese, I can only guess their names based on Romanized *pin ying* which I often embarrassingly mispronounce. While my Chinese name is to a certain extent foreign to me, since my return to Hong Kong, I have adopted "Lucille Lok-Sun Ngan" as I have come to know myself by both Chinese and English names. Since English renderings of Chinese names are often inaccurate, I have placed a hyphen to join the two characters of my Chinese middle name together, being worried that westerners may not know which is my surname. The journey of the changes in my name does not quite end here. Being recently married, as a woman, it is customary to adopt one's husband's surname. In this way, the transformations of my name allude to the continual negotiations of my identity as a migrant, and as a woman, through the course of my life.

During a lunch gathering with some close family friends in Hong Kong, there was an intense conversation about the diminishing respect shown by children brought up overseas because of their unfamiliarity with the Chinese culture. People were quite distressed that their grandchildren and children who grew up overseas have adopted the western social norms and are addressing them (their seniors) by their names instead of their Chinese family titles. These titles are practiced forms of address in Chinese families that represent the particular relationship and hierarchy for members in a Chinese family. One person confessed that he has accepted his son-in-law calling him by his first name since he is white, but his grandchildren who are Chinese and half-Chinese (mixed-race), as he put it, "must show respect for the older generations." He insisted that even though they may have grown up overseas, they are still Chinese. The family order regulated by generation, age, and gender has been an important Confucian ideology that has continued influence on Chinese families today. Cultural unfamiliarity of such sorts—of not having a full-fledged identity—situates returnees and their children in a peculiar position, leaving them estranged and having feelings of being misfits in their own culture.

As a sociologist, I can understand that the bemusement with regard to my identity has been due to the intersection between similarity and difference in the process of figuration and refiguration of Chineseness arising from the crossing of routes and roots. The Chinese identity is an "imagined" social construct and is inherently political. It is conditioned through a process of relational positioning by which individuals engage in identity construction, maintenance, and transformation in the social and cultural spheres of life. Paradoxically perhaps, my biography and feelings of liminality—of being suspended in between the East and the West—led to my interest in pursuing my undergraduate and graduate studies in sociology in Australia. My cross-cultural encounters compelled me to ask many questions. What happens to the identity of subsequent generations of early Chinese migrants whose parents, grandparents, and great-grandparents may have been born, brought up and raised in Australia? How do those with long-term residence in Australia "construct," "do," and "perform" Chineseness? How is Chineseness negotiated in different stages and generations of the immigrant's life trajectory? Do Chineseness or racial relations dissipate in the course of long-term residence? How does the sense of identity of subsequent generations impact on their everyday experiences through the life course?

During my research in Australia, I was privileged to partake in the lives of long-settled ABCs where I met parents, siblings, friends and kin of my informants. My ongoing association with the community, enriched by sharing many leisure activities, including dinner parties, museum and heritage tours, lunches, coffee, seminars and talks, allowed me to understand their lives, their sense of identity, their hopes and aspirations. While learning about their lives, I became part of the discourse; ideas were exchanged like ping-ping, bouncing off each other. The wealth of knowledge and depth of insights gained from my engagement with the community have led to a greater understanding of myself as a Chinese Australian. This book has evolved from a child's puzzlement and perplexed identity, to a sociological research that examines the multidimensional nature of identity formation in the lives of long-settled Australian-born Chinese in Australia.

Chan Kwok-bun

I was born in China in 1950. I grew up in Hong Kong and left the city in 1969 to study in Canada as an 18-year-old foreign student. My undergraduate and graduate studies in sociology were in three different Canadian universities, moving from Canada's west coast to the east. Throughout my studies, I did not take a single course in migration or race and ethnic studies, perhaps evading these subjects and not wanting to know I could be and indeed was a victim of racism. I wrote my masters thesis on stress, illness, and coping within the disciplines of medical sociology, psychoanalysis, and psychiatry, and my doctoral dissertation was about wife abuse, which examines feminism and sociology of the family, marriage, and gender in North America in the 1960s and 1970s. Neither of these two academic exercises had anything to do with being Chinese or constructing Chineseness, the subject of this book. It was perhaps a case of selective inattention and intentional avoidance—at both experiential and intellectual levels.

Like all good, prodigal Chinese sons, I returned to Hong Kong to see my parents, brothers, and sisters, each and every time I got a university degree. In those days, for a poor, self-sufficient foreign student who left home for the first time in his life to study in a snow-clad country thousands of miles away (I bought in Hong Kong a one-way ticket as it was cheaper and I didn't expect to be able to come home within months, unlike thousands of Hong Kong students studying in Canada nowadays who would go home for Christmas or Chinese New Year every year), coming home was a luxury, but also a duty for me. Buying a return air ticket required me to wash dishes in a restaurant for at least one month. I was more than glad to do so though I was not conscious at the time that I was "performing Chineseness." My father and my mother, whom I am very fond of, were happy to see me grow up and do something good for myself, perhaps also for the family.

My big family of two parents and eleven children (I am the youngest child) escaped in 1951 from mainland China to Hong Kong as refugees. My father was a self-made millionaire, a landlord, and a restaurant owner who, like thousands and thousands of land, business, and property owners, quickly became a target of persecution under the communist regime. Father was locked up by the same peasants he helped through dry and rainy days. Hong Kong then was a British colony. The bulk of its people were struggling to make ends meet. Not wanting to put all his eggs in one basket, father sent his two eldest sons in 1952 to his rich relatives (who owned casinos) in Vietnam to receive an education. My two brothers went to school, learned English and French, married local-born Chinese women, had children, and became settlers in an Indochinese country. Neither of them returned to Hong Kong. I remember I was forced by father throughout childhood to write letters to tell them the ins and outs of the Chan family in Hong Kong. I hated it, and so did my kid sister. Those letters were literally written in tears, with father holding a stick and threatening to hit.

In 1976, Saigon fell, Vietnam-turned communist and the ethnic Chinese took to the sea as boatpeople, which caught the world's attention. My two brothers wrote home, to Hong Kong, for money to buy tickets to get on an unseaworthy boat built by gangsters illegally in a village. Father wrote to me in Canada to help him to save his two sons (he did not say "my two brothers")—a request I as his son could not decline although, when I last saw my brothers in Hong Kong, I was about 1 year old. In 1978, I got my doctorate and became an assistant professor of sociology in Montreal. Not aided by my siblings in Hong Kong, I alone sent money to my brothers who had fled Vietnam by boat and were sojourning in an Indonesian camp. I worked with the Red Cross to find them in the camp and bring them to Canada. Single-handedly and overnight, I became a sponsor of four adults (my two brothers and their wives) and six teenage children. One Sunday afternoon, while holidaying in New York City, I received a long distance call from an immigration officer. He said my relatives had arrived in Montreal, Canada. I flew back on the first available flight. When I received them in a transit camp in French Montreal in a cold Quebec evening, they were total strangers to me. Still single myself, I had suddenly become a carer for ten people. Perhaps not surprisingly, in hindsight, I had the first car accident in my life—a seven-car collision on a Montreal highway on a cold Saturday afternoon.

Decades later, brothers' children grew up and received a Canadian education which was and still is an envy to the rest of the Chan family in Hong Kong. Like many Chinese children in North America, my oldest brother's son became a doctor and his daughter, an accountant. Life has treated them well, really well. In 1982, I decided to return to Hong Kong to get married and host a wedding banquet as this would please my aging and ailing mother and bring her luck—or so I believe as a Chinese. Weddings were and still are expensive exercises. I reminded my oldest brother of my loans to him. He was angry that I even asked, saying I read too many sociology books in English, received too much western education, and had stopped "being Chinese." His point was that a true-blooded "real" Chinese would not ask his family to pay back. Money that is passed between hands in a Chinese family is a gift, an obligation, a sign of love and compassion, definitely not a loan, or a fake loan that does not need to be paid back. I should feel ashamed of having lost my "Chineseness" during my years in the West—to receive a white man's education; I got an education and a job, but I had lost my identity. Till today, the "loan" or, I should say, the "gift," remains outstanding in a double sense, depending on whose side one is on and one's construction.

While I said in the above that I purposely avoided studying or writing things Chinese when as a university student, this did not prevent white Canadians, including my university colleagues in sociology and other social sciences, from reminding me I am Chinese and insisting on my race, ethnicity, or culture—on my face, my skin color. All those years in Canada, as a sociologist, I did not teach a single course that had anything to do with migration, race, and ethnic relations, China and things Chinese. Yet I was treated by Canadian society inside and outside the university as a Chinese first, a sociologist or even a male second or third. My race was my master identity. Everything else about me, good or bad, was secondary. Although I completed all my university studies in Canada, learning Canadian sociology to make sense of and to write about Canadian society, my colleagues did not seem to be able to resist the temptation of asking me all the time about things Chinese: the many Chinatowns that decorate the Canadian cityscapes, Chinese food, tea, Mid-Autumn Festival, Lunar Chinese New year, foot binding, male domination and female victimization, the Great Wall, communism, Chairman Mao—and the list continues and repeats itself, over and over again. I have become a China expert, even a sinologist, though my knowledge of things Chinese is probably no better than that of a cook, a grocery storekeeper, a laundryman in Chinatown. But all this doesn't matter, not at all. I am a Chinese, whether I want to be or not. Identity is socially prescribed, bestowed, imposed—never a matter of personal choice.

By the early 1908s, my sociological writings took an ethnic turn. I edited a special issue titled "Coping with Racism" for a journal, *Canadian Ethnic Studies*—my first venture into the field. I also published a host of journal articles on racism against the Indochinese refugees in Quebec. I wrote my book *Smoke and Fire: The Chinese in Montreal*, a historical and ethnographic study of racism, for Hong Kong's Chinese University Press. Beijing University Press put out a Chinese edition shortly after. So did Beijing's China Social Sciences Publishing House with any special issue, "Coping with Racism." It was a journey of no return. All these years of avoiding the subject and suppressing the consciousness of it came to an abrupt stop, followed then by an implosion, an eruption, like a pressure cooker that has blown its top.

As it happens, to my brother I am not a Chinese, a fake Chinese (even when I insist I am), but to Canadian society I am a real Chinese (even when I insist on being approached and treated otherwise).

My journey does not end there.

In 1987, I moved my family out of Canada. I taught at the National University of Singapore between 1987 and 2001 and became head of its sociology department. Singapore is 75% Chinese but being, displaying, doing, and performing Chinese in this small city-state is ethnic chauvinism. The English-educated Singaporeans have long constituted the city's economic, political, and intellectual elite. At the sociology department of the university, many staff and students of ethnic Chinese descent do not habitually read, speak, or write Chinese, at least not in public life. Chineseness in the public domain would need to be muted, subdued, joked about, played with, disguised, even hidden. One face, many masks. Chineseness is like a mask, to be put on and off, depending on the audience. Identity is for performing. It is relegated to the domestic sphere, almost forgotten, but if it is ever remembered and used, it is an afterthought, a kind of "by the way," a practice among the elderly, the working class, the new immigrants; in a grocery store, a restaurant, a coffee shop; during weddings, birthday parties, festivals.

I "returned" to Hong Kong in 2001 to take up a headship at the sociology department of Hong Kong Baptist University, then a chair professorship of sociology and a directorship at the David C Lam Institute for East–west Studies. David C Lam was a prominent politician in British Columbia, Canada, and his institute is a place in which to interrogate the popular discourse in ethnic and racial matters. Hong Kong, my hometown where I grew up, to my shock and suffering, is less free, less open-minded, less democratic, less egalitarian, than I thought. I experienced a shock of arrival, a myth of return. A comparison between Singapore and Hong Kong would make exciting writing in sociology, politics, culture, geography and political economy. More and more so since the British handover of Hong Kong in 1997 to China, the city is undergoing a process of resinification, which has its many intended and unintended consequences. One of such consequences relates to what it means to be Chinese in Hong Kong. For a sociologist like me who operates mainly within the university environment, being Chinese and behaving like a Chinese has everything to do with compliance, conformity, even obedience, and all for the sake of keeping peace, order, and harmony—yes that (in)famous word "harmony"—in a mainland Chinese manner. Or harmony with "Chinese characteristics." With its famous Chinese penchant for bureaucracy, managerial control, and hierarchy, a university head of department, a dean, a director, a vice-president, and certainly a president preside over their professors and intellectuals—certainly also all the students because students are children to be taught by elders who know better. In Hong Kong, more so now than, I suppose, when I left it to study in the west as an 18-year old 40 years ago, being Chinese has much to do with reading the boss's mind, shining his (more likely a his than a her) shoes, and not rocking the boat. As it happens, creativity, innovation, independence of the mind, being critical, outspokenness, linguistic eloquence have become, as they say, academic—fit only for consumption in the classroom, in scholarly books, in seminars or conferences which have little to do with real life and real living. One violates these norms at one's peril.

At one moment the professor stands in front of hundreds of students in the lecture theater eloquently and self-righteously preaching that sociology's mission is to deconstruct the taken for granted, the status quo, the given. As he speaks, the students take copious notes so as to reproduce them in essays, term assignments, exams. The university is a factory that produces knowledge on an assembly line and students are its ever-obliging clients or consumers. Or, following the British psychiatrist R.D. Laing, it is a slaughterhouse that prepares standardized canned food for the market. Professors have become the frontline butchers. Students are their products, in uniform tins of meat. At another moment, once outside the classroom, deconstruction has its own costs, for professors and students alike. The flipside of the demise of sociology is the ascent of the Hong Kong and China versions of Chineseness and their respective political, economic, cultural, mental, even existential, connotations. Sociology, or at least the more progressive or radical version in the tradition of Marxism, which ironically is the only manifest (but not latent) ideology in town across the border of the city, is displaced by an administrative discourse on constructing, doing, and performing Chineseness. The university is a house of divided self, a schizophrenic personality, a split mind, or it is a place for pretending, hiding, saying one thing one moment, and doing something else another moment. Such switching is done rather smoothly, every day, on the campuses.

People in Hong Kong have thus learned to construct and do their Chineseness by taking hints from the north, from Beijing. Harmony has long become a hegemonic word that, borrowing Foucault, disciplines and punishes. As their colonial masters departed, in 1997, their "grandparents" up north arrived—in spirit, in ideology.

A revolving door of power, control, other-directedness keeps swinging.

There is also this question of where I am from, or, as people insist, "Where I am *really, really* from." While in Canada or the States, I was from China or Hong Kong, neither of these two places meaning much to the Americans, Quebecois, and Canadians then, even now, other than all those cheap products made in China they bought, used for a while, threw away, and bought again—and the cycle starts again—because they couldn't find better, cheaper products made elsewhere. In 1970, I was at the Vancouver airport in Canada, catching an onward flight from Edmonton, Alberta, to Los Angeles in the USA. I was to join my childhood neighbor there and work in his boss's Chinese restaurant for my summer job—a must if I were to live and continue my university studies. As always, I was in a long queue, watching pensively an American immigration officer, a white male, doing his routine work of asking questions of where one is from, where one is going, why, doing what, staying for how long, and with whom—but only to the colored people. When it was my turn, the officer made me empty all my pockets, in public, saying he wanted to know how much cash in total I had on me. As an innocent, inexperienced 19-year old, I did the wrong thing: I asked him why I had to do that. My Canadian professors taught me to ask the "why" question boldly. He retorted: "Chinese would do funny things when they run out of money." This short sentence of 11 words was uttered aloud in front of a long queue of passengers—white and not so white—then all as onlookers witnessing a spectacle. These words were burnt onto my mind, like an inscription, a red hot rod scathing my skin.

Two years later, in Toronto, Canada, while driving to York University, where I studied for my doctorate in sociology and lived (in the students' hostel where I was a don), I was stopped by a policeman. He asked the inevitable question of where I was from, referring to my place of birth outside Canada. I had told him like I told many curious, well-intended Canadians, I was born in China, grew up in Hong Kong, came to Canada for my university studies, and became a landed immigrant of Canada in 1973 while finishing my masters degree in sociology at University of Western Ontario. He probably decided somewhere in my short biographical narrative that I was too much a "smart cookie" for him. He wanted to do a search of my car. Always naturally, I asked him why. He sharply retorted, "Have you heard of drugs? The Chinese have a big part in it. You are lucky I won't turn your car upside down, though I have the power to do so. If I want to, I can rip open all the seats, I can do a body search on you." Luckily, for me and for him, he didn't.

In Singapore, the local Chinese remembered me as someone from Hong Kong. They asked me questions of all sorts about Hong Kong, and Hong Kong only— rarely about Canada where I had spent as many years as in Hong Kong: 18 years of my life. Singaporeans call people from Hong Kong "Hongkies"—a derogatory term which suggests clannishness, money-mindedness, cash hunger, capitalism, rudeness, even shrewdness. Rain or shine, the eternal questions for me while in Singapore were: Have you gone back to Hong Kong lately (not Canada) for your holidays? When will you return to Hong Kong (again, not Canada)? Then, when I left Singapore to return to Hong Kong in 2001 to teach and take up a headship at the Department of Sociology, Hong Kong Baptist University, I found that I was committing an act of betrayal in the eyes of a former colleague at the National University of Singapore: "Singapore has treated you so well all these years." I was ungrateful, I had betrayed Singapore, and this was a sin to someone who is Chinese.

What happened upon my "return migration" to Hong Kong? Between 2001 and today, the same questions have been asked of me as when I was in Singapore, "Have you gone back to Singapore (not Canada) for holidays? When will you return to Singapore (again, not Canada)?" Oh, and I almost forgot another often-asked question: "Have you sold your house in Singapore?" You shouldn't, you know house prices in Singapore have gone up. Hongkongers or, for that matter, the Chinese the world over, including mainland Chinese now, must ask questions about real estate, property, land ownership. Yes, they must.

Yet in Hong Kong, even among the academics, racism is not part of the conversation in everyday life, nor in the scholarly critical discourse. In the eight local universities, race, ethnicity, and migration do not typically find their ways into courses being offered. In fact, a university course in race and ethnic relations does not exist here. Throughout the 1970s and the 1980s, except scattered works by expatriate scholars sojourning in the city, local academics did not write much about the plight of the Indochinese refugees then languishing in several refugee camps and transit centers in Hong Kong. In contrast, Hong Kong media portrayal of crimes, delinquencies, and gang fights were an important part of the local imagination and social discourse on their Indochinese neighbors—more often than not in a negative manner—thus the hostility of Hongkongers toward them.

While at the National University of Singapore, I guest-edited a special issue on the Indochinese refugees for the *Southeast Asian Journal of Social Sciences*, which is based in the university's department of sociology.

Then, in 2001, upon joining the Department of Sociology, Hong Kong Baptist University, I designed and taught for two semesters a new course called "Migration and Identity." A third-year course, its enrolment was meager and, judging from their term assignments and tutorial presentations, the students' interest was lukewarm. I subsequently dropped it, in disappointment.

Hong Kong as "Asia's World City" did not have a law to prohibit discrimination on the basis of race and ethnicity until recently, which is very late. A law to ensure a minimum wage was passed only two years ago. In several rather significant ways, Hong Kong's globality is infamous in its lack, even absence sometimes, which includes lack of public policies to combat poverty. The city's Gini coefficient of 0.53 earns the city a place in the world record.

Over the past 10 years of my university life in Hong Kong, I have seldom talked about racism, ethnic prejudice and discrimination, human rights, etc., among my family, friends, and colleagues. There were two exceptions in the past 3 years: first with my niece, an immigrant in Australia, and second with a French-Canadian, an old friend of mine who was visiting me from Montreal, Quebec. My niece was born and grew up in Hong Kong. Like thousands of other Hongkongers who left the city before the handover of the British colony to China in 1997, she migrated to Australia with her husband. A real estate agent who has made good money over the years, she insisted Australia's history of racism is over and done with. Chinese immigrants, she said, enjoy equal opportunity at all levels just like everybody else. Personal failures—and successes—are of one's own doing, and achievement is a consequence of hard work and self-discipline, not skin color, not ethnicity—which is why she is now still in Australia, in spite of a global trend of return migration of Chinese back to Hong Kong, Singapore, Taiwan and mainland China. When I told her many Hongkongers couldn't make it in Australia, she questioned my sources and, on methodological grounds, discredited research findings reported in studies. As to my old friend from Quebec, Canada, my experience with her was a lot more conflict-ridden and intense. When I told her official statistics and sociological research, including mine, were saying streets of Hong Kong are filled with returnees from Canada—in fact more so than from any other western countries—she was visibly upset. When I told her Hongkongers are coming back because of racism and blocked opportunity in Canada, she, like my niece, challenged my data, my research methodology, and my motive of research. Then she threw the last straw that broke the camel's back: she accused the Chinese-Canadian returnees of being ungrateful to Canada, her country of birth, who may even include me. On both occasions, with my niece and with my friend, the sociologist that is me took great pains to explain the tools of social sciences and his motive of research but, lamentably, with no success. To local Singaporeans and Canadians, the Chinese are ungrateful; they are traitors.

In both cases, racism against the Chinese was denied, by a native-born white Canadian or by a newly arrived Chinese immigrant in Australia, since there is apparently no racism in both white countries and the Chinese immigrants' opportunities for upward mobility are not blocked, well, at least not now. Chinese returnees are seen as ungrateful on the one hand and not working hard enough on the other hand. It is their own fault. Indeed a classic example of blaming the victim. At one moment, Hongkongers are welcomed by Canada and Australia as they bring along with them skills, connections, experiences, and wealth—they are also world famous for being diligent, self-disciplined, and achievement-oriented. At another moment, when they, not wanting to be unemployed and relying on government handouts for long, having strong signs of work ethic, decide to go home, they also take their economic capital away—which could well be a sore point for the native Canadian, and the Chinese immigrant in Australia who has decided to stay. As it happens, the notion of Chineseness is imputed different, even contrasting, meanings during different stages of the life trajectories of immigrants. Meanwhile, the global tension between the stayers and the movers, the local and the global, the whites and the nonwhites, continues.

Acknowledgements

This book would not have been possible without the support of many people. First are my informants in Australia and the Chinese Australian communities and organizations. Without them my research could not have been conducted. In particular, I would like to express my gratitude to Reg Mu Sung and Doreen Cheong who generously shared not only their personal stories and precious family archives but also spent much time and effort in writing their autobiographies for this book. Also, I would like to thank Andrew Davidson and Grant McCall, my supervisors and staff in the School of Social Sciences and International Studies at University of New South Wales, who provided guidance and valuable advice on my research. Andrew opened my eyes to sociology and has been a source of inspiration since my undergraduate years. Wang Gungwu, Manying Ip and David Ip, my external examiners, deserve a special mention for their useful comments and feedback. Thanks also to my co-author Chan Kwok-bun for his encouragement, intellectual stimulation and exchange that sharpened insights and ideas for this book. And to Tony Green for his helpful editorial comments. Last but not least, I thank my family for their love and support.

Lucille Lok-Sun Ngan

I started writing about racism since my years in Toronto and Montreal, Canada, in the 1970s. The subject continues to grab me morally, emotionally and intellectually throughout my subsequent years in Southeast Asia and now Hong Kong. Producing this book with my co-author, Lucille Ngan, enables me to carry on my struggle; this time the spotlight is on long-established Australian-born Chinese who count amongst the 4th, even 5th generation and beyond. My two years of collaboration with Lucille have given me some new insights into an old problem. For that, I remain indebted to her, the Chicago school of sociology, and the writings of Simmel, Mead, Park, Stonequist, Schutz, Berger, and Goffman. Many things change, yet others, like the ebb and flow of the tide, remain an "unchanging same", haunting the human race in their many guises for centuries. The Chinese of Australia, like their brothers and sisters in the Chinese diasporas the world over, have taken it all in their strides–in plight but also in delight. My many rounds of exchange with Lucille–and Doreen Cheong and Reg Mu Sung who contributed autobiographical chapters to this book–will stay in my memory as a testimony to the fruitfulness of intellectual cooperation.

Chan Kwok-bun

Contents

Chapter 1
Introduction: Chineseness and the Chinese Diaspora

I left home young, I returned old;
Speaking as then, but with hair grown thin.
Children, meeting me, do not know me;
They smile and say:
"Stranger, where do you come from?"

'Coming Home', by He Zhizhang

Throughout history, "Chinese" communities have spread all over the world—with some 12 million Chinese moving out of China since the 1820s onward, striving with mixed results to adapt themselves to different social environments (Skeldon, 1995b). While members of the Chinese diasporic communities often make gradual transitions from being a migrant to becoming an integrated member of the host society, as they take root in a land far away from the original home, they may at the same time also feel, maintain, revive, or reinvent a connection with their prior home in various ways. In the process of integration, what emerges is a complex synthesis of a diversity of ethnic cultures, resulting in the union of two or more group cultures, but this does not necessarily lead to homogeneity. The process of cultural collision opens up new possibilities of identities and belongings.

Prior to the nineteenth century a number of diasporic Chinese communities were already scattered overseas even though, in China, and until 1893, Chinese immigration overseas was fundamentally one of prohibition. However, the majority of those overseas saw themselves as only living temporarily abroad, and thereby presenting a political and cultural discourse of return. By the end of the nineteenth century, under the Qing court, the political attitudes toward overseas movement changed, and living abroad was no longer considered a treason or crime. Chinese who were successful overseas could become an asset to the Chinese empire through the skills and expertise they acquired, albeit that the lifting of the ban on foreign travel in 1893 was in reality only a removal of a defunct symbol, as there had been illegal movements all through the past. Nevertheless, this act gave official recognition to diasporic Chinese

L.L.-S. Ngan and K.-b. Chan, *The Chinese Face in Australia: Multi-generational Ethnicity among Australian-born Chinese*, DOI 10.1007/978-1-4614-2131-3_1,
© Springer Science+Business Media, LLC 2012

for their contributions, and the Chinese government encouraged them to identify not only with their local provincial hometowns but also with China and the Chinese civilization. What is important, as Wang (1985: 70) reminds us, is that the vast majority of those of foreign nationality, and their subsequent generations who have been far distanced from China, still consider themselves to be ethnically Chinese or are considered so by others. This was the beginning of a period that marked the celebration of Chineseness, a sense of unification and security for Chinese overseas (Wang, 2000: 64).

The old western projection of "being Chinese" often entailed some form of common racial collectivism. It was imagined that "Chinese" inhabited a single cultural territory bounded by the political nation-state of China and that Chinese people shared stereotypical physical characteristics. If this one-dimensional notion of a single "Chinese" identity had long satisfied western political and philosophical needs to categorize foreign people, it was never adequate to encompass the variety of identities it sought to define, especially within a diasporic context. The "Chinese" could equally be qualified historically by internal geographical markers (north, south, east, west) as well as by external national labels ("Australian," "Malaysian," "Filipino" or "American"), without signifying any underlying consciousness or unified opinions regarding ethnic or cultural identity (Wang, 2001: 182–199). More important in the formation of diasporic communities were differences among Chinese people themselves, as revealed by subethnic markers like dialect, dietary preferences, customs and habits, locality, and parochial ties to particular provinces or districts within provinces. These are old differences that predate the transnational influences of the contemporary era.

For long-settled diasporic Chinese, other factors have also influenced their formation of identities. These include varying perceptions of culture and class, strategic accommodations at different times and places, at local, national, and transnational levels, and length of settlement in the new country. Recent Chinese immigrants from Hong Kong, Taiwan and mainland China as newcomers and outsiders, who bring new (or renewed or reinvented) ideas and traditions about "being Chinese," also impact on the identity of long-settled Chinese communities. Interactions between old and new Chinese communities result in a hybridity that "articulates" East and West (culture), past and present (time), here and there (place), global and local, and center (China) and periphery (Chinese diasporic communities). The interaction or intersection of all these factors has led to a situation in which the construction of identity for migrants and their children often occurs in a state of liminality—that is, a feeling of being beyond, suspended in-between cultures, or in borderlands. This factor further transforms any collective notion of a shared Chinese identity among diasporic communities, often imparting "a sense of being a people with historical roots and destinies outside the time/space of the host nation" (Clifford, 1997: 255).

Where Australia is concerned, diasporic Chinese settlement has a long, varied, and at times unpleasant history, with the first large-scale emigration largely from Canton occurring after the discovery of gold in Victoria and New South Wales in the mid-nineteenth century. In particular is the progressive change from the White Australia Policy (1901–1950s) to the policy of integration (1960s) and multiculturalism (1970s onward)—policies which have had profound influences on Chinese settlement.

External Historical Events

Throughout Australia's history there has been a concerted effort to restrict non-white immigration, particularly that of the Chinese, driven by a pursuit of racial purity. Anti-sentiment to the early Chinese settlers, largely from the Canton province, was a result of massive influxes of Chinese in Australia during the Gold Rush era, which led to social fears of a "Chinese invasion" into Australia. The White Australia Policy entrenched the racism and xenophobia of the government through excluding nonwhite people from Australia. It was the official policy from 1901 to the 1950s, and elements of the policy survived until the 1970s. The exclusion of Chinese immigration was enacted severely through the legislation of the Immigration Restriction Act in 1901. One of the tools for exclusion was the notorious dictation test for immigrants entering Australia. The test could be given in any European language so a Chinese migrant who wanted to live in Australia could be tested in French or English, which made it virtually impossible for Chinese to remain in Australia. Rice, a staple food for Chinese, was heavily taxed; Chinese workers were paid less than the whites and they were also limited to a few occupations (Fitzgerald, 2007). There was also strict restriction on the entry of Chinese women. Ideas of white privilege, prestige, and racial hierarchy embedded in the White Australia Policy brought a spatial order that placed Chinese and aboriginals at the bottom of the spectrum. During this period, there was only a small Chinese population in Australia and they were unified and excluded as one homogenous group.

After World War II, Australia launched a massive immigration program, believing that the nation must either "populate or perish." The idea was to bring in British migrants and, where that failed, Europeans who were "white" and believed to be the next most likely to be assimilated into mainstream Anglo-Celtic Australian society. The entry of Asians and Jews continued to be severely restricted by the government although the White Australia Policy gradually eased from the 1950s onward as, for example, with the abolition of the diction test in 1958. Immigrants were expected to assimilate into an English-speaking, Anglo-Celtic culture by shedding their languages and ethnic culture to become indistinguishable from the host population. This wave of immigration as well as an increasing acknowledgment of Australia's social responsibilities as a member of the international community greatly changed the previous monoculture and the conservative character of Australian society. The Australian government began to review its approach to assimilation, and integration became the official policy. This meant that migrants were allowed to maintain many features of their ethnic culture, and ethnic languages were allowed to be freely spoken. In addition, almost all anti-Chinese laws were repealed in all states after World War II (Choi, 1975).

Although immigration laws were relaxed, one of our informants, Jerry, who was born in Australia in 1942, shared with us his childhood experience in the 1950s in

Sydney[1] where racial discrimination toward Chinese was still severe. Jerry made the observation that, "in those days there was none of this "easy street" that the Asian kids have now."[2] He maintained that there was a racial hierarchy that generated discrimination toward the Chinese: "At the top of the spectrum were the whites. Then you had Chinese, blacks and then the mixed-race." Being Chinese was a burden as "there was so much pressure living in the white world and living in the yellow world and being nowhere." Because of Jerry's family's status as refugees from Papua New Guinea he had to endure a complicated migration process during his childhood, including deportation from Australia and continued appeals to return. Racial discrimination, unpleasant migration experiences, his sexuality as a gay man, and pressure from his family (see Chap. 6 for detailed discussion) eventually led to his attempted suicide when he was 24.

From the 1970s onward, Australia began to adopt an official policy of multiculturalism, and Chinese migrants as well as other "nonwhite" people were allowed to settle in Australia. Growing migrant populations from all over the world gave greater visibility to the importance of social and cultural diversity. With increased national expenditure on assistance to migrants, migrant groups began to form formal associations to maintain their ethnic cultures and to promote the survival of their heritages and languages within mainstream institutions. The changes in policies dramatically altered ideas about race and culture affecting Chinese immigrants' experiences of identity.

Inevitably, those who grew up in this new era of cultural diversity constructed expressions of their cultural identity which were different from those of migrants in the earlier exclusionary period. Our informant, Danny, a third-generation Australian-born Chinese (ABC),[3] born in 1981, showed a more positive childhood experience about being Chinese in Sydney in the 1990s:

> At boarding school, I was probably the minority, in terms of race. There were many Chinese but not in boarding school. I felt slightly discriminated against only because people just sort of assume that you fit into a typical Chinese group based on your race. So people judged firstly by your appearance and ethnicity comes into it. But it hasn't been on a big scale, it was just small. But I had no problems admitting I am Chinese. I was just not the typical nerdy type!

While looking Chinese was still a mark of difference for Jerry, the comparison between Danny's and Jerry's childhood experiences shows that the negotiation of Chineseness is largely contingent on external social circumstances. In other words, a cohort's placement in historical time indicates a great deal about the opportunities enjoyed by and the constraints placed upon its members. Individuals growing up in different periods of Australian history have different experiences. This has contributed to the similarities and diversities of experiences within the Chinese community in Australia.

---

[1] Capital city of the state of New South Wales.

[2] Meaning that Asian children nowadays have an easier life compared to early immigrants.

[3] For the sake of brevity "Australian-born Chinese" will be referred to as "ABC" and will be used throughout this book.

However, it needs to be noted that while the White Australia Policy was administered nationwide from 1901 up to the 1950s, there were variations in the intensity of social exclusion toward Chinese in different localities within Australia through this period. For example, the account of our informant, May, also a third-generation ABC, illustrates that although the White Australia Policy had negatively impacted on the experience of Chinese settlement in Australia, not all living in that period experienced the same degree of discrimination:

> When we were evacuated from Adelaide to Sydney because of the war I can remember people teased us in the streets like "Ching Chong Chinaman. Ha! Ha! Ha! Born in a teapot, christened in a jar!" ...Anyone Chinese, they would do that. That was only in Sydney. When we went back to Darwin[4] we never experienced that. There were many more Chinese and we were business folks, so more elite. There were also lots of aboriginals too. That's why we never felt it. When I got married and went to Hong Kong people kept talking about the White Australian policy. I was ignorant about that, I didn't even realize that it had existed because we had never had an experience of that. It was never spoken about. But now I realize what it was. There was not much discrimination in Darwin. Even in Adelaide I wouldn't call it discrimination, I would call it curiosity. They were respectful.

In Darwin, Chinese settlement was different from other metropolitan cities because successful integration of Chinese into the host society took place after World War II. For many years, the Chinese formed the majority of the population, although by 1966, there were only some 400 Chinese in Darwin (Australian Heritage Commission, 2002). With a population of 9,943 Chinese in 1966, Sydney, in contrast, had a much larger Chinese population than Darwin (Choi, 1975: 69).

In the case of Darwin, successful integration can be linked to the city's geographical locality. It was relatively distant from other urban areas and has received little immigration of Chinese even after the war, only one-fourth of the Chinese population being foreign-born and many being third- or fourth-generation Chinese (Choi, 1975). As a result, in contrast to other Australian cities, the Chinese in Darwin were widely dispersed throughout the closely knit society without any apparent social tension with the local whites. In so far as they retained many of their traditional cultural traits and their physical distinctiveness, they were not completely assimilated (Inglis, 1972). Not only did the Chinese work in a wide range of occupations and show little concentration in any particular one, Chinese had been elected as members of local councils and the government.

Our informant May explained that when she was growing up in Darwin in the 1940s, the White Australia policy remained largely unnoticed to the extent that she "didn't realize that it had existed." When May moved from Darwin to Adelaide[5] for tertiary education after high school she felt that the social environment was vastly different:

> At that time I was the only Chinese girl at Teachers College in Adelaide and that was when I felt different. But up in Darwin, it was a small town and of the sixteen of the class, eight of us were Chinese. The mayor was Chinese and most of the business people were Chinese. So we felt equal. There were lots of Chinese and they were very prominent. And living with the aboriginals, it was so multicultural up there, you never thought of being different.

---

[4] The capital city of the state of Northern Territories.

[5] Adelaide is the capital city of the state of South Australia.

Rob, another informant who spent his childhood in two localities, Darwin and Sydney, articulated similar reasons behind the vastly differing attitudes in Australia during the 1930s:

> In Darwin in those days, Chinese were the majority there. The other foreigners were a few Malays, Japanese and Filipino and also Aborigines. The few Australians that were there were single men who worked in a permanent job but they were all spread out. We had problems getting work, but we never had discrimination there because we were all Asians. The truth was that the white people caused the discrimination... There was no discrimination against Chinese in Darwin but when I came down south in Sydney, just before the War, people were very racist. I think it's because there were hardly any Chinese people in Sydney in those days... They were all spread out.

Our informants who grew up in Darwin indicated that they were first confronted with racial discrimination when they relocated to other urban parts of Australia. For example, in Sydney, while the city had a relatively larger Chinese population than other states in Australia,[6] the Chinese were often discriminated against (Choi, 1975: 70). A contributing factor, as noted by Rob, was that the Chinese in Sydney were sparsely dispersed in middle-distance suburbs and outer suburbs and so they were often the minority in their local communities. In contrast, the Chinese in Darwin resided within the city of Darwin with a "racially and ethnically very heterogeneous population" (Inglis, 1972: 279). As such, individuals of a common birth cohort living within Australia may not necessarily share similar life experiences.

Ethnic Composition

The early Chinese settlers were largely from Cantonese origins, mostly male and middle-aged. In contrast to the migrants who arrived in the first 100 years, the second half of the twentieth century saw a growth in subethnic diversity as migrant numbers expanded. Nevertheless, even though the majority of early migrants were Cantonese, their subethnic makeup was diverse. People from districts such as Chungshan, Toishan, and Kaoyau were often isolated from each other because of differences in the local dialects they spoke (Choi, 1975: 3–16). Today, Chinese Australians are even more diverse: Taiwanese, Hong Kong Chinese, and Shanghainese, for example, are among the fastest growing segments of the Chinese Australian population. There has also been a general shift away from the largely working class origin of the late nineteenth and early twentieth century Chinese. Many of those from Hong Kong and Taiwan are skilled or business migrants who departed due to the political uncertainty of the future of Hong Kong after the 1997 handover of the British colony to the People's Republic of China, and amid fears of military intervention in Taiwan from China, respectively. Those hailing directly

---

[6] The three states, NSW, Victoria, and Queensland had over 80% of the Chinese population in 1947 (Choi, 1975: 51).

from mainland China include the independent professionals or skilled migrants and also students who left around the time of the incident in Tiananmen Square in 1989. While considerable social and economic diversity remains within the Chinese Australian population today, many post-1965 Chinese immigrants are from a professional and highly educated background. The contemporary Chinese Australian community is therefore divided along several socioeconomic and cultural terrains, including that of generational differences in Australia. As such there is really no single or any one Chinese identity at all. As Chan (1999: 6) argues, "there is not and never was, a single community we can call the Chinese community in Australia."

Long-settled ABC who are the subject of this book form a unique group within the broader community of Chinese Australians, and their negotiations of the "Chinese" element of their identities are different from other Chinese residing there. According to the 2001 census, Australians with Chinese ancestry made up 3% of the total Australian population and were the largest group among those of Asian descent. Of those with Chinese ancestry, 5.2% were third-plus generation, i.e., they were Australian-born and born to Australian-born parents, making up a population of 27,930. The second generation made up 20.7% and overseas-born, 74.1%. The third-plus generation is likely to increase substantially in the future, with more second generations reaching marital age and increasing numbers of Chinese migrants settling permanently in Australia. Added to this, the variations in sociocultural factors such as intercultural relations and ethnic composition in different localities have differing impact on the formation of identity resulting in varied experiences of Chineseness among the Chinese community in Australia.

This book is based on co-author Lucille Lok-Sun Ngan's research that saw her carrying out participant observation in the Chinese-Australian community and conducting in-depth interviews with subsequent generations of early Chinese migrants in Sydney, Australia, during 2005 and 2006. The book explores how subsequent generations negotiated their Chinese identity in their everyday life interactions with diasporic Chinese communities and the mainstream "White" community. As descendants of early Chinese migrants, their families have resided in Australia for over three generations; however, historically, the general tendency has been to treat "Chineseness" and, in a broader sense, "Asianness" as a common unifying factor that connects everyone of Asian descent (Gilbert, Lo, & Khoo, 2000). Despite an individual's birthplace, generational longevity, cultural inclination, or sense of belonging to Australia, Ngan's respondents acknowledged that some members of the local "host" community still routinely subsume them under the homogenizing categories of "Chinese Australian" or "Asian Australian." The monolithic projection of a stereotyped "Chineseness" distorts complex and changing Chinese cultural realities, and its persistence over time has reified it into a set of widely held assumptions that multi-generational Chinese have to deal with. More recently, a dialectical tension has developed within subsequent generations of ABC: between their Chinese cultural heritage, with its sense of identity colored by subethnic influences, and more recent experiences of a radically changed idea of Chinese identity—one in which nationalist desires for greater modernity and homogeneity simultaneously confront the new realities of transnationalism and a borderless Chinese diasporic community.

Identity Construction

The conflicting impulses and influences of the cross-cultural encounters make diasporic life potentially fraught with contentions over belonging and difference. Identity construction and its relationship with social integration is a complex process and there is no single theory that can describe the sense of identity of immigrants nor explain their differential identification as they construct their lives in different societies. Co-author of this book, Chan Kwok-bun's (2005a) conceptual framework on the outcome of cross-cultural encounters provides a starting point to explore the different identities of immigrants as they interact with a foreign culture. One outcome he details is *essentializing*, as groups in contact emphasize their respective differences by constructing stereotypes of the self and the other which become a breeding ground for racism. A second outcome is *alternating*, where both cultures are kept separate and compartmentalized "in their minds," and immigrants alternate their identities depending on the situation. A third outcome is *assimilation*, where migrants completely integrate into the mainstream society and eventually lose their ethnicity, thus becoming like members of the dominant group. The general assumption is that most ethnic groups will assimilate and acculturate by the third and later generations. The fourth and fifth outcomes, *hybridizing* and *innovating,* are characterized by shifting formations of identity. While immigrants are initially unlike their neighbors in fundamental ways, in a process of entanglement between the locals and them, the foreigners, they are able to work at, on and through their differences. In the course of time, they develop a common identity through cultivating similar cultural interests and a shared sense of history and community. Simultaneously, transformation takes place as they negotiate their identities, thus opening up many exciting possibilities, as found among our informants in this book.

Hybridization takes many forms and has been formulated by sociologists, anthropologists, and theorists in cultural studies as a means to problematize the complex process of identity formation of migrant communities. There are two sides to the process of cultural maintenance, construction, negotiation, renegotiation and exchange: an upside and a downside. The downside, or the inner turmoil, of the migrant is best illuminated in Park's (1928: 892) classical concept of the "marginal man":

> A cultural hybrid, a man living and sharing intimately in the cultural life and traditions of two distinct people; never quite willing to break, even if he were permitted to do so, with his past and his traditions, and not quite accepted because of racial prejudice, in the new society in which he now sought to find a place. He was a man on the margin of two cultures and two societies, which never completely interpenetrated and fused.

Thus it is "in the mind" of the marginal man that cultures intersect with one another. The impossibility of complete integration, the feeling of belonging to nowhere, suspended between two or more cultures, alienated from the mainstream *and* ethnic communities, existing simultaneously in two places, all contribute to the feelings of displacement and ambivalence of the migrant. Yet others accept hybridity, take pleasure in change, and benefit from their cosmopolitan outlook, creativity and innovation, and diversified cultural knowledge. The pluralization or fragmentation of identities is not necessarily "wounded attachments" but can be positive and enriching structures of belonging and identification—the upside of hybridization (Chan, 2011).

The diasporic literature has taken up the idea of hybrid identity construction largely in relation to first- and second-generation migrants and to the sojourner's sense of roots in a diasporic setting (see, for example, Ang, 2004; Charney, Yeoh, & Tong, 2003; Kuah-Pearce & Davidson, 2008; Pe-Pua, Mitchell, Iredale, & Castles, 1996). Somewhat lost in the debate over Chinese diasporas and identities are the experiences of long-settled migrant communities. Their experiences are usually discussed in terms of the melting-pot concepts of assimilation and integration that assume ethnic identification decreases and eventually disappears over successive generations. As we argue in this book, our qualitative research on long-settled ABC reveals a contrasting picture of ethnic identification. Wang (1991b: 2) rightly suggests that Chinese identity "is living and changeable; it is also the product of a shared historical experience whose record has continually influenced its growth." While Chinese identity varies in different locations and there are myriad ways of being Chinese, the fact is that the term Chinese is "real," allowing individuals to interpret, construct, and reconstruct themselves—and the culture of which they are a part (Anderson, 1999).

Aims of the Book: Exploring Identity as Chineseness

This book argues that while the identity of long-settled ABCs is continually undergoing transformations in different contexts and situations, the experiences they encounter throughout their life courses—within the family, Australian society, and Chinese diasporic spaces—carve and graft Chineseness into their lives in a diversity of ways. Consequently, despite generational longevity and strong national and cultural identities grounded in Australia, Chineseness is *still* a significant part of their identity—whether they willingly choose to identify with it or not. Although the notion "Chinese" commonly functions as an essentialist construct, the sites and processes by which Chineseness is invoked or evoked is contingent upon its significance in different contexts and situations; *therefore it is inherently political.* The focus on the process of identity formation has important ramifications for understanding the arbitrariness and artificiality of Chinese cultural discourse as well as the social experiences of the long-settled ABC community in Australia.

The primary goal of our book is to examine how long-term effects of migration impact on the process of identity formation of Chineseness. We focus on two major areas: at a philosophical and theoretical level, we deconstruct and reevaluate the concept of "Chineseness"; and at a social and experiential level, we explore how successive generations of early Chinese migrants experience and negotiate Chineseness in their everyday lives.

While long-settled ABC in Australia are the focus of this study, the social processes and practices which they engage in across their life courses are shared by the wider Chinese diasporic community. Similarly, it is not an exaggeration to say that while the narratives collected in our interviews are unique, the numerous issues interwoven in them are not just those of the Chinese diaspora but are also found in the experiences of diasporic people of other ethnicities and races as well. Our study addresses the particular and the universal simultaneously. As such it provides a bridge of understanding over cultural gaps and many "troubled waters" of race, ethnicity, and culture, even civilization.

Meeting Ngan's Informants

To understand the conception and construction of Chineseness among Australians with Chinese heritage, co-author Ngan conducted in-depth interviews with 43 multi-generational ABC in Sydney and participated in their community activities during 2005 and 2006; her ongoing association with her informants built rapport for continued dialogue after the interviews. Ngan focused on exploring those with long-term residence in Australia, as they are a unique group who are different from the broader community of Chinese Australians with their diverse historical, political, national, and cultural backgrounds. We call those who were born in Australia and have at least one parent also born in Australia (i.e., three or more generations of a family living in Australia) long-settled ABCs. It must be noted that while the categorization according to birthplace is conceptually neat, the definition quickly proves problematic in the face of empirical realities, due to complex migratory movements, marriage patterns within the family, and life trajectories. We will discuss this complicated condition in greater detail in the section below on "Complexity of Generational Groupings."

Ngan's initial strategy to contact informants involved identifying relevant social and cultural community organizations and participating in their activities. She attended social meetings, dinner parties, leisure outings, community gatherings, forums, seminars, conferences, and museum tours. A number of the informants' families who had settled in Australia in the late 1800s had achieved prominence through the generations. Often their family histories were recorded in museums. Observations and conversations in a natural setting unobtrusively provided a deeper understating to complement what was learned in the interviews. Ngan contacted several Chinese community associations as the initial points of contact; two specific community organizations were particularly appropriate since the majority of their members were long-settled ABCs. Common to both organizations was that the primary language was English, and one of their key aims was to promote discussions of the history of Chinese communities in Australia. However, this meant the majority of their members were elderly retired people, who felt that, in their later years, they had the freedom from family and work commitments which allows for self-reflection and the time to pursue their interests in these organizations. To increase diversity in the sample, Ngan adopted a second strategy, which involved advertising the study in places without a particular Chinese cultural focus or Chinese membership such as university student groups, student magazines, or hospital or community notice boards at local shopping centers. The snowballing technique was also adopted to recruit participants. Informants acted as intermediaries by contacting other friends and relatives within their own social network whom they knew fitted the sampling criteria.

With a topical questionnaire in hand Ngan talked with her informants about their family migration history, their conceptions of homeland and their sense of belonging, their understanding of Chinese community groupings within the Australian context, the way they situated themselves within these social categories, and the social significance of "being Chinese" in different contexts and at different life stages. As a sensitive means to understand the experience of Chineseness Ngan adopted a dialogical approach, which took on the appearance of informal everyday conversation during interview sessions. By emphasizing their generational longevity, she could evaluate how their sense of Chineseness impacted on their social positioning among Chinese diasporic groups in Australia. With much generosity, family history was often shared with her through the presentation of artifacts such as family photographs, family trees, birth certificates, poems, calligraphies, books, and historical documents.

Interviews were not one way. Informants were as curious about Ngan's migration experience as she was with theirs. Ngan had to negotiate her role as a cultural "insider" as she was studying an identity that she shared with her informants, albeit in a peculiar way. At other times, after the revelation that she migrated to Australia as a child, Ngan was perceived to be a cultural "outsider"—a sameness in origin but an otherness stemming from her "relatively short presence" in Australia (compared to our informants whose families have been in Australia for over three generations). Some informants said that they would try to avoid using typical Australian idioms during the interview, fearing that Ngan may not be familiar with the colloquial language. On the other hand, some informants perceived Ngan as a cultural "insider," and when Ngan told them that she was exploring the notion of Chineseness, they reacted with an agreeing nod and with comments such as "Most research on the Chinese in Australia has been done by [Anglo] Australians. Only Chinese can really understand the nuances of our own culture." Several informants admitted that they knew they would be more at ease in sharing their experiences because Ngan's familiarity with the Chinese culture would allow her to understand how they came to the views they had about certain issues. Ngan became a part of the discourse. Being perceived as sharing a common heritage—a sameness originated from an "imagined community" (Anderson, 1983)—yet being also an outsider at the same time allowed her to be in a position to develop more in-depth questioning and genuine engagement with the informants.

Ngan was fascinated by the projects and invaluable artifacts that many of her informants generously shared with her during her fieldwork. In 2011 Ngan contacted her informants to seek their interest in contributing these artifacts to this book, together with a short biography of racial incidents they had encountered in their own lives. These visual materials and mini-autobiographies form Chaps. 3 and 4 of this book.

Table 1.1 Our study by gender, age groups and migratory generation of long-settled ABCs

Migratory generation	Age groups							
	Male				Female			
	18–29	30–44	45–61	62+	18–29	30–44	45–61	62+
Third	Marco Danny	Rodney		Ralph Jerry		Vera	Sarah Jean	Mary Tanya May
Fourth	Dave Nelson Martin Dean	Leon Bruce Sean	Pete Sunny Don	Andrew George	Jean	Janice Jessi Catherine	Daisy Debra Dianne	Sandy Donna Lilly
Fifth +	Bill	Andy	Rob Gerard Alan		Mandy Bella	Loucia Jenny	Ada	

Dividing the sample by gender and age gives the following proportions: 22 males and 21 females whose age groups included 10 aged over 62, 12 aged 45–61, 11 aged 30–44, and 10 aged 18–29. In terms of generations distant from China, 11 informants were third generation, 22, fourth generation, and 10 were fifth generation or over (Table 1.1). In regard to their educational background, 35 had post-high school education, seven had completed high school education, and only one did not complete high school. Most of those with tertiary education were professional people, comprising academics, bankers, traders, pharmacists, government officers, and librarians. According to a 1968 Melbourne study which surveyed 285 "Australian-born full-Chinese" and 152 "part-Chinese," most of the adult ABCs were descendants of well-established early Chinese migrants who were financially capable of supporting their offspring's higher education; thus many of them would have had the privilege of being able to move into professional occupations (Choi, 1975: 91). The educational qualifications of those interviewed for this study support this; as a whole, the attainments, current occupations, and residential suburbs of our informants who lived within the Sydney metropolitan area indicate that this sample of long-settled ABCs had middle to high socioeconomic status. All interviews were conducted in English as it was the primary language spoken in the informants' homes. Only a few could converse fluently in a Chinese dialect.

Despite all informants' families having lived in Australia for over three generations, only 14 of them had mixed ancestry. Of the 26 who were or had been engaged in a long-term relationship, barely one-third (nine) involved a Caucasian. It should be said that Ngan's sample of informants is not representative of the pattern of inter-marriages in Australia where, according to a 2004 study, approximately 85% of all third-plus generation ABCs were partnered with spouse of a different ancestry and, more precisely, 68% of them were partnered with a spouse of Australian or Anglo-Celtic ancestry (Khoo, 2004). This relatively small number of mixed-race individuals probably arose from Ngan's selection method, which aimed to include individuals with strong feelings about their Chinese heritage as well as those who were indifferent to it. Some of her participants had initially worried that their sense of Chineseness in everyday life might be inadequate, that they were "not Chinese enough" for her study, but once assured that their social experience would still be important to her research, they agreed to participate. Those who declined to take part said they were not interested in the subject. Furthermore, some respondents were confused about her research topic and expressed comments such as "we are just Australians with Chinese heritage." For many, "Chinese" as a concept is so widely taken-for-granted by them that it did not require explanation. While Ngan tried to explain that she was studying the processes involved in the construction of identity, many assumed that she was a historian or a genealogist and that her main objective was to study their family history. This highlights a limitation in our sample, as individuals who declined to be interviewed generally felt that Chinese identity issues did not matter to them because Chineseness played no salient role in their everyday lives. Most such individuals came from an interracial family background. As a result, our sample was generally skewed toward a group that was conscious of their Chinese heritage.

In attempting to deconstruct the essentialist notions of Chineseness, Ngan found herself also holding onto preconceived stereotypes. Some of her informants had a "Western" physique with untraceable Chinese features and she recalled her bemusement initially upon meeting one such informant. Trying to hide any hint of surprise, she quietly thought to herself "she looks nothing like a Chinese." As a researcher who examined the construction of the Chinese identity, Ngan would admit that she was also conditioned by normative social constructs of "Chinese." Such reflections reaffirm that social constructs have slipped into the unconscious even though one may be consciously questioning the processes involved.

The qualitative nature, methodological limitations, and sample size of our study mean our findings would not be representative of the experiences of the long-settled ABCs in Australia. In this respect, rather than making general conclusions about the social experience of the community, this book explores the uncharted realities of the diasporic experience through the microsociological lenses of multi-generational ABCs. To preserve their anonymity, all informants were given pseudonyms in this book.

Complexity of Generational Groupings

The general tendency of defining migrants according to birthplace has been based on conceptually neat categorizations. For example, according to the Australia Bureau of Statistics (2001), overseas-born immigrants are classified as "first generation"; people who are born in Australia but have one or both parents who are overseas-born are categorized as second generation; and those who are born in Australia whose parents are also born in Australia are labeled as long-settled Australians. Under such a classification system it is not possible to differentiate and segregate between third and higher order generations in the 2001 census data (Khoo, 2004). Moreover, the mutual exclusivity of each generation is problematic in the face of empirical realities when classifying ABCs with long-term residence.

Definitions based on generation and birthplace classification can never be totally clear-cut as there will always be cases situated in zones of liminality. It was clear from the start that the migratory and marriage patterns of long-settled ABCs are not a straightforward matter and are far more complex than what is often assumed. Many Chinese migrants of the early twentieth century were sojourners as they moved back and forth between China and Australia. One of the reasons for such movement was due to the early discriminatory migration policy that banned Chinese women from going to Australia. As a consequence of the unequal gender distribution of Chinese migrants, men often returned to their homeland to search for a bride, and children would thus be born in China (Choi, 1975).

For example, in the case of Andrew, one of our informants, although the previous three generations from the paternal side of his family have resided in Australia, he was the first to be born outside of China. Andrew's great-grandfather migrated to Australia in the late 1800s and later returned to China to marry as "there were hardly any Chinese women around at the time." His grandfather was born in China but subsequently returned to Australia as a young adult. Upon reaching marital age, Andrew's grandfather also returned to China to get married and subsequently his father was born overseas. Andrew's father later migrated to Australia as a young adult and settled there permanently. He married a Hong Kong-born migrant in Australia, and that is where Andrew was born. In short, Andrew is the fourth generation away from China but a second-generation ABC. For the purposes of this study he is considered as a fourth-generation ABC. In other words, classification is based upon generational distance from China calculated from the side of the family which has the longest residence in Australia.

Complex migratory movements can also be highlighted by the continuous migratory journeys not only between China and Australia but also in a third place of settlement. For example, for a number of the participants, their family migratory movement also included Papua New Guinea. From 1921 the territory was formally under Australian civil administration until 1975 when it gained independence. During this period, citizens were given Australian citizenship, and a number of Chinese immigrants in Papua New Guinea moved to Australia in search of a better life as economic prospects were more promising there. For some Chinese families the migratory journey was a departure from China to Papua New Guinea, then to Australia, and such complex movement can be demonstrated by the family of our informant, Nelson. His paternal great-grandfather migrated from China to Papua New Guinea in the late 1800s for commercial reasons. His grandfather was born in Papua New Guinea but went back to China for education and married his grandmother. The couple later returned to Papua New Guinea where his father was born. Both his grandparents and father were given Australian citizenship under the Australian mandate, and in the 1960s his father moved to Australia to study and married his mother, a first-generation Hong Kong immigrant. Nelson was later to be born in Sydney. Nelson is technically the fourth generation to be away from China but a second-generation ABC, but for the purposes of the study he is identified as a fourth-generation ABC.

In highlighting the complexity of classification, one can see the difficulties of presenting generational groupings in a precise and systematic form. The significance of gaps in an individual's family migratory and birthplace history reveals the complications of typologies. Similar problems regarding presentation of generational indicators have been discussed by Tan's (2004a: 49) intergenerational study on Chinese Australians, where she reports "…generational indicators are so complex it is extremely difficult to identify these accurately and present them in any clear, coherent way." Nonetheless, noting the complexity of generational groupings of respondents provides an understanding of the significant advantage in employing a qualitative approach—that is, a potential to identify a diversity of unseen variations within individual circumstances, particularly within family migratory movements.

While it is important to know the complexity of our informant's migratory movements, given that the focus of our book is on how life course experience and spatial linkages with the cultural homeland—as they are received and interpreted by individual—would shape the sense of identity, our analysis will not go into a detailed analysis of the "depth of generations." Our informants represent the general experience of those with long-term residence in Australia whose families have resided in Australia for over three generations.

Long-settled ABCs and Chinese Australians

We acknowledge that identifications such as "ABCs" or "Chinese Australian" may not satisfactorily address the identity of our informants. Different cultural connotations are associated with different categories and they may be in contrast to an individual's own sense of identity. For some, the label "ABCs" represents a greater inclination toward one's Chinese heritage, while for others, the emphasis is on being Australian. Similarly, this applies to the term "Chinese Australian." For the purpose of this book, we have adopted the term "long-settled ABCs" to refer to the descendants of early Chinese migrants who had settled in Australia and who comprised the main subjects of this study. This term designates people who were born in Australia and whose families had resided outside of China and in Australia for three or more generations. The term "long-settled ABCs" is employed to highlight the long-time, indeed multi-generational, settlement and establishment in Australia. In contrast, "Chinese Australians" is used more widely to refer to Australians who ethnically identify themselves as Chinese, regardless of birthplace or length of residency in Australia. By distinguishing between these terms through emphasizing birthplace and, more importantly, length of generational longevity in Australia, we seek to set apart the "long-settled ABCs" as a unique group from the wider community of Chinese Australians that is comprised of a diversity of diasporic Chinese groups of different historical, political, national, and cultural backgrounds.

Themes of Chineseness

This book is comprised of eight chapters including an introduction and a conclusion. The book's chapters present a number of interrelated perspectives on the formation of identity and the social experiences of long-settled ABCs, all of which concern the conceptual themes of space, time, and locality. These three related themes are the basic components that constitute the condition in which identities are established through cultural practices and negotiations across the life course.

Chapter 2 forms the analytical framework of this book. We explore the current postmodern theorization of identity construction and hybridity as a means to understand the fluid formation of Chineseness. We also highlight the significance of using the life course orientation as an analytical framework to examine the negotiation of identity construction.

Chapters 3–7 provide a reportage of fieldwork that brings to the fore construction and operation of identity as Chineseness through the lives of long-settled ABCs within the social and cultural spaces they inhabit.

Chapters 3 and 4 consist of mini-autobiographies of two long-settled ABCs. As authors of their own biographies, they write about the personal racial encounters throughout their lives. Their autobiographies are complemented by original archival photographs illustrating their everyday lives as ethnic minorities living in the white-dominated society of Australia. As the saying goes, a picture paints a thousand words. Through their own voices and their collection of photographs we capture "visually" what Chineseness means to them.

Chapter 5 draws attention to the social phenomenon that, regardless of whether subsequent generations choose to identify or deny themselves as "Chinese," Chineseness represents an inescapable "reality" they have to, and must, confront due to societal discourses of social recognition and essentialism. Through our informants' daily experiences we show how the prevailing racial, cultural, and social discourses of authenticity based on physicality and language consolidate subdivisions within Australia and across the diasporic Chinese community.

Chapter 6 focuses on the context of the family and discusses how Chineseness is represented and configured across the life courses of our informants. We discuss how factors such as gender roles, sexuality, marriage, filial duties, memories, and sexuality influence the cultivation of Chineseness and socialization of subsequent generations.

Having established that the formation of Chineseness is a fluid process contingent upon social and cultural contexts, biographical and historical times, and socially constructed age-based identities, Chap. 7 examines the hybrid identity of subsequent generations and its relations with decentered transnational linkages. We utilize two distinct notions of hybridity—namely, "double consciousness" and "third space"—as means to explore the hybrid space in which long-settled ABCs are situated. In doing so we highlight that, while underlying both approaches is an intellectual decentering that is built upon notions of difference and otherness, as well as an attempt to abolish the reliance on unitary notions embedded in assimilationist frameworks, ironically, the very logic of these conceptions has led to a reinstatement of sameness and a redrawing of exclusionary lines. We point out that, while the transnational framework has been central to our understanding of the construction of identity for recent Chinese migrants, those with long-time establishment do not necessarily engage in conventional transnational practices. The negotiation of Chineseness by subsequent generations is continually influenced by decentered linkages of memory, desire, nostalgia, and imagination with the homeland. We also argue while the general emphasis of "hybridity" has been on its negative experiences or downside, with a focus on the manipulation and reshaping of identities according to circumstance and audience, or a sort of making the most of the situation, these supposedly negative experiences can also lead to contentment and pleasure—the upside—and thus the plight and delight of hybridity.

Chapter 8 concludes the book with a discussion that retraces the underlying processes of identity construction as Chineseness and Australianness that impact on the experiences of multi-generational ABCs in Australia. In a quickly globalized world—or Anglicized, even Americanized, depending on one's political persuasions—that is compressed in time and place, the celebration of hypermobility of ideas, cultures, people and capital, and the porousness of borders and boundaries may be premature. It could even be a myth, a utopia that is yet to arrive because the ship of hope for the millions and millions of racial minorities, whose families have settled in the western world for three or more generations, like the subjects of our study reported in this book, is still not in sight. The Chinese face, the faciality and physicality, the body, continue to serve them a grim reminder of their differentness, if not inferiority. But humans seldom take things lying down. They never did. They never will. Meanwhile, they strategize, they role-play, they pass, they don masks, even pretend, they put their best foot forward, so to speak—thus the subtitle of our book, "Multi-generational Ethnicity among Australian-born Chinese." The hyphen that separates the book's main title and its subtitle focuses our gaze on the chasm between social constraints on the one hand and human creativity on the other. Meanwhile, what happens in between is what the sociologist Anthony Giddens calls structuration or efforts at survival, construction, and deconstruction of the real and the social and, if lucky, even rising above it all. The racial person is a juggler, an actor, always on stage, in public. One face, many masks. The balls he throws up in the air are his myriad masks or roles and persona. Once in a while, a ball may drop, or it may not—thus the dramatic, theatrical, and unexpected quality of the game of race. When he succeeds, he is in ecstasy. When he fails, he is embarrassed (in a Goffmanian sense), or even feels shame. The game of race continues because of the stubbornness of race and racism. Some bad things in life just won't go away.

Chapter 2
Constructing and Performing Chineseness

I am Chinese because by definition I am. My cultural roots are
Chinese. If you ask me what country I come from, it's Australia,
but my cultural background is Chinese. That is by definition,
but I consider myself as an ABC. If you are asking me what
makes me think I am Chinese, I don't know!

Quote from informant, Rodney

The idea of identity is one of the most important organizing principles of modernity—
and, certainly, postmodernity. It has provided an overarching conceptual framework
to understand larger areas of social life. However, the traditional essentialist concept
of identity, which tends to conceive a single aspect of identity as the fundamental
essence of an individual's experience, has come under attack because of its inability
to capture the dynamic, processual, and fluid nature of identities. Identities are constituted differently in different historical and social contexts. Identity is always *in context*. For example, although "Chinese" identity functions as a socially constructed
category, it can be argued that it is not a genuine ethnicity. Chineseness is not an inert
fact of nature, just like any other racial collectivity, it is not merely there, but is a
bundle of ideas that have histories and tradition of thoughts, imageries, and vocabu-
laries that have given it "reality" and presence in and for the West (Said, 1978).
Similar to other overseas work on the Chinese diaspora such as Tong and co-author
Chan's (2001b) volume on the Chinese in Thailand, Leung's (2004) research in
Germany, Man's (2004) work in Canada, Greif's (1974) and Ip's (2003) studies in
New Zealand, the diasporic Chinese in Australia, like any other Chinese community
overseas, are embedded in complex communal relationships constructed along
divisions of birthplace, language, gender, generation, birth cohort, occupation, and
political and religious affiliation. These divisions change in time and space across
the life course, carving out dynamic sociocultural spaces for different members of
the Chinese diaspora, which in turn form their sometimes common, at other times
dissimilar, experiences and self-perceptions.

L.L.-S. Ngan and K.-b. Chan, *The Chinese Face in Australia: Multi-generational*
Ethnicity among Australian-born Chinese, DOI 10.1007/978-1-4614-2131-3_2,
© Springer Science+Business Media, LLC 2012

Since the analysis of Chineseness is predicated on the centrality of collective constructs in shaping social life, "being Chinese" to a large extent also means living within the norms of the Chinese life cycle which is largely influenced by Confucianism, the ideology that has dominated Chinese thought, morals, and values for nearly two millennia—while Confucianism has also had a strong cultural influence on other East Asian countries such as Japan, Korea and Taiwan, and Southeast Asian countries such as Singapore and Vietnam. However, the assumptions of orderly patterns, static cultural norms, and firm boundaries in life are problematic because changes through the life course are inevitable, consequently leading to a diversity of life trajectories. This is evidenced in Chinese diasporic studies where variations of experiences have long been well documented. Similarities and diversities exist in "Chinese" cultural continuity and cultural transformations, as well as in expression of cultural identities. It is thus important to understand that each Chinese society has its own cultural conception of Chineseness which is invariably different from those in Chinese communities elsewhere. Not only does the meaning of "Chineseness" of these diasporic communities change, the cultural practices in China are also changing in each locality through the internalization of localized traditions. In fact, global cultural forces including Chinese culture from overseas also influence the local culture in mainland China. The transnational networks and linkages that migrants sustain with their previous places of residence through cultural, social, economic, and religious activities, as well as other decentered connections, have a direct influence on the construction of Chineseness. Diasporic Chinese of different generations and birth cohorts have also developed distinct cultural expressions. In these differing contexts, the notion of "Chinese" can take on a wide diversity of meanings. The inadequacy of this single word, "Chinese," commonly used to represent an extraordinary multiplicity of meanings, has become a source of social and political tension.

The shift toward a postmodernist perspective on identity characterized by individualism, fragmentation, uncertainty, and fluidity has already gained much credence in understanding the experience of migrants. It insists on the need to deconstruct the conceptually flawed and politically pernicious essentialist conceptions of identity. The prominence of such phenomena is discerned in the countless discussions examining the nature of identity formation, where synonymous metaphors such as "flows and streams" (Urry, 2000) and "liquid modernity" (Bauman, 2000) have been used to challenge the inadequacy and disorderedness or disorderliness of the collectivist cultural framework. The distinctiveness of the postmodernist approach is in its treatment of the concept of difference, where it either internalizes difference so that the individual is seen as "fragmented" and "contradictory," or attempts to subvert difference by showing that "difference" is merely a discursive illusion (Moya, 2000b: 68). Although it is correct that identities are not determined by any one social collectivity, nevertheless, the major limitation of the postmodern perspective is in its inability to sufficiently account for the social and historical specifications of ethnicity and race and their relation to cultural production (Nguyen, 2000).

If we eradicate the collective notion of Chinese based on its fluid and varying character, we lose an important mode of identification which has always been intertwined with and inseparable from people, land, history, and cultures. Yet defining what

"Chineseness" means in a static sense fails to illuminate our understanding of relations between identity and social incorporation. What is important is to understand how Chineseness enables diasporic Chinese to make sense of their lives and negotiate their identities between East and West, North and South. This book of ours explores the notion of "Chineseness" through the experiences of long-settled ABCs in Australia whose families have resided in Australia for over three generations—by deconstructing and reevaluating the concept of "Chineseness" through the experiences they encounter throughout their life course—within the family, Australian society, Chinese diasporic spaces, and mainland China.

Identity as Social Construction

The topic of cultural identity, as many argue, remains one of the most controversial and intensely debated subjects in sociological and cultural studies. Concepts of identity offer ways of conceptualizing individuality, community, and solidarity and have provided a means of understanding the social relations of human beings within and between different cultures (Abu-Lughod, 1991; Chambers, 1994; Hutnyk, 1999; Papastergiadis, 2000; Young, 1995). Interestingly, while much has been written about identity, there has been a tendency, particularly among postmodernists, to delegitimize the concept itself by revealing its ontological and political limitations (Moya, 2000a). Our postmodernist critique of identity here should be understood partly as a corrective to a prior social tendency toward essentialism.

The problem with essentialist conceptions of identity is their tendency to posit one aspect of identity as the single cause that determines the social meanings of an individual's experience. Essentialist notions are challenged because they often ignore historical and social changes and neglect internal differences within a group—by only acknowledging the experiences that are common to everyone (Moya, 2000a). The complications of essentialist conceptions quickly become exposed as one begins to unravel the concept of "identity" and its association with "race," particularly for diasporic communities, as we shall discuss in the next section.

Countering the collective construction of identity is the postmodernist perspective, which is in part a corrective to the previous social and scholarly tendency toward essentialism and which seeks to deconstruct the conceptually flawed and politically pernicious essentialist conceptions of identity. Nguyen (2000: 171) defines postmodernism as:

...an intellectual position characterized by an epistemology of racial skepticism that takes truth and objectivity to be always socially and discursively constructed, mediated by power, discourse and desire.

This definition is common of the view on cultural identities held by postmodernists, who perceive identities as fictitious or unreal because the self cannot be fixed and definitively defined (Moya, 2000a). For such people the essentialist ideal of achieving ordered, orderly, full, static, homogenous identity is one that is doubtful.

Postmodernism argues that the complication of shifting identities is distorting the imagery of unity. The fluid movement of identity is seen as a journey that is often open and incomplete and where there is no fixed identity. Chambers (1994: 25) explains:

> So identity is form on the move, identity is formed at the unstable point where the "unspeakable" stories of subjectivity meet the narratives of history, of a culture. In that passage, and the sense of place and belonging that we construct there, our individual stories, our conscious drives and desires, acquire a form that is always contingent, in transit without a goal without an end.

Chambers suggests that the self is continuously transforming and is open to questioning, rewriting, and rerouting. In this context, the formation of identity is seen as a hybrid process where the self becomes a flexible zone, opening up multiple discourses (Mathews, 2000). It involves complex transformations, and the self in this respect is made of past memories and future anticipation linked to an ever-transforming present (Hall, 1996). As such the self enters into a state of hybridity in which no single narrative can confidently claim to represent the truth about the real world (Bhabha, 1994; Chambers, 1994; Chan, 2011).

Postmodernists, in particular, insist that experiences and histories cannot represent the truth. They hold the view that "identities are fabricated and constructed rather than self-evidently deduced from experience—since they claim that experience cannot be a source of objective knowledge" (Mohanty, 2000: 31). Therefore there is no single frame that unites these experiences and histories, which implies that there is no privileged representation of reality, nor is there a language in which the truth about the real world can be confidently asserted (Hawkes, 1992). Thus, a fully objective perception of individual entities is not possible as any individual is bound to create something out of what he or she observes (Berger, 1984). Hawkes (1992: 17) notes that the true nature of things does not lie within the things themselves, but rather "in relationships, which we construct and then perceive between." In other words, experience alone is not a reliable source of knowledge because it is a social construction that is fluid in nature and thus cannot be a foundation of social identity.

The unconscious shifts in the social imaginary of a global system are producing changes in identity and culture that are beyond the boundaries of the conventional sociological frameworks, consequently destabilizing the foundations of the nation-state, which was built upon the rigid notion of sameness and difference. Bauman (1998: 38) argues that, "the present situation of the world looks rather as a file of scattered and disparate forces, sedimenting in places difficult to predict and gathering momentum impossible to arrest." The "dystopia" of late modernity has come about as a result of the transformations of social frameworks. They have moved away from the once-anchoring concepts of unification, which conveyed hope and determination of order making and a sense of belongingness, to a fluidity which is shaped by uncertainty and disorder. The impact of progressive waves of transnational movements has led to a distortion of time and space such that there are no longer any clearly defined identities. As Appadurai (1997: 26) contends, "the world we live in now seems rhizomic and even schizophrenic, which is calling for theories of rootlessness and alienation on one hand, and the fantasies (or nightmares) of virtual connectedness on the other." The general sense of the present condition is that a sense of security and belonging through communitarism has become unattainable.

People are thus left to deal with existential questions which once seemed to have concrete answers. The general awareness of this phenomenon has transcended into the *angst* of modern society.

Although the postmodernist debates on the theoretical ambiguities of identity have gained much credence, socially embedded essentialist notions have been and are still serving as the fundamental organizing principle of human conducts. Chambers (1994: 25–26) explains:

> Still, I would suggest, we are beginning to learn to act in the subjunctive mode, 'as if we had' a full identity, while recognizing that such a fullness is a fiction, an inevitable failure. It is this recognition that permits us to acknowledge the limits of ourselves, and with it the possibility of dialoging across the subsequence differences… This fictive whole, this 'I' as Nietzsche would have it, a life-preserving fiction, one that conserves us, and saves us from the discontinuities of the unconscious, from schizophrenia, self-destruction and the entropy of madness. It is this knot, the interminable tying together of the stories across the 'resistance to identity at the very heart of psychic life,' that holds us together.

The fact is that not only is identity imposed, prescribed, and bestowed by the other, but for many people identity also feels "real" and is a source for making sense of their social experience. Since collectivized notions of identity are crucial in giving meaning to everyday life their impact should not be underestimated. As Mohanty (2000) argues, a good theory of identities does more than simply celebrate or dismiss the various uses of identity; rather, it provides explanation of where and why identities are disabling *and* where and why they are enabling.

Relational Nature of Identity

Cultural identity (or any identity) gains its significance by relational positioning through the local and global settings of life. Such conditioning is based on the authentication process of labeling and representation of the "other" through essentializing cultural attributes (Pickering, 2001). But the qualification of such constructed "ideas" cannot be seriously studied without their "configurations of power," as negotiation of racial identities involves a hegemonic relationship with the Other. As Said (1978: 12) rightly points out, "the world is made up of two unequal halves, Orient and Occident" and yet these collective entities do not have any ontological stability as each is made up by the identification of the Other.

Underlying this construction of identity categories is the ongoing sense of how the self conceives of itself and labels itself (Giddens, 1990), which intersects with three interacting processes—that is, how we perceive ourselves to be, who we want to be perceived as, and what the other perceives you to be. Paradoxically, the tendency is to focus on that which divides the "self" from the "other," yet to focus on difference is something we all share (Sax, 1998). Such a process of othering is based on "allowing the other an apparent aura" which inherently involves the calculation of relationship between the self and the other (Trinh, 1991: 186). A person's identity will vary depending on the context and the questions asked of identity in a particular instance, and in this respect, a postmodernist perspective argues that a fully objective perception of individual entities is not possible as any individual is bound to create something through relational positioning between the "self" and the "other." Identities are therefore not simply established by the "facts" of an individual but rather by the perceptions of these socially constructed "facts." In other words, cultural identities in some ways are "fictitious" because the selves they claim to represent cannot be pinned down.

The instability and heterogeneity of identity have prompted critiques of the essentialist conception of identity where the tendency is to posit one aspect of identity such as "race" as the sole determinant constituting the social meaning of an individual's experience. Identities are constituted differently in different social and historical contexts as discussed previously; so, for example, a working class "Chinese" woman living in mainland China might experience Chineseness very differently from a middle-class "Chinese" housewife in Australia. Even if the two women were living in close proximity to each other—for example, the Shanghainese house helper/maid and the Hong Kong immigrant housewife living in Canada—their experiences of Chineseness will be different because of their social status. Furthermore, if both women were living in Australia but in different historical times, their experiences of Chineseness would also be very different. An obvious comparison would be between women living in the early 1900s during the era of the White Australian Policy as compared to Chinese women presently living in Australia where the official policy is one of multiculturalism. As such, it is difficult to describe coherently the social meanings inscribed in those experiences in the same terms, which suggests social meanings attached to "race" (or ethnicity, depending on the context) are invariably different. These examples illustrate that, contrary to an essentialist view, collective identity categories are neither static nor homogeneous.

The heterogeneity and relational nature of identity can be further understood through group membership. A person can concomitantly belong to different social groups, which combine with and mutually constitute one another. This idea was illustrated by our informant George—a gay Australian-born Chinese:

> I figured that being gay has given me another dimension. I am a gay Australian and I am a gay Chinese. I can identify with an even broader community of people…There used to be just an Australian gay community. I now realize that I am not alone in this world anymore. I am now a person that belongs to a wider international Asian network of gay people.

The meaning of membership in one group, such as maleness, could mean something different in another group, such as Chineseness, or yet another group, such as homosexuality. The consequence is that one cannot understand the self as the mere sum total of just so many separate parts (maleness + Chineseness + homosexuality), but rather it is the reciprocal influence of different parts. Hames-García (2000: 105) explains the totality of such relations in the establishment of the self:

> Politically salient aspects of the self, such as race, ethnicity, sexuality, gender and class, link and imbricate themselves in fundamental ways. These various categories of social identity do not, therefore, comprise essentially separate 'axes' that occasionally 'intersect.' Such 'salient aspects' of the self expand one another and mutually constitute each other's meaning.

Thus, the subjective experience of any social group's constituent membership depends fundamentally on relations to memberships in other social groups. Fluidity stimulates the fusion of identity and movement where the central question arises: How do individuals interpret, construct, and reconstruct themselves and the culture of which they are a part (Anderson, 1999; Chun, 1996)?

Indeed the way in which identity is established largely depends on how the self and the other are interpreted. Interpretation and construction of identity depends fundamentally on relations of power between social groups. The authority of relational positioning is highlighted by Chow (1998: 12) in her assessment of the significance of the Chinese language:

> For the white person, in other words, competence in Chinese is viewed as a status symbol, an additional professional asset; for the Chinese person, a competence in Chinese is viewed rather as an index to existential values, of which one must supply a demonstration if one is not native Beijing. And of course, if one is not a native Beijing and thus not bonafide by definition, this attempt to prove oneself would be a doomed process from the beginning.

The social expectations percolating from a particular identity—whether "white" or Chinese—are subjected to relational positioning which changes according to social contexts and situations. The significance of an essentialized characteristic—in this instance, language—is valued differently: for the "white" person it is a status symbol, whereas for the Chinese it is an index of existential values. Because identities are constructed through relational positioning, there is no objective or essential part of an individual that can be considered as a concrete identity. Identities evolve through interactions and therefore are always in a state of being reconstructed and reshaped. As such, identities should always be considered in context. However, this does not necessarily make them less real to the participants.

Accepting Diversity, Accepting Solidarity

Although the postmodernist approach is useful in understanding the constructed nature of identity and in contextualizing the present global condition where boundaries of collectivities seem to be increasingly blurred, it has not adequately carried out the important task of evaluating the political implications of identity. The major contradiction of the postmodernist approach is that its celebration of difference unintentionally creates a kind of universalizing sameness such that we are all marginal. Dunn (1998: 29) explains:

> Unfortunately, despite a growing rejection of identity politics in favor of a politics of difference, a postmodern move intended to avoid essentializing and stabling connections, difference has remained inadequately theorized. In most postmodern writing, difference has become another essentialism and universal, whether through inclusionary or exclusionary strategies.

To hold the kind of skepticism toward experience as the postmodernists have pursued would lead to a strange conclusion that the experiences of members of societies are irrelevant to explain their moral and political growth (Mohanty, 2000).

Although the postmodernist argument that identities are not homogeneously determined by any one social collectivity is correct, it however misses the important point that social collectivities such as "race" and "ethnicity" are relevant to the construction of identities. The irony is that postmodernism cannot conceive a way to ground identities without essentializing them.

As highlighted previously, identity is conditioned through ongoing interactions between the "self" and the "other" which involves a process of relational positioning. People can identify a person of Chinese background because of certain predefined signifiers—Chineseness is not Englishness, not Frenchness, and so on. The boundaries of inclusion and exclusion are thus based on essentialist constructs which are vital elements in shaping and giving meaning in social lives. Thus, cultural identity is rarely a question of who one is as an individual, despite appearances to the contrary, but always of who we are, as a group (Chun, 1996). The substance of any identity is based on the reality that individual security can only be attained in a social setting in which the security of one individual depends on one's association with others (Carter, 2004). Scholars such as Ang (on Asianness) and McKinney (on Whiteness) theorize on the basis of identities which are innately tied to the social collectivities such as ethnicity and gender that make up their individual social location, and this contradicts the postmodernist rejection of identity. In this respect, essentialist or collective identity categories provide important modes of articulating and examining significant correlations between lived experience and social location.

The postmodernist approach lacks an analysis of how the social categories that make up one's social location are relevant to one's experience as well as how those experiences inform cultural identities. The major limitation of postmodern perspectives on theoretical collectivities then is its inability to sufficiently account for the social and historical specifications of ethnicity and race and their relation to cultural production (Nguyen, 2000). Such a critique of the postmodern perspective of identity is opportune and relevant as it highlights the significant weaknesses in the postmodernist framework by drawing attention to the intellectual and political limitations of employing such a framework in the racial context.

In short, the limitations of both the essentialist and postmodern approaches have tended to overestimate or underestimate the political salience of actual identities. As Moya (2000a: 7) points out, neither "essentialist" nor "postmodernist" theories of identity are able to adequately analyze the epidemic status and political salience of any given identity or provide the resources to ascertain and evaluate the possibilities and limits of different identities. We argue that despite the ambiguities of identity, essentialist notions *still* serve as the basis of the social organization of human beings—something which has been largely unaccounted for in the postmodernist literature. It must be emphasized that we are not attempting to rehabilitate an essentialist notion of identity—the critiques and fallacy of essentialism have been well explored. What we propose here adheres to Moya's (2000a, 2000b) argument, which is to acknowledge how social categories of "race" and "ethnicity" function in individual lives without constricting individuals to those social collectivities. Instead of delegitimizing essentialist identities as the postmodernists have pursued, it is more fruitful to examine the strategic forms of essentialism; that is, to seek an understanding of how individuals construct and deal with social determinants which are "real," and therefore binding, in everyday life. Thus, as Alcoff and Mohanty (2006: 6) articulate, the theoretical issue concerning identities "is not whether they are constructed but what difference different kinds of construction make." In this respect, we argue the negotiations of Chineseness across the life course can result in varying life trajectories; therefore, recognizing its changes has the promise of enhancing the understanding of the "real" impact of identity on individual lives.

Identities are not simply imposed by society, as individuals also construct their own identity that enables them to better understand and negotiate the social world. Individuals will internalize and enculturate the social norms and values of the particular cultural group that they belong to. As Kuah-Pearce (2006: 225) maintains, they will "interrogate and engage in not only the material but also the ideological orientation of the cultures and structures of the society that they are in." As such, identities are the locus by which social, political, and cultural constructs are played out, reinforced, and sometimes challenged. "Social identities can be mired in distorted ideologies, but they can also be the lenses through which we learn to view our world accurately" (Alcoff & Mohanty, 2006: 6). It is thus a false dilemma to suppose that we should accept pernicious uses of identity or pretend they do not exist.

Chinese as Identity

In their habitual obsession with Chineseness, diasporic theories often encounter a kind of cultural essentialist ideal that draws an imaginary boundary between China and the rest of the world—a fascination with an authenticity that can only originate from China. Although increasing emphasis is placed on cultural differentials, the persistence of essentialist ideology still resonates in diasporic discourses. The theorization of Chineseness often entails the notion of "cultural China," which assumes that Chinese diasporic communities do have in common certain cultural symbols and that they originated from China. Scholars have insisted that Chinese diasporic communities perform different Chinese cultural practices in different localities and that the localized Chinese tradition of a diasporic community is the Chinese tradition that has become localized or that is locally created. Although this perception assumes volatile realities of ethnicities by acknowledging the variations of "Chinese" cultural practices throughout the world, the emphasis on China as the original source contradicts the essence of change and flow of modernity. It highlights a fascination, even romance, with a pure and authentic culture that must originate from China. Such discourse is a modified claim of homogeneity, but one that is made through notions of a cultural China.

The process of decentering, pivotal to the development of diasporic theory, has been articulated in Tu's (1994a) collection entitled *The Living Tree: The Changing Meaning of Being Chinese Today*. This collection challenges the holistic boundaries that normally define Chineseness and encapsulates a notion of "cultural China" by emphasizing the periphery as the center. Tu (1994b: 13) argues that cultural China consists of three continuous interacting universes: first, mainland China, Taiwan, Hong Kong, and Singapore; second, overseas Chinese communities; and third, the international communities of intellectuals and professionals generally concerned with China-related matters. These universes refer to a common interest in a single cultural sphere which transcends socially constructed boundaries. It attempts to decenter the discourse of a geopolitical China by emphasizing the "periphery as the center" in making sense of what it means to be Chinese in the present world. In Hsu's words (1994: 240):

> The center, be it geographic, geopolitical, social-economic or even cultural-ideological possesses a gravitational force which pulls from the peripheries whatever else are scattered therein … This force in turn causes the formation of new spheres of peripheries by influencing elements and resources scattered around it.

While this notion of a "new" kind of cultural space challenges the traditional centrist conception of Chinese identity insofar as it aims to refute the static and rigid, the stereotypical and conventional definition of "Chinese," the orientation toward a discourse of "cultural China," is in itself ironic. The privileging of the periphery—the diaspora—is nevertheless constructed within the boundaries of a shared cultural background and common ancestry. Ang (1998: 230) argues that Tu's notion of "cultural China" as a discourse is "motivated by another kind of centrism, this time along notionally cultural line."

The presence of "cultural China" in relation to the "older center" is similarly highlighted in the concept of *huayi*, which designates people of a variety of nationalities who are ethnically and culturally "Chinese" (Wang, 1991a). A number of scholars have maintained that the study of diasporic Chinese today must take into account of the historical and cultural experiences of those who left China in the early periods, as their descendants formed the majority of those who are still identified as "Chinese," however defined (Cohen, 1994; Elvin, 1994; Wang, 1991b, 2000). The general suggestion is that although the meaning of being Chinese is continually changing, there are still "core" characteristics—"the fruits of 3,000 years of continuous history"—embedded in the notions of Chineseness today (Wang, 1991b: 3). While acknowledging the historical significance in identity formation, the current conception of diasporic Chinese nevertheless indicates another kind of essentialism accentuated by collectivized notions based on common ancestry and a shared cultural background. As forms of uncertainty characterize the world today, the fantasy of a "pure" culture warrants a discerning reassessment.

Within the parameters of diasporic Chinese studies, there is the persistence of an essentialist approach adopted by some scholars toward their objects of study. Even in a period of what Bauman (2000) terms "liquid modernity" where concepts of "race" and "ethnicity" are being delegitimized because of their ontological and political limitations (Moya, 2000a), essentialism continues to resonate under the guise of "progressive" theoretical discourse (Chow, 1998). Despite the ambiguities of the concept of Chineseness, the image and reality of it is creating a sense of unity among members of the Chinese diaspora. Gilroy (2004: 99) explains the process of unification as "… a fundamental part of how [people] comprehend their kinship—which may be an imaginary connection, though nevertheless powerful for that." The distinctiveness of identity is that it is able to create an imaginary community that can be transformed into notions of solidarity. Thus the concept of "Chinese" reflects the shared essentials of race, ethnicity, and culture which make binding (and blinding) connections possible.

Authenticating Chineseness

In exploring the hegemonic discourse of "Chineseness," an important question that has become necessary in understanding the experience of diasporic Chinese is "Who is and who is not Chinese?" The pigtail in Thailand, for example, which Skinner argues as an assumed symbol of being Chinese, is in fact not an outward manifestation or a signifier of being Chinese. Tejapria (2001)'s excellent analysis that scrutinizes Skinner's arguments on the pigtail as a signifier of Chineseness during the late nineteenth and early nineteenth centuries of Siam, points out that the Chinese were never considered foreigners as long as they were subordinate to the social order of the phrai-kingly state. In addition since only Chinese could smoke opium, many non-Chinese faked their ethnicity by having a pigtail in pursuit of such interests. The pigtail as ethnicity is an invention—a social construction that is subjected to transformation and negotiation.

The establishment of racial collectivities is essentially based on naturalized and idealized notions of a socially constructed community which Anderson (1983) describes as an "imagined community." This process inherently involves some form of stereotyping which is an evaluative form of labeling and representation of the "other" through imposing order, and fixing meaning as natural and given (Pickering, 2001). As Kibria (1998: 942) contends, "because racial membership is widely believed to be given as a biological matter, the presumed traits of race and the institutional conditions and inequalities with which they are intertwined, can also be seen as natural, inherent." As such, the general determination of "what is" and "what is not Chinese" is predicated on the hegemonic discourse of authenticity which is inevitably associated with racial markers. The collective habit of associating "markers" with the notion of "Chinese" assists in defining racial boundaries and they become the authoritative stamp of authenticity—an inevitable hierarchy of cultural representations. Ang (2001: 30) explains:

> Chinese identity becomes confined to essentialist notions of Chineseness, the source of which can only originate from China, to which the ethnicized Chinese subject must adhere to acquire the stamp of authenticity.

The lingering pervasive hegemony of authenticity creates a hierarchical classification that stratifies the position of the diasporic Chinese given their embeddedness in a larger system of power. The distinguishing feature of such racial markers is that they reflect relations of power, in particular the ability of the dominant group to construct and impose identities upon others (Kibria, 1998).

The diaspora literature has generally argued that the collectivized notion of "Chinese" has been continually constructed and reconstructed as a result of the lingering dominant hegemony of Western culture (Ang, 2001; Chow, 1998), and the discourse of Chineseness often reflects stereotyping of ethnic subjects externally imposed by the mainstream recognition of non-Western representations. The way in which the West affirms its moral supremacy is precisely by way of ethnic, national labels and the implication on ethnic minorities, Chow (1998: 4) argues, is a continual struggle for recognition:

> Against the systematic exclusivism of many hegemonic Western practices, the ethnic supplement occurs first and foremost as a struggle for access to representation while at the same time contesting the conventional simplification and stereotyping of ethnic subjects as such.

Even when such "access" to the mainstream society is achieved, representations are continually constructed under the influence of Western hegemony. To this extent, knowledge of the Chinese culture and civilization often becomes the preeminent basis for establishing a Chinese identity for the diasporic community. This undeniably is associated with the spoken language (as well as other cultural forms such as physicality and food).

However, it is also important to consider that although racialized collectivities are stratified by Western ascriptions, in-group members also play an important role in establishing their own hierarchy of identities. Kibria (1998: 940) explains:

> By definition, given their embeddedness in a larger system of power, racial categories reflect the externally imposed designations or assignments of dominant groups upon others. But racial definition is also shaped by the action of the categorized group itself. That is, within the limits of prevailing structure of opportunity and constraint, racialized groups work to shape their own identities.

As such, we suggest it is equally important to question the politics of recognition that is shaped by the action of the categorized group itself. The theorization of Chineseness in other words would be incomplete without a concurrent problematization of Chineseness within the stratified position of "Chinese" within the Chinese diaspora.

Ethnic identity and ethnic relations are far more dynamic than the rigid poles of ethnic purity. Inquiries that focus on ethnic purity or complete assimilation shadow the centrist conception of the Chinese identity insofar as it still conceptualizes "Chinese" within the conventional static and rigid structure. We therefore seek to examine in this book the politics of recognition and the social significance of markers of identity in different contexts and situations.

Chineseness and Language

As we argued in the preceding chapter, language is often articulated to determine one's connection with one's identity and is also seen as a link to one's cultural heritage. Tan (2004b: 122) suggests that the literacy of diasporic Chinese is vitally significant for their negotiation of Chineseness. Those who were educated in

Chinese and are literate in Chinese can have access to and are in greater touch with the historical and cultural heritage of China. The ability to speak and write Chinese denotes a source of "superiority." Tan suggests, for this group, when they visit places in China, they have intimate associations:

> In the first place, the Chinese perceives China as the land of his ancestors and a land of his very civilization. Secondly the Chinese-educated Chinese does not just do sight-seeing. The historical places in China remind him of certain places of Chinese history which he has read about. They may remind him of certain poets and their poems, or of certain heroes and sages which he has become familiar with through reading. In this respect, the Chinese-educated people of Chinese descent have certain cultural similarities with other citizens of China but the similarities end there. Subjectively, the ethnic Chinese perceive themselves as people of different nationalities or as not belonging to China.

Underlying Tan's argument is the assumption that the "Chinese-educated people of Chinese descent" share similar connections with China because of their educational background and language ability. Their ability to read Chinese means that they can have access to the historical and cultural heritage of China (ibid: 122). For illiterate Chinese, Tan (2004b: 122) has this to say:

> For the illiterate, Chinese is merely the land of their ancestors and they may have historical memory of ancestral site there or even be proud of their ancestral land. For those who are familiar with the historical and literary tradition of China, China of course means more. While those not literate in Chinese may have learnt about the history and even literature of China, the Chinese-educated generally know more and feel more intimate with the historical and literary traditions of Chinese; they have their great cultural identification with the overall civilization of China. There is a difference between one who merely admires the beauty of a historical site and one who thinks about a certain Tang poem (for instance) upon seeing the sites or monuments. The cultural identities of the Chinese are very much influenced by their language of literacy.

To Tan, "cultural identification" and intimacy with China are dependent upon literacy, and as such language ability and those who are literate will have much closer affiliation and thus are more Chinese than those who are illiterate. However, we would argue that this assumption between language and identity is fallacious.

Take for example co-author Ngan who cannot read and write Chinese. Although she is not fully literate in the Chinese language, she nevertheless embraces Chineseness wholeheartedly which can be demonstrated by her research interest in Chinese diasporic communities and perhaps even more strongly, by her return to her homeland in Hong Kong despite growing up in Australia. When she was a child, her parents perceived language as a skill, a practical matter, rather than a source for cultivating Chineseness. Ngan migrated to Australia from Hong Kong as part of an astronaut family at the age of 7, so her Chinese language level was around the Primary 2 level when she departed. In the first couple of years after arriving in Sydney, her parents ensured that she concentrated on learning English as they didn't want her to fall behind in her schooling. Her father in particular felt it was more important to master at least one language fully than to be only half-way competent in two languages. Nevertheless, at home they would converse in Chinese, watch Chinese movies, and her mother would also read traditional Chinese poems, which contributed to her continued maintenance and cultivation of Chineseness.

It was only after a few years from their arrival in Australia that Ngan's mother encouraged her to attend Saturday Chinese school because she felt bilingual skills would be an asset for her daughter's future. However, because Ngan had stopped learning Chinese characters for several years, she was much further behind in written Chinese than her friends who left Hong Kong at an older age and therefore had much better language skills. Most of her peers at school also went to the language school that she attended but due to her language level Ngan was always sent to classes with children much younger than her, while the rest of her peers attended the same class together. As a young adolescent striving for conformity and belonging, being separated from her peers was emotionally dispiriting—a situation which was exacerbated by the fact she was also the odd one out in class (in terms of physical size and age as the other children were much younger). As a result, she did not want to attend these Chinese lessons. From her mother's perspective, while she would have liked her daughter to learn Chinese, driving her to and from Chinese school was an extra chore on top of the many household responsibilities that she had as a lone parent and so she did not insist on Ngan continuing her classes. From her father's perspective, he preferred his daughter to learn traditional Chinese because it was the written form in Hong Kong. To him traditional characters are more "authentic," but the school that Ngan attended only taught simplified Chinese. The combination of these factors discouraged Ngan from pursuing Chinese.

Certainly Ngan's attachment to Australia and her inability to read and write Chinese often situated her in a peculiar zone of in-betweenness, of not being an Australian, who by implication should be white, nor being Chinese who "by definition" should be literate in the Chinese language. However, intimate relations with the Chinese heritage have been unconsciously established through a variety of channels such as transnational family ties and social networks maintained with the homeland, movies and popular music about China, childhood memories and dreams, authentic Chinese food cooked at home, and the routine practice of Chinese festivals. Relations with homeland involve not only education and literacy but also other factors such as memories, emotions, desires, nostalgias, imaginations, family ties, even innocence. The prevailing theoretical framework of using language as a centering device for cultural attachment must thus be contested because of what it lacks.

It is interesting to note that in Tan's analysis of the Babas in Malaysia he contradicts himself about language as an important source of cultural identification. The Babas, who identify themselves as Chinese Peranakan, are descendants of some of the earliest Chinese settlers who married Malay, Siamese, and Balinese women. This category of Chinese Peranakan speaks Baba Malay as their language and writes English, and due to the loss of their original Chinese language, the Babas place much emphasis on traditional Chinese customs and religion, or at least their adaptations of them. The point of interest is that while language is a crucial symbol of ethnic identity, its loss does not necessarily mean the loss of an ethnic identity. Tan argues that the Babas have remained Chinese despite not speaking any Chinese dialects. In fact, since it is an adaptation or reinterpretation, it could be, again, an invention. While the Chinese label persists, the meaning of that label has changed as the Babas become *a different kind of Chinese*—one that does not fit neatly into the collectivist paradigm of Chineseness. Subjectively, whether one speaks a Chinese language or not does not make one more or less Chinese, as there are different ways of "being Chinese." Tan (ibid: 133) himself concludes that, "while language is a crucial symbol of ethnic identity, its loss does not necessarily mean the loss of an ethnic identity." However, despite their self-identification as "Chinese," the Babas are often confronted with derogatory attitudes by the wider Chinese community. Because of their language loss, their non-Baba Chinese friends often tease them as not being real Chinese, as being fake Chinese. Due to adaptation, integration, and localization with local communities through time, the identity of diasporic Chinese often contradicts stereotypical notions of "Chineseness," thus highlighting the fact that language ability as a centering device of Chineseness is problematic.

The pervasiveness of the diasporic imagination of "being Chinese" through language ability is articulated in Ang's (2001: 30) semi-autobiographical paper:

> So it was one day that a self-assured, Dutch, white, middle-class, Marxist leftist, asked me, 'Do you speak Chinese?' I said no. 'What a fake Chinese you are!' was his only mildly kidding response, thereby unwittingly but aggressively adopting the disdainful position of judge to sift 'real' from 'fake' Chinese.

From this excerpt, it is evident that to a "white" person, competence in Chinese is an index to the existential value of someone who is "Chinese." Such then is a paradoxical construction of "Chineseness" in terms of a system of values that arises with Westernized ascriptions. In such cases of language loss, one would attend to Ang's (2001: 30) argument that it "is a condition that has been hegemonically constructed as a lack, a sign of loss of authenticity." However, what Ang seemingly misses out is that although the collectivized notion of "Chineseness" has been continually reconstructed as a result of the still dominant hegemony of the Western culture, the process of authentication is also shaped by the collusion or cooperation of in-group members. As such, one could also speculate if Ang would have reacted differently if the question had been asked by, say, a person from Beijing.

Many diasporic Chinese who don't speak Chinese when in China are judged in a similar way. Consider the inherent racial prejudice based on essentialized ideals toward Chinese returnees in Hong Kong. Ngan was looking for a job at a university in Hong Kong after her return to her native place. During the interview she was asked if she could read and write Chinese, to which she replied that she does not. She then learned from a reliable source that she did not get the job because she (a Chinese person) could not read and write Chinese. The job was eventually given to a mainland Chinese, an authentic, "real Chinese" who speaks Mandarin. Of course, one could easily dismiss racial bias with reasons related to competencies, skills and the necessity of Chinese fluency, but the fact that similar and even higher ranking positions in Hong Kong's several universities have been offered to white people who do not speak, read, or write Chinese, and that this was the main point for their rejection of Ngan's application, highlights a double racial standard faced by some Chinese returnees in Hong Kong. There is a cultural expectation and demand by in-group members that a Chinese must be literate in the Chinese language. Returnees, particularly immigrants' children who grew up overseas and thus are not fluent in the Chinese language, are jeopardized by a double expectation that is only placed upon Chinese-looking people. This "racial incident" invokes the specter of "internal colonialism."

The standardization of the Chinese language as Mandarin is another aspect that highlights the limits of the theoretical framework of Chineseness. A seemingly simple question of "what is standard Chinese?" quickly draws our attention to the complexity of Chinese diasporic politics. Most commonly, Mandarin has been adopted as the official language and its hegemony can be displayed by its authority over all other Chinese dialects (Chow, 1998). However, there are a multitude of other "subordinate" dialects' that are spoken by the Chinese population within and outside China. An excerpt from an autobiographical essay by Tham (2001: 44), who has been living in diasporas, illustrates this phenomenon:

> I personally thought that the people from the Chinese embassy were different from us, because the embassy staff spoke to us in Mandarin, which most of us local Chinese did not understand…I accepted that they were Chinese, but just as we considered ourselves a subset of the Chinese race, I considered them China Chinese.

The fluency of Mandarin has become a cultural authentication of Chineseness, a recognition that is certainly contestable. From Ngan's personal encounters, the usual form of "evaluation" of her "Chineseness" begins with the question of "do you speak Chinese?" Rarely, does she get asked about a specific dialect such as Cantonese or Chiu Chow. Speaking "Chinese" is almost unquestionably equated with speaking Mandarin, which is a stereotypical feature of being Chinese. The ability to speak the "Chinese" language—Mandarin only—is viewed as an index to the existential value of Chineseness. Moreover, as discussed above, Ngan's father's preference of traditional Chinese over simplified Chinese also illustrates a hierarchal stratification of Chineseness, where the former is seen as more authentic or desirable than the latter.

Chow (1998) argues that in Western societies, fluency in Mandarin has become a cultural authentication of Chineseness—a recognition that is certainly contestable. The concept of Chineseness does not generally entail knowledge of just any kind of Chinese language, but specifically competence in Mandarin. The standard speech that most "white" scholars will learn, when they intend to learn "Chinese," is Mandarin because of its ascription within the discourse of Chineseness. On the contrary, what Chow seemingly misses is that many foreign scholars choose to learn Mandarin among other dialects because of the practicality and advantages associated with fluency in the official language of China. Mandarin, but not dialects such as Cantonese, is often taught at universities. It is also the second most convenient common language transnationally for the Chinese worldwide—English being the first (Tan, 2004b).

The ideology that China is the land of the ancestors of the people of Chinese descent and the original source of Chinese civilization has both historical and cultural relevance to the Chinese everywhere. The lingering pervasive hegemony of authenticity creates a hierarchical classification that stratifies the diasporic Chinese. Therefore, we argue that it is also important to understand that, although racialized collectivities are stratified within a broader social spectrum where stereotypical identities are often imposed by the dominant groups, in-group members also establish among themselves their own hierarchies of identities. As such, within the prevailing rigid structure of identity, racialized categories not only reflect the wider ascription by the dominant groups—Western ascriptions, per se—but also reflect internal stratification (and discrimination) among as well as between in-group members.

Physicality and Recognition

Physicality has always been an existential condition for ethnic minorities, and one which has been hegemonically constructed as an initial sign of identity, regardless of the particularities of personal history[1] (Ang, 2001). This is particularly significant for diasporic Chinese who live in a Western environment where the mainstream society is dominated by "whites." In the Western world, the notion of Chinese is synonymously associated with Han Chinese, without regard to the other 55 Chinese ethnic minority groups who do not look stereotypically Chinese—round faces, short in build, and with "slanty" eyes. Such a process of unconscious labeling has become a usual practice in multicultural Australia where representations of Chinese people are often reinforced by the bombardment of media's manipulated images such as exotic Chinese banquets, "nerdy" Chinese students, and thrifty Chinese people. Such stereotypical representations limit the degree of cultural diversity implied by the boundedness of labels. As such, although multiculturalism has transgressed in favor of cultural diversity, ironically it is actually maintaining the boundaries between the diverse cultures it encompasses and also the boundaries circumscribing the nation-state as a whole. Ang (2001: 16) explains: "...multiculturalism is nothing more and nothing less than a more complex form of nationalism aimed at securing national boundaries in an increasingly borderlessly world." Although multiplicity has become a salient feature of identity, people still seem to have an expectation that you have to be either part of one group or another and you cannot be part of two or more. On such a platform, members of the diasporic community are forced to go back and forth between different identities—which situate them in a space of liminality.

Ang (2001) argues that for Australians of Chinese descent (as well as other "non-white" backgrounds), no matter how "Australian" or "Westernized" one feels, physical appearance—which includes facial features, skin color, and height—becomes the definitive racial marker. Language, we argue, is cultural as much as it is physical. When written, language is physical as "black" on white paper and audible when spoken. For some, this reinforcement may be natural while for others they may feel it is an identity imposed upon them. Confrontation with ethnicity is often inescapable in the face of an insistence on origin, which takes the form of this exchange:

Where do you come from?
Australia.
No, where did you *really* come from?

---

[1] By "personal history" we include factors such as length of residence, place of birth, and ethnic background.

"Australia" seems never to be an acceptable answer, and its instant rejection reveals at once that the question is not about hometowns. The repeated questions almost always imply, "you couldn't be from here," which equates nonwhites with aliens (Lee, 1999). Ang (2001: 29) described these inclinations of specificity as "the disturbing signals for the impossibility of complete integration (or perhaps naturalization is a better term), no matter how much I (pragmatically) strived for it." Ethnic identity is reinforced by external appearance, as cross-cultural borders cannot be easily transgressed, which alerts us to the underlying process of othering through differences.

Here, we would like to consider a personal incident encountered by Ngan that can be echoed by many individuals of ethnic minorities in the West. She was at a European restaurant in the lower North Shore region of Sydney with a group of ex-high school friends of "Chinese" descent. Perhaps more precisely, they were the "parachute children"[2] of Hong Kong "astronaut families" who left at the peak migration period of the late 1980s (Ho, Ip, & Bedford, 2001; Pe-Pua et al., 1996; Skeldon, 1995a). We will explain the point of such specification shortly. As with any other social gatherings, they chatted away in the most comfortable language shared by the group, which at that event was Cantonese. Looking rather annoyed, a "white" man (accompanied by several of his "white" friends) sitting across from their table, came over to them and asked them to keep their voices down. Although he might have genuinely felt they were loud and did not even think about racial prejudice, their reaction to his request was an immediate suspicion of racial discrimination. They were deviant in that context because the language they spoke was Chinese and the way they looked was Chinese. Perhaps that made them rather intolerable? If they were "white" and spoke English, would their behavior be less disturbing for this "white" gentleman? The dialectic of sameness and difference in this context involves a process of naturalizing the other into broad generic categories ("whiteness" or "Chineseness") based on physical attributes. Of course, similar encounters like this are shared by many people around the world, where migration has become an increasingly global phenomenon. Such confrontations could be seen as a sign of difference much like what Ang (2001: 28) called the "inescapably of Chineseness," inscribed as it was, on the very surface of our bodies and our language. This incident shows the potent effect of the physicality of language. One could further argue that such behavior percolates from the enduring hegemony of white supremacy. However, if the context had changed, if they were in a Chinese restaurant, inhabiting a "Chinese" space, Ngan would be quite certain that the gentleman would not have made such a request. As such, tolerance and social expectation are contextually, and situationally, based and the discourse is acted out by both sides. In other words, although racial categories are stratified within a broader social spectrum, they not

---

[2] The peak period of immigration from Hong Kong to Australia was around the late 1980s to early 1990s, before its handover to China in 1997. Many Hong Kong immigrants migrated as family units whereby one or both parents along with their children settled permanently in Australia. In many cases the father returned to Hong Kong for work purposes, while the rest of the family remained in Australia. The terms "astronaut family" and "parachute children" describe the family arrangement of these Hong Kong migrants in Australia (Pe-Pua, Mitchell, Iredale, & Castles, 1996).

only differ contextually but are also impacted by a dialectical process of othering, in which both sides play the game.

Comparably, we would like to narrate another similar experience where Ngan was dining in a fine Chinese restaurant in Sydney. Her friends brought to her attention a group of overseas Chinese tourists from the mainland, who were mixing lemonade with some fine red wine. (She was referring to the wine as "fine" because, when they ordered, they said loudly that they wanted the best wine of the house.) Cultural practices, as Tan (2004b) suggests, are recreated through transnational cultural flows together with local forces in different parts of the world as people construct new ways of living. Such differentiation in cultural behavior led Ngan to feel a desperate sense of disassociation, not from "Chinese" per se, but from a particular category of "Chinese" she saw as different from herself. While this is not the place to recapitulate modern Chinese cultural practices in detail, we highlight it here to underscore the complexity of recognition. Our point is not to criticize or make judgment about the supremacy of certain cultural practices—the purpose of such illustrations brings with it a shift in perspective such that, in differing contexts, different stereotypical identities are not only imposed by the dominant groups as in-group members also establish their own categorization of identities. In a broader social spectrum, due to the Western hegemonic construction of the Chinese imagery, those who "look" Chinese would be generically labeled as "Chinese" by Western observers. However, as illustrated before, the meaning of and the association with "Chineseness" invariably change for diasporic Chinese in different localities who are living with other Chinese. The contextual nature of Chineseness thus highlights the inadequacy of the prevailing paradigm of physicality as a determinant of the Chinese identity. Yet, unfortunately, its power and potency persist.

The current obsession with emphasizing Western hegemonic discourse in racial questions is very much an outgrowth of postcolonial theories. To confront Chineseness as a theoretical problem, it is not sufficient to only point to the Western ascriptions as such. In other words, the theorization on Chineseness would be incomplete without a problematization of Chinese identity as understood by in-group members within the broad framework of Chinese diasporic studies. As Gilroy (2004) asserts, there is an urgent need for a change in the social understanding of race, embodiment, and human specificity. A broader context of social identification through dialectics of sameness and difference needs to be considered in the politics of recognition.

Whether there is a "core" in Chineseness is debatable; what is more important is to understand the dynamics of identity and its social significance in different contexts. Thus, a broader context of Chineseness and its multidimensional nature must be addressed. Accordingly, our book does not see "Chineseness" in a static sense; a nonproblematized approach will not provide a deep understanding of the significance of identity. Chineseness is an "imagined" construct and *is inherently political as identity is always in context.* As such, if Chinese identity and its discourse are social constructions, why bother to question what they are? It is perhaps more pertinent to question what it takes to be recognized as "being and belonging" (see Levitt & Glick-Schiller, 2004) and the social significance of "being and doing Chinese" in different contexts.

Hybridity

The notion of hybridity has largely been formulated as a means to problematize the complex process of identity formation of recent migrant communities. In particular, it challenges the ideal of homogeneity embedded in early assimilation models which projects that, through a process of assimilation, ethnic and racial groups would be integrated into society's institutions and culture such that minority identities would eventually disappear (Cornell & Hartmann, 1998: 44; Tong & Chan, 2001c). Such a process of assimilation or what has otherwise been described as acculturation, Anglo-conformity, or conversion suggests the loss or negation of one culture because the migrant has been uprooted and has buried his previous identity. Rivas and Torres-Gil (1992: 94) argue that most ethnic groups will assimilate and acculturate by the third generation, thus becoming like members of the dominant population. In Thailand, for example, the popular opinion is that the Chinese tend to slant toward social assimilation rather than conflict. Skinner (in Tong & Chan, 2001c) argued that the majority of descendants of Chinese immigrants in each generation merge with Thai society and become indistinguishable from the native population to the extent that fourth-generation Chinese are, in all practical considerations, Thai. The combination of Thai government policies and a lack of formal Chinese education is alleged to have contributed to such a process.

In the Australian context, the idea was that a much wider group of people could become part of Australian society and be able to share the Australian way of life. While there was acceptance that complete assimilation might not be achieved in the first generation, as Markus (2001: 17) notes, "assimilation remained the long-term objective." Even as late as 1969, Bill Snedden, the minister for migration, suggested that, "integration implies and requires a willingness on the part of the community to move toward the migrant, just as it requires the migrant to move to the community." He was adamant that Australia must remain a homogenous culture with a single culture (Snedden cited in Markus, 2001: 17). The assumption is that a natural linear process occurs that eventually leads to complete integration into the mainstream society, and the consequent erasure of "ethnicity" such as Chineseness is perceived as the price of assimilation (Martin, 1978; Wilton & Bosworth, 1984). In common parlance, the perception is the more Australian one becomes, the less Chinese one will be.

However, due to transgressions of ethnic boundaries and dynamics of social environment, the formation of identities of diasporic communities is increasingly complex and cannot be defined simply in bounded homogenous notions. A number of studies have highlighted the liminal experience and hybridized identities of diasporic Chinese in Australia, with particular focus on first-, 1.5-, and second-generation migrants (Ang, 2001; Davidson, 2004; Pe-Pua et al., 1996). Tong and Chan's (2001a) research on Chinese migrants in Thailand demonstrate that contrary to Skinner's assertion of complete integration of Chinese by the fourth-generation, assimilation has not taken place. Ethnicity, they remind us, is both primordial and situational, expressive and instrumental, and is often used in the center of one's own ethnic group, in the private place, but it is also amenable to construction where the ethnic actor can strategize and manage their ethnicity according to situations in the public place. Challenging Skinner's ideas on the assimilation of Chinese migrants in Thailand, Tong and Chan (2001c: 34) argue:

> ... theories of assimilation often over-exaggerate the absorptive power of the majority group and its culture; oversimplify the process of social change in terms of its directionality and dimensionality; and tend to view minority groups in terms of the simplistic dichotomy of either having been assimilated or not.

While the notion of hybridity confronts and problematizes the unsettling boundaries of identities, the identity of later generations is still largely subsumed under the traditional models of assimilation, which expect ethnic identification to decrease over successive generations. Consequently, this has led to a lack of in-depth research and theorization on the identity formation of descendents of early Chinese migrants in Australia.

Moreover, contributing to the lack of research on different Chinese groups (and Asian groups), particularly the subsequent generations, is the general tendency of treating "Chineseness" and, in a broader sense, "Asianness," as a common label which connects or subsumes everyone of Asian descent (Gilbert, Lo, & Khoo, 2000). Subsequently, historical migration conditions and specific issues that different Chinese diasporic groups face within mainstream Australian society become subsumed under the homogenizing categories of "Chinese Australian" and "Asian Australian." This practice is problematic as it serves to reproduce and reinforce Oriental conceptions of "China" and "Chinese" and, more broadly, "Asia" and "Asians" already embedded in the mainstream Australian discourse, the latter *bracketing* all people of "yellow" skin together as a singular (as opposed to plural) group (Ang, 2001).

The diversity of life experiences throughout the life course is in itself made up of transitions which involve changes in identity, both personally and socially, thus opening up opportunities for behavioral changes resulting in varying life trajectories. Across the generations, the formation of identity takes place as part of an ongoing process in which certain aspects of the "original culture" are maintained or reclaimed while other aspects and expectations of the previous generation that appear irrelevant are modified, resisted, or discarded (Alba & Nee, 1999; Nagel, 1994). In this manner, subsequent generations reconstruct hybridized forms of Chineseness in ways of their own choosing that are relevant and meaningful to their identifications. Hence the image of a Chinese identity is a cultural product that can be established in various ways depending on one's social and cultural locations.

Hybridity as an idea and a concept has largely been formulated as a means to problematize the complex process of identity formation of recent migrant communities (e.g., Ang, 2001; Chan, 2011; Charney, Yeoh, & Tong, 2003; Davidson, 1991, 2004; Kuah-Pearce & Davidson, 2008; Ma, 2003). The postmodern literature maintains hybridity is a notion of crossroads and borderlands, which implies a blurring of boundaries as a result of unsettling of identities. The hybridity concept is often used as an analytical tool to explain the relational positioning of identity and to analyze complicated entanglements of identity and marginalization of many members of the ethnic minorities (Ang, 2001: 34). Ang (2001: 194), for instance, defines hybridity as "a means of bridging the multiple boundaries which constitute 'Asian' and 'Western' in identities as mutually exclusive and incommensurable."

Various perspectives of hybridity such as "double consciousness" (Gilroy, 1994; Nagata, 1979) and "third space" (Bhabha, 1991, 1994; Hall, 1996) have received much currency in understanding the multiple and liminal identities characteristic of members of diasporic communities, which shape social incorporation in fundamentally different ways. It has been acknowledged that diasporic communities often maintain a social and cultural foothold in two or more ethnic environments. More often than not they find themselves developing two or more identities in transnational spaces, which they learn to move between, from one to another. Their tolerance of different cultures and their mental agility can open up many new possibilities and the concept of "double consciousness" reveals the hybrid character of modern ethnicity and its profound effect on the diasporic communities.

The fluidity of ethnic and cultural boundaries is maintained through the interpretation of cultural phenomena in accordance with the requirements of a situation. On the one hand, the formation of identity is influenced by the degree to which families and ethnic communities draw on the social-control properties of ethnic boundaries and identity. In this respect, the family plays an important function in the construction and maintenance of ethnic identity through celebration of traditions and rituals and through the intergenerational influence of cultural values and morals. On the other hand, influences from the wider community can lead some immigrants, particularly immigrant children, to reject their family's ethnic identity while gravitating toward socially accepted lifestyles of the mainstream society (Wolf, 1997). Often the types of social networks outside of the home environment (such as friends from schools) have a direct impact on the establishment of identity. In this context, the experiences of marginality—of straddling two or more cultural contexts—become a necessary life condition (Chan, 2011).

While this postmodernist notion of hybridity represents a new kind of cultural space that challenges the traditional centrist conception of identity as a single entity, the orientation toward a discourse of "double consciousness" is in itself ironic. The privileging of multiple "groups" of identity is nevertheless constructed within the boundaries of a unified and collectivist paradigm. Such discourse is motivated by another kind of centrism—this time along the conglomeration of multiple groups of identities. As such this notion of hybridity still largely depends on the fact that an identification of where one fits in society is highly correlated to identity categories.

An alternative postmodern concept of hybridity problematizes boundaries and argues that they are an opening within which different elements encounter and transform each other. In this respect, hybridity is a dialectical identity construction with the original and its counter identity yielding a third new form of identity in a boundless site articulated by Bhabha (1991: 211) as the "third space":

> For me the importance of hybridity is not to be able to trace two original moments from which the third emerges, rather hybridity to me is the 'third space' which enables other positions to emerge. The third space displaces the histories that constitute it, and sets up new structures of authority, new political initiatives, which are inadequately understood through received wisdom.

To Bhabha, hybridity is not a consequence of other "pure" collectivities inter-mixed together. More precisely he explains that third spaces are "discursive sites or conditions that ensure that the meaning and symbols of culture have no primordial unity or fixity; that even the same signs can be appropriated, translated, and rehisto-ricized anew" (Bhabha, 1994: 37). In other words, the third space is a site of innova-tion where identity is negotiated and where a person's ambiguity, complexity, and hybridity are situated. This notion opens up possibilities for new structures of authority and for new interpretations of identity as temporary, dynamic, and fluid.

As such, an analysis of identity formation should not begin with two or more pure cultures and then a tracing of their historical movements of hybridization. While hybridity can be perceived as both the assemblage that occurs whenever two or more elements meet and the initiation of a process of change, we cannot take discussions of cultural difference as if there really were different cultures to be stud-ied discretely in the first place (Huddart, 2006: 126). Cultures are always conse-quences of historical process and they are fused by the movement of groups in different territories through time and space. Thus, according to this perspective, one can argue that Singaporean Chinese are in many respects a hybrid. This concept may be used to conceive the complicated entanglements of cultural boundaries—as highlighted in Ang's (2001: 194) experience:

> If I were to apply this notion of complicated entanglement to my own personal situation, I would describe myself as suspended in-between: neither truly Western nor authentically Asian; embedded in the West yet always partially disengaged from it; disembedded from Asia yet somehow enduringly attached to it emotionally and historically. I wish to hold onto this hybrid in-betweenness not because it is a comfortable position to be in, but because its very ambivalence is a discourse of cultural permeability and vulnerability which is a necessary condition for living together-in-difference.

Such "hybrid in-betweenness" is a new form of identity suspended in a space of liminality in which complicated entanglement of identity is positioned. The post-modern concept of hybridity also stresses that identity is not the combination, accu-mulation, or fusion of various components—rather it is an energy field of different forces (Anthias, 2001; Papastergiadis, 2000; Werbner, 1997). The emergence of a floating identity is a result of the combination of different forces which further exposes the limitations of essentialist social constructs.

Indeed this perspective of hybridity provides an alternative account to multiplic-ity. However, such an orientation toward a discourse of "in-between" is similarly as ironic as the previous discussion on the oscillation of identity. Contrary to Ang's analysis of hybridity that identity is a "complicated entanglement" such that it can-not be definitely defined, we argue that it is possible to develop reliable knowledge about the world and about how and where one fits into that world (Mohanty, 2000; Moya, 2000b; Nguyen, 2000). In Ang's situation, the way in which she positions herself in relation to "imaginary" cultural boundaries (suspended "in-between," nei-ther "Western" nor "Asian") demonstrates that she is clear about where she fits according to restricted essentialist categories, although the meanings of these con-structs themselves are dynamic. Nevertheless, these imaginary constructs are still serving as the organizing principle of life.

The analysis of the different processes of hybridity is purely in abstract theoretical terms, and individuals may experience variations of these processes. Some may identify with several cultural groups in a particular situation while feeling caught in-between at another time. Some may even feel that they do not belong to any cultural group at all. However, the manner in which members of diasporic communities position themselves according to specific collectivities suggests that essentialist structures *still* shape our perceptions of the real world.

As such, despite postmodernist attempts to delegitimize identities, collective notions *still* prevail in the carving of identities in daily life. We emphasize that in understanding identities we cannot totally dismiss the historical and social significance of cultural collectivities, as they are tools that enable us to account for the role of multiplicity in an enabling way. The fact is that identification of where one fits in society is *still* highly correlated to identity categories.

Moreover, hybrid identities are often presented one-sidedly, as negative struggles, as they exert a detrimental impact on social mobility. Quite certainly such negative experiences are undeniable for some. However, missing from the debates on hybridity is an interest in those who have accepted hybridity in their lives. In the subsequent chapters we will illustrate that, contrary to the common assimilationist assumption, subsequent generations continue to encounter complicated experiences of identity. The relevance of studying diasporic "Chinese"—in particular subsequent generations who often are identified as part of a distinctive minority—is that their racial and ethnic identities are frequently in a state of flux, situating them in a state of liminality. In many cases, regardless of their time of residence, they are continually viewed through a prism of otherness (Ang, 2001; Tan, 2004a). It is the very essence of such conflicting experiences that cultivates the analysis of identity constructions.

Gender, Sexuality, and Life Course Trajectories

Since Chineseness is a collective social construction, to a large extent "being Chinese" also means living within the "norms" of the Chinese life cycle, which is socially determined. As Kuah-Pearce (2006: 225) contends, "within a Chinese society that continues to embrace Confucian values, the social self is expected to conform and act to social expectations. The communal self is enculturated to fit into the cultural paradigm and enact roles expected of the self." In all societies including Chinese society, there is an insistence on social conformity, especially in the moral values and actions of their members. The self is thus subjected to various levels of pressure—to ensure that it falls within the social expectations of a "moral community."

Traditionally, ideologies of the Confucian social philosophy determined the roles and expectations at every stage in the life cycle of a Chinese. In the Confucian tradition, certain relations between family members are bestowed a position of paramount importance—in particular senior members of a family are accorded a wide range of powers in their relations with juniors. Both parties to a relationship are circumscribed by rules of correct behavior, which entail rights and responsibilities for each (Bond & Hwang, 1986). *Xiao* or filial piety, which principally defines children's moral duties to their parents, has been understood in the Chinese tradition as the root of morality and it is, in Weber's (1951: 157) words, "the absolutely primary virtue" which precedes all other virtues in China. The significance of *Xiao* in the lives of Chinese is similarly noted by Wang (1991c: 169): "Whatever else may be uncertain, there was no doubt that loyalty and filial respect were the duties par excellence in traditional China." Traditionally, through education and indoctrination, the younger members of the extended Chinese family learn and accept the responsibility that they will care for the financial and social wellbeing of the elderly members in their family. The elderly expect being taken care of as their right, and families face pressure from the wider community to meet their obligations. Such reciprocal relationships were and still are considered a distinctive Chinese family cultural value (Ryan, 2003: 64).

Gender ideology also differentiates the filial duty between sons and daughters. According to Choi (1975: 12), in a traditional Chinese cycle, marriage is perceived as an obligation of sons to their parents. One of the main purposes of marriage is the fulfillment of the sacred duty of producing male heirs for the perpetuation of the ancestor's lineage for the security of the parent's old age. The family, and particularly the parents of the husband, is the focus of life in traditional Chinese culture. It is considered that a woman not only marries, but that, as a wife, her primary responsibility is to take care of her husband's parents, even more than her husband (Williams, 1999: 10). In this way, it is particularly important for sons to marry a Chinese daughter-in-law who understands and upholds Chinese family roles. Marriage is often arranged by one's parents, as it is considered too important a duty to be left to the inexperienced young.

The focus on men and the importance of family lineage can also be found in the experience of Chinese migration to Australia. During the late 1800s, there was strong objection against the migration of women for the fear that the whole family would be lost, as the role of a married woman was to keep the family together (Choi, 1975: 12). As it happened, Chinese men migrated to the Australian goldfields in search of gold while their wives remained with their children in China, waiting for their husband's return with wealth and fortune. Men were expected to make money abroad and remit it back to their home villages in China to promote the interest of their lineage. The gender role of Chinese men as dominant income earners for the family and women as the keeper of the family, has persisted well into the contemporary era, where a similar pattern can be found in a recent type of immigration from Hong Kong to Australia. In these "astronaut families" the father returns to Hong Kong for business purposes, while the wife remains and looks after the rest of the family in Australia (Pe-Pua et al., 1996).

Due to the sexual ideology, Chinese women's economic and social contributions to migration were considered trivial as they were routinely viewed as dependents of male migrants or as a passive participant in migration (Ryan, 2003). Because of the inequality in the construction of sexuality, the two genders have not received the same proportion of visibility. Although it is obvious that there have been significant changes in social conventions about sexual roles through the women's liberation movement and policies of equal access,[3] etc., a persistence of traditional sexual ideology still remains deeply embedded—one which differentiates the behavior of males and females (Hochschild, 1989). The construal of "gender strategies" or gender-related decisions is deeply bound with the perpetuation of traditional gender ideology. Traditional sexual stereotypes are deeply engrained in culture and the extent to which sexuality is internalized can be highlighted by the persistence of gender roles from the past to the present. Chow (1991) writes that the internal self is already mapped out for a Chinese woman as 2,000 years of definitions, expectation and clichés have already determined what she always is. Thus, notions of sexuality have a direct impact on the carving of identities, which simultaneously affect choices that individuals make in their everyday lives.

More recently, the contemporary diasporic literature dealing with interracial relations has paid increasing attention to the gender imbalance and the objectification of Asian women who are often characterized by hyper-femininity and submissiveness. The focus has largely centered on the ambivalence of the Asian woman who is the objectified subject (Ang, 2001; Ip, 2002; Ryan, 2003). While it is crucial to understand the experience of the objectified, to adequately encapsulate the entirety of the self/other relations, objectifications within Asian communities are also necessary. Largely neglected in the literature are the attitudes of Asian men who are also part of the "gaze." The discourse of the White Australia Policy has led to a lowering of the social status of Chinese men, which has persisted into the contemporary era. There was a deliberate desexualization of Chinese men to keep them away from Anglo-Celtic women. The hegemony of White superiority ushers in an emergence of a subculture in which Chinese men are perceived as "not quite real men, as they fail the (Western) test of masculinity … particularly the 'macho' version" (Hibbins, 2006: 291). This marginalization is exacerbated by the typical feminized representation of Chinese men as physically smaller than "white" men, which is an example of hegemonic masculinity. In the case of sexuality, Chinese men are often depicted as asexual. As ambivalence pervades the daily life of diasporic subjects in multicultural societies, examination of ambivalent moments of both male and female subjects has much relevance in understanding the construal of identities.

Certainly there is a longstanding literature on the philosophy of Confucius and the western presentation of Asian women; the concern here, however, is to highlight its influence in Chinese familial values, gender ideologies, and the social roles

---

[3]Generalized notions of masculinity and femininity have implication not only in the way identity is negotiated but also in social research and public policies. In the public arena, gender implications can be highlighted by the perusal of equal access—whether it is gender, language, or culture—to government services and programs. However, simply applying fair treatment to all groups is insufficient as different gender groups may need more assistance to ensure more equitable outcomes because they have been historically disadvantaged—e.g., women trying to break into a traditionally male industry.

of individuals as they age. According to Chinese philosophy, age transition is perceived as a series of fixed states which imply social and moral obligations—and as a pattern that is to be repeated through the generations. However, what is the experience of those who never marry, are interracially married, or are homosexual, as well as those with disabilities who are nursed by their elderly parents? These individuals cannot be accounted for as part of the "normative" Chinese development as portrayed in the traditional paradigm. Furthermore, those who departed from China for a substantial period of time often found cultural values and gender identities regarding duty for the aged to be increasingly influenced by the cultural values of the host country. As Uhlenberg and Mueller (2003: 124) explain, "the significance of any specific family environment may vary markedly across societies and across time…" It is important to stress that no single Chinese identity is more authentic than others—the Confucius ideology only makes up part of the Chinese imaginary. Nevertheless, while the concept of Chinese identity is not neatly definable, there is indeed *a* singular notion of Chineseness, whatever that may be.

The experiences an individual has are likely to have been largely determined by his/her social location, which consequently influences the formation of an individual's cultural identity (Moya, 2000b). For example, there are different expectations for nonmigrant background children and for immigrants' children of Chinese families. Most of those with a migratory background develop better foreign language ability than their parents and are required to assist in daily communicative tasks, which supposedly would be done by adults. The change in social context means that children of migrants are taking on a certain responsibility at a much earlier age than is required by the social norm. This can be highlighted by the study conducted by Pe-Pua et al. (1996: 59) on Hong Kong astronaut families and parachute children in Australia: immigrant children have taken on a much larger amount of domestic responsibility in Australia compared with what was expected of them back home in Hong Kong—particularly if their mother could not speak English well. As children, they were taking up responsibilities such as banking, dealing with bureaucracy, and doing repairs around the house that normally were chores for the adults. Their experiences suggest that there is considerable variability in the ages at which individuals enter into new social roles. Riley, Abeles, and Teitelbaum (1982: 13) contend, "… aging must be seen as series of continually changing—and mostly changeable— experiences involving and often transforming individuals and society…" The formation of identity thus is closely linked with the different trajectories resulting from interactions with various factors (e.g., institutional, social, cultural) of an individual's life course.

It is well documented that a diversity of experiences and identities exist in different diasporic Chinese communities; thus it is important to understand that each Chinese society has its own distinctive cultural conception of Chineseness. Moreover, different generations and birth cohorts have also developed distinct cultural expressions, beliefs, and sense of belonging. In particular, we will demonstrate in later chapters that subsequent generations who are influenced by historical events and social contexts of local societies no longer live within the "norms" of the Chinese life. The once-clear and definite patterns of life have become uncertain as such, while new analytical frameworks are sorely needed to understand the complex nature of shifting cultural identities.

The theoretical orientation of the life course through life stages is a particularly useful framework for analyzing the hybridity of Chineseness of long-settled ABCs. This approach dwells on the diversity of experiences in the course of people's lives and focuses on the interpretation of different stages of life (see, for example, Alwin & McCammon, 2003; Elder, Johnson, & Crosnoe, 2003; Hareven, 1996; Hockey & James, 2003). The aging process is a significant resource through which individuals construct their biographical narratives as well as their interactions with others, which are intricately linked to the establishment of cultural identities and belongingness. Yet despite the importance of the aging process, there has been relatively little research on how ethnic identities of members of Chinese diasporic communities are, in practice, made sense of by individuals in relation to the wider social and cultural norms of aging. The few studies that have examined the relationships between life course and ethnicity include those by Rivas and Torres-Gil (1992), Levitt (2002), and Smith (2002). Social factors such as family, sociocultural context, gender, and sexuality bring with them cultural ramifications resulting in different life trajectories. These factors which surround the negotiation of identity within the life course must be considered to adequately comprehend how people shape their identity. We have adopted the life course orientation to which Chap. 6 turns, to understand the fluid and dynamic construction of Chineseness among long-settled ABCs.

Chapter 3
The Voice of a Woman: Doreen Cheong

*I believe that we all "don masks" throughout life with the only
distinction being that with maturity and experience, you become
more adept at identifying the occasions where you feel the need
to "don a mask" and the other instances where you feel there is
no necessity to "play a game."*

Doreen Cheong

Doreen Cheong

L.L.-S. Ngan and K.-b. Chan, *The Chinese Face in Australia: Multi-generational
Ethnicity among Australian-born Chinese*, DOI 10.1007/978-1-4614-2131-3_3,
© Springer Science+Business Media, LLC 2012

Before proceeding to our thematic analysis of data we gathered in long, in-depth interviews with our respondents, we shall present autobiographies of two Australian-born, long-settled ethnic Chinese, in this chapter and the next. Sociological biography is a powerful research tool which was first commented upon by Robert Merton (1988), who was joined by a group of American sociologists reminiscing on their academic careers and their coming-of-age as sociologists, in the book, *Sociological Lives* edited by Martha White Riley. Co-author Chan Kwok-bun (2005b) used the method in an autobiographical essay in which he retraced his life history, specifically in terms of what he called "racial incidents" or daily encounters with racism while he was a Chinese foreign student from Hong Kong, and later, a professor of sociology in French-speaking Montreal, Quebec, Canada. Chan, with co-author Ngan, who retraced her racial encounters as a 1.5-generation Chinese immigrant growing up and living in Sydney, Australia, and later as a "returnee" in Hong Kong, a society which was both familiar yet foreign to her, added a "new chapter" to his autobiography in one of the two prefaces to this book. In an intriguing and revealing manner, the sociologists and their respondents joined hands in interrogating their own life histories. While the ever-intruding sociologists are asking others about their lives, they cannot help being curious and inquisitive about their own ethnic and racial conditions. We write about others to know ourselves, this time aided by self-interrogation which is neither a natural nor a wanted thing, thus the occasional usage of therapy and psychoanalysis.

In this autobiographical chapter, our respondent Doreen—a fourth-generation Australian-born ethnic Chinese—recalls her school years when she strove hard to excel academically to gain the acceptance and approval of her white Australian school mates, to gain back an identity which was robbed of her, and to cope with the shame of being Chinese: different, inferior, the other. Her sense of shame did not vanish upon passing through the doorsteps of home. Behind closed doors, Doreen battled with being a girl in a Chinese family that placed boys on the pedestal in the name of family continuity. Racism outside the family and sexism inside it constituted a double jeopardy for her—a double otherness. Is Doreen Chinese or is she not? Both her family and white society insist she is though she might at times choose to be otherwise. Racial identities are socially bestowed, even imposed, inscribed, burnt onto your skin, like a Mark of Cain. Ethnic Chinese, at least during the days of Doreen's childhood and adolescence, disapproved of interracial marriages, being fearful of giving birth to "half-castes"—the racial hybrids who, in the Chinese parlance, were "neither humans nor ghosts," the marginal men and women who wanted to belong to the Chinese and white worlds but were rejected by both, thus their double victimization. As an expression, "half-caste" suggests a stance against fusion, hybridity, mix and match, and in praise of purity, noncontamination, nonpollution. The Chinese in the mainland have a long history of celebrating the pure, the uncontaminated—thus the national and historical phobia of cultural invasion or pollution; of mixed marriages. Hybrids lived lives in suspension and had "the worst of all possible worlds": as much as the Chinese were victimized by racism and social exclusion, they themselves were not particularly fond of mixing with their white neighbors either, and vice versa. The racial divide was as deep as it was visible as both sides colluded to keep building walls and putting up fences. As years, decades, even centuries went by, immigration, multiculturalism, trade, geopolitics, political economy, globalization, capitalism exerted their impact on race relations. Our respondent, Doreen, continued to speak about her role-playing behavior. One face, many masks. She dons the masks and puts on and off her persona, depending on the nature of her audience, inside and outside her home, her community. She performs ethnicity, or she performs Chineseness and Australianness. She rehearses, to strategize, to manage others' impressions of her, to cope, to increase her social desirability and respectability.

Performing or doing ethnicity, which stresses ethnicity or race is both a thing, thus a noun, which is hard to change (e.g., when will people all over the world, including Americans, stop calling Obama the black or half-black president?) but also a verb, meaning nonwhites are actively doing things—to survive, to excel, to "cope," to do the best they could under the circumstances, sometimes triumphantly, other times tragically. Nonwhites in history and all over the world do not take racism lying down so they "perform" or "do" ethnicity.

Doreen Cheong's Autobiography

"Sing Choy" … "Ching Woo" (Choy clan from the village of Ching Woo) were the four words that I was made to rote learn as a toddler. With these words etched indelibly on my mind from an early age, the die was cast to tie me inexorably to my Chinese ancestry and which, as I grew up, would give rise to the tensions resulting from being juxtaposed with very different values and customs…my Sydney world. Moreover, my physical appearance, and specifically, my face, was not Anglo-Australian and thus, it was essential, as has been so convincingly argued by Chan Kwok-bun (2005a), for me to adopt a "one face, many masks" approach so as to make a more socially desirable impression when I engaged with others.

Firstly though, I need to put my life's story into its chronological context, so let me begin by telling you about my paternal forebears. My great grandfather, Choy Yuen Gum, arrived in Sydney in the late 19th century from the village of Ching Woo which is situated over an hour's train journey from, and is west-central of, Guangzhou. This region is called Gu Yiu/Gao Yao and the people from this area traveled to Australia in large numbers and, it has been said, were the largest group of Chinese to settle in Sydney, prior to 1901. Their dialect was distinctive yet similar to Cantonese. It was only their able-bodied men folk who came; they being seen to be the best chance to earn sufficient monetary rewards to repatriate to China so as to take these families beyond their subsistence existence in the agrarian-based village. Many of these men left wives and extended families in China and, from what I have been told and observed, my forebears were Confucian in their upbringing and values. Children were required to pay respect to their parents, to their elders and traditions, and to display filial piety. This would manifest itself as obedience to the values and moral standards of their parents and in not questioning their viewpoints.

I believe that these long-held cultural traditions and values are the mainspring behind the collectivist nature of the Chinese psyche. It was accepted without questioning that sons looked after their aged parents, including often having the extended family all live under the same roof. Therefore, having many sons was seen to be very auspicious for a family. Moreover, there was much rejoicing if male children were born, as this would allow the father's name to be carried forth to the next generation. Sons were not only a type of social welfare insurance for parents in their old age but there were the practicalities arising from being another pair of hands to work in the fields. This favoring towards males could also translate to having the most nutritious morsels being served to them at dinner, readying them for the next day's hard work, and it was not unusual for the women to go hungry during the hard times. Recently, I have been given a genealogy chart covering eight generations of the paternal side of my family. However, the chart only names male descendants, with there being no female offspring listed.

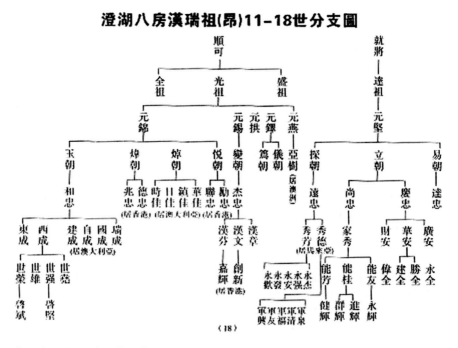

Genealogy chart of the Choy family with my father, War Choong, being the fourth generation after Zun Hor at the top.

Not being overly skilled in areas of Western-style work when he arrived in Sydney, my great-grandfather, Choy Yuen Gum, found work as a cabinet maker. During the late 19th and early 20th centuries, there were a plethora of cabinet-making workshops in Sydney, located around what is now Wentworth Avenue, East Sydney and Botany Road, Waterloo. Increasingly during the 1920s, the cabinet-making sector was becoming a non-viable industry, thus, the Gu Yiu Chinese looked for other employment opportunities. Many of them turned to market gardening, vegetable hawking or remaining in the countryside and establishing general stores. These "low level" occupations were the only roles available to the Chinese once gold digging was no longer practicable. This has parallels to the situation today where we see each new wave of non-white unskilled immigrants take up jobs at the lowest stratum of the labor market. Until after World War 2, it was the Chinese who were the ethnic group on the "lowest rung" of the occupational ladder.

My great-grandfather, Choy Yuen Gum, was a sojourner. He had no intention of settling permanently in Australia. After improving his economic circumstances, his plan was to return to his family and village in China, to spend the rest of his days there. His youngest brother, Choy Yuen Yin, also migrated here about the same time, and this seventh brother settled here, married an Anglo-Australian woman, had four children (a daughter and three sons, including twin boys) and lived until he was 97 years old. In the fifty years until the White Australia Policy was introduced in 1901, hundreds of thousands of Chinese came to Australia, and in 1881, for example, it is claimed that it was not unusual to have around 2000 Chinese arrive over a matter of weeks. This "flood" of Chinese immigrants gave rise to a xenophobic fear amongst the Anglo-Australian population, of being taken over by the "yellow hordes" from China. This was the basis for the stricter immigration laws, which included the requirement for new Chinese arrivals to sit for a "dictation test" in English, and the introduction of the White Australia Policy in 1901.

Great grandfather, Choy Yuen Gum (centre) with his son, Choy Jerk Chiu on his right hand side and a Choy nephew on his left (photo taken in the 1890s).

Prior to 1901, some Chinese men brought their Chinese wives to Australia and raised their children here. Interestingly, many of these Australian-born Chinese children were often taken back to China so that they could be become familiar with their Chinese roots and culture. Some males stayed for many years, marrying Chinese girls before returning to Australia. On the other hand, as eligible single Chinese women were a rarity in Australia, many Chinese men like my Uncle Yuen Yin, the seventh brother of my great grandfather and my great-great uncle, married an Anglo-Australian. While his was a "mixed" marriage, my memory of him was that he retained many of his Chinese characteristics. Moreover, his values and traditions appear to have strongly influenced the views and behavior of his Eurasian sons, as they were very compliant and accommodating people throughout their lives.

My three Eurasian great uncles, Uncle Charlie, Uncle Albie and Uncle Willie (the sons of Choy Yuen Yun).

Unusually for the period, Uncle Yuen Yin was bi-lingual, being literate in both Chinese and English. For more than 20 years, he was the manager of a Chinese trading company, Tiy Loy, an unlisted public company. This business, established in 1887 and located in Botany Road, Waterloo, primarily sold Chinese goods to the Gu Yiu people. It also facilitated the repatriation of funds to their families in China where a similar establishment was located near Ching Woo. I recall my father regularly repatriating funds to China for his mother and immediate families through this company. Tiy Loy is still operating, having relocated to Chinatown, Sydney, in the 1930s. However, in recent times, it has not operated as a general store, being more active with its investments in commercial properties.

My great great uncle, Choy Yuen Yin

Following the introduction of the White Australia Policy, the Chinese without Australian citizenship returned to China, and it is said that, by 1901, only about 3000 Chinese remained in Sydney. The arrival and departure dates in Sydney of my forebears are vague, due to difficulties in obtaining more accurate details as it was not unusual for the men from our village to use the pre-1901 migration papers and names of those who had returned to China permanently, as it had become virtually impossible to obtain a visa through legitimate channels. Therefore, while I know the correct Chinese names of my great grandfather and grandfather, if I were to conduct a search of official archives, shipping schedules or other records, it is not likely to be productive because of my not knowing the names they used to come to Australia. For example, my father, Choy War Choong, was known on all official documents in Australia as Ah Lee.

It was customary for the relative living here to organize/sponsor his son(s) to Australia. My great-grandfather was able to bring his second son, my grandfather, Choy Yook Chiu, and his fourth son, Choy Jerk Chiu, here. Choy Jerk Chiu settled in Australia after bringing his wife from China to join him and raised a family of five children in Australia. He was also a prominent figure in the Chinese community, including being an office bearer of the Chinese Chamber of Commerce for many years. I recall that he and my great-Aunt often had me stay with them, either overnight at week-ends or during school holidays so that I could be exposed to a little more refinement than living on the market garden and running "wild" with my brothers.

Me when I was ten-years old and was flower girl at the
wedding of my great-Aunt's daughter, Hazel.

Growing up on the market garden, I led a tomboy existence with my brothers.
Bare-footed, we would often race each other over about a 200-yard distance to the
front gate and back. Subsequently, when I attended the State primary school, I was
winning 50-yard races with ease and ended up representing the school at regional
athletics meetings. Being seen as a "winner" was a wonderful feeling and was probably the first time that I felt truly accepted by my Anglo-Australian school-friends.
Sadly, this was not an interest or an ability which continued beyond my early teens
as I had discovered how much I loved reading and other more passive activities.

My grandfather, Choy Yook Chiu, left behind a wife and only child, my father,
Choy War Choong, and did not return to China, dying in New Hebrides (Vanuatu)
on the homeward journey. My father had been educated in China and, for a period
in the early 1920s, had worked in a department store in Shanghai. However, Uncle
Jerk Chiu thought that there were better economic opportunities in Australia and,
hence, in the late 20s, brought my father to Sydney.

My father, in coming to Sydney, left behind a wife and two children (a boy and a
girl). After working hard for a few years, he returned to China in the mid-1930s with
sufficient funds to marry a second wife. It was customary for Chinese men to build
a new home for their new bride, separate from the home of the first wife, yet co-
habiting with both wives. During this period, a second son was born to the first wife
and the second wife also became pregnant. The second wife is the lady who is my
mother.

Photo of my father (circa 1940s)

My mother did not have an easy childhood. She was born in a village in the Gu Yiu region, near Guangzhou. However, at a very early age, her father passed away and her widowed mother, not being able to keep both my Mum and her younger brother, allowed my mother to become the foster daughter of a childless friend of the family. Whilst my mother regarded this lady like a mother, there were insufficient funds for her to have any formal education and, from early adolescence, my mother worked in the paddy fields to help out. At sixteen years old, she married my father, possibly following a visit to a marriage broker by my father.

My mother when she made her application
to come to Australia (circa 1939)

Father decided that there were better money-making opportunities back in Sydney, so he left China once again to return to Sydney in about 1937-8, leaving his wives, his children and his mother behind. About a year later, and after my elder brother was born, my mother came to Sydney to visit my father. My elder brother was left in the care of his paternal grandmother. My mother, having purchased the name and Australian migration papers of another Chinese woman, was granted permission to stay in Australia for only one year. Fortunately for her, she became pregnant with me and World War 2 in the Pacific region had commenced which meant that her return to China was deferred until after the war ended. In 1945, I think there were three Australian-born children and the immigration authorities allowed my mother to stay in Australia. However, they only granted her residency of one year at a time until the late 40s, after which she was told she could stay indefinitely.

Like his predecessors, my father also saw himself as a sojourner, believing that, eventually, he would return to China with his Australian-born family. To this end, he saw no point in learning to speak English although he could read the language. My mother could speak English although her speech was heavily accented. As she had had virtually no schooling in China, she was illiterate in both Chinese and English, but she readily adapted to her new life in Australia without relinquishing her Chinese traditions and way of life. Like my father, she strongly supported the education of her children. Nevertheless, they also both wanted their Australian-born children to not lose their "Chineseness" so that when the family returned to the village in China, their relocation would be seamless and they would readily adapt to their new life. As part of this process, my siblings and I were also given Chinese names which we were reluctant to acknowledge or use although my father had spent much time creating our names so that they would have a poetic resonance. However, at home, I was usually called "Dor-lin" by my parents: a variation on my given name "Doreen" but it may have also incorporated part of my given Chinese name, "Lin Fong" or it may have been due to my parents not being able to pronounce the English sound of "r." My sister, Julie, was mostly called "moi moi" by my parents and, occasionally, by her siblings when she was a child. Interestingly, one of my Anglo-Australian beaux liked to call me "Lin Fong" but this may have been due to the "exotica" of such a name or an opportunity to demonstrate a closer level of intimacy than that which I had with my other friends. By my siblings and outside the home, I have always been called "Doreen" or "Dor." During my childhood and adolescent years, I certainly did not want to be identified as Chinese so I would not have wanted to be called anything but a western sounding name.

Until I started school, I only spoke Cantonese. As the only Chinese child at the local Catholic school (until my younger brother joined me the following year), I was teased and called names. Not wanting to be different from the other children and being ashamed of my color and the very different way that my family and I lived by comparison to my school friends, I denied my ethnicity. I remember playing with some school friends on one occasion and, on the following day, being told by one of them that she wasn't allowed to play with me because her mother had told her that "you and your family live on the smell of an oily rag."

Such an explicit expression of non-acceptance was not strange as many Chinese living in Sydney at the time did little to affiliate with their Anglo-Australian neighbors. However, this early experience, which I later knew to be racism, hurt me deeply and I think the seeds of wanting to be accepted were sown then. This manifested as a strong need for approval, from my parents, my school teachers and to a lesser extent, from my friends. Thus, I learned to work doubly hard at school and to "role play" in my interactions with others so that I would be treated favorably and, hopefully, be accepted as one of them.

On reflection, I believe that all through my life, I have made a determined and conscious effort to appear on "top of the situation," even if it meant role-playing, at times. Personally, I do not regard role-playing as a form of "manipulation" as, generally, it is accepted that most people wish to behave in a socially acceptable way so as to make a positive impression. Further, through role-playing, one can often internalize and imprint that behavior by frequency of practice so that eventually that way of behaving becomes "second nature." In other words, role-playing is widely accepted as a strategy to cope with situations when one is lacking self-confidence or seeks enhancements to social status.

An example of "role-playing" is an incident which I recall from my first year at the State school, when we were asked to read from the school magazine as part of our half-yearly exams. I was dismayed to have only received a very average mark for reading. Ashamed at doing so poorly, I practiced reading aloud in my bedroom and by the end of the year had made a marked improvement. As I wasn't given feedback on why I had done so poorly, I suspect it may have been due either to my accented or "strine" English. Speaking well was (and still is) important to me and, to this end, at high school, I joined the Drama Society. Moreover, this growing interest in speaking well resulted in being asked to speak at high school speech days, with the Drama teacher often coaching me to improve my enunciation and presentation. Mrs. Evans was like an elocution teacher and I have much to thank her for.

My class in my last year at high school (1955). I am on the right hand side of the top row.

Again, as a young adult, I learned to become more socially confident from role-playing. As a committee member of the Chinese Women's Association Younger Set, we were charged with the responsibility of persuading some of the more timid men who attended our dances to partner us in the barn dance and, thus, to get them up to dance and to circulate. This required some courage as my fellow committee members and I were, basically, reserved in nature but, for the sake of the success of the function, we assumed "a brave face" and appeared more extroverted than we felt. Some of my fellow committee members were more reluctant to "circulate" than others but, as young adults, we didn't feel embarrassment if we couldn't persuade the "wall flower" to join us on the dance floor and would "move on" to find a more willing participant.

Chinese Women's Association, Younger Set, taken in 1985. From left to right: Rose Jung, Shirley Fong, Bettina Tuck-Lee, Margaret Wong-See, Phyllis Jung, Dianna Tingyou, Peggy Low, May Young, Doreen Choy Lee, Eva Ma Howe.

Another example that I recall of role-playing was when, as a young mother and needing to establish a new circle of friends in my local neighborhood, it was important that I presented myself as someone with similar values to the rest of the community. This often meant getting involved in school fund-raising activities, volunteering my services to the school canteen, having my children become involved with activities similar to the other Anglo-Australian children such as playing sport, getting involved in the local scout group and attending Sunday school!

Further, when I commenced work as a junior consultant, role-playing as a confident and competent professional was a necessary strategy to "cover" the apprehension I felt when I met with the senior executives of client organizations or with my more senior colleagues.

Role-playing was not the only strategy which I adopted to gain approval or to be accepted as "one of them." I recall that when I was about 10 years of age, my teacher was stern and somewhat authoritarian and, while I didn't dislike her, I was afraid of "getting into her bad books." As she often caught the same bus as me, I would offer to carry her briefcase to the classroom so that she would think I was a well-mannered child. Another instance of trying to make a good impression was to add to the childish hand-written notes, whenever I had to explain an absence from school or to give parental permission to attend a school excursion. I wrote these notes on behalf of my parents as they could not write in English and I would finish by saying that the teacher was doing a wonderful job with me. This additional comment was made on my own initiative because I had overheard the teacher tell another classmate that the letters from her parents were very kind and I wanted for my parents to be seen no differently.

An anecdote which illustrates the two cultures to which I was exposed from an early age was my parents' non-observance of Christmas. During my first year at school, I was learning to sing Christmas carols and was told about a person called Santa Claus. After being told that this person visited your home on Christmas Eve and, if you had been a "good child," your stocking, which you had left on the windowsill, would be filled with toys. I rushed straight home to do just that. I couldn't find any stockings so I pinned my father's sock to the sill. Awakening on Christmas morning, I was so disappointed to find that the sock was empty and, on going out to play, saw that all my friends had new toys. When I asked why Santa had forgotten me, one of the responses was "Santa wouldn't visit your place because he might drown in one of your garden's creeks." Here was an example of implied racism and the reluctance of my parents to accept the traditions of their new domicile. It took another Christmas to come and go before I learned the truth about Santa. There were few toys around our home as toys were considered by my parents to be an unnecessary luxury. Infrequently, my father would bring home a toy (usually a truck or car but never a doll) from the markets for us as he was a kind father.

Fortunately for my family, we had some very generous neighbors who were very forthcoming in providing assistance when any official papers required completion, for doing handy man jobs and for giving us a never-ending supply of "hand-me-downs." On thinking back, I believe their benevolence towards us was likely to have been due to a sense of "paternalism" towards a family whom they saw as disadvantaged by comparison to themselves. Another neighbor was a competent seamstress and made many woolen jackets and matching skirts for me and short pants for my brothers to wear to school. I suppose my love of sewing for my baby sister, including making an appropriate outfit for her to wear at her first day at school, was possibly influenced by the actions of that kind neighbor. At high school, I enjoyed my dressmaking lessons and made all of my own clothes until life became too busy when I became a young mother. I was also starting to see that dressing stylishly not only had a "feel good" component but could also contribute to one's improved social standing in the community. To this day, I still love clothes and looking smart.

My father worked as a market gardener, mainly at Kogarah, during his working life in Sydney. I recall that he worked from sunrise to sunset, whatever the weather. Rarely would he take a break from work, only making an exception for Chinese New Year. His hard work was rewarded when, in the late 1940s, he saved sufficient funds to buy the previously leased market garden of 2-3 acres. My mother, unlike Anglo-Australian wives who focused their efforts on child-rearing and house-keeping, worked beside my father in the garden for much of the day, only returning to the homestead to cook the evening meal. However, in the late 40s, father also sponsored the migration of his eldest son (from his first wife) and his brother-in-law to come and assist, thus, increasing the adult male labor force threefold.

As my mother had only known a life of hard work during her childhood years, she could not accept the Western way of "just letting children be children" and allowing them to play and so, from an early age, my siblings and I were the extra pairs of hands and had to do our share of the work in the garden. During peak growing times, my siblings and I were also commandeered to help in the garden, scrubbing the dirt off bunches of carrots, radishes, etc., or stacking the cut cabbages and cauliflowers into gradings as preparation for being taken to the vegetable markets. These would have been normal chores for young children in China, but how I resented those demands. My father attended the market at least twice and sometimes three times per week. As he couldn't drive, an Anglo-Australian neighbor was employed to drive the vegetable-laden truck to and from Haymarket on these mornings.

Once I started school, my English improved and my conversations in Cantonese at home grew less and less. I recall my father threatening not to speak to me unless I spoke in Cantonese. However, his words fell on deaf ears. My stubbornness persisted until I realized, at about 15 years of age, that I could have been bi-lingual had I con-tinued to speak Cantonese at home. That opportunity for fluency and for extending my vocabulary was lost because my Cantonese had stalled at a kindergarten level.

My increasing fluency in English also resulted in my doing the household shop-ping at the local shopping centre rather than my mother relying on the services of kind neighbors. This was the time when wartime ration coupons were used to pur-chase necessities like butter, sugar, tea, etc., and there was many a time when, walk-ing through the paddocks where dairy cows grazed and many opportunities to explore presented themselves, I lost the precious coupons and felt the wrath of my mother's anger. She was a strong advocate of corporal punishment and didn't spare the rod. Seeing how free my Australian friends were and the fun that they were hav-ing, I often rushed to play with them after school rather than doing chores around the house. By such behavior, I was constantly being punished by my mother as she regarded me as a rebellious and difficult child.

My mother, true to her Confucian based values, was very pleased to have borne four sons and only two daughters. I was the second-born and my sister, the sixth. From a young age, I was well aware that, in the eyes of my mother, being a female child put me at a huge disadvantage. As a daughter, my role was to accept with grace that my brothers were superior. I was constantly told by my mother that they carried their father's name and that boys stayed close to their parents and looked after them in their old age.

My siblings and me taken at my mother's 80th birthday dinner.

I vividly recall my young brothers and father going off to the city to celebrate Chinese New Year and coming home with their pockets full of silver
coins. It was customary to give children money during the Lunar New Year
Festival. However, I was told by my mother that, as a female child, I could not
go with them. With my brothers being so bountifully rewarded, I strongly felt
at an early age that "the system" was very unfair and was very resentful of this
discrimination. This was reinforced at the start of each new school year when
my brothers were always bought new school clothes and I wore the "hand-me-
downs."

The birth of my sister brought me much joy as the household till then had
been so boy-centric. As my mother was busy working in the gardens, I looked
after Julie from about three months of age. She was like my little doll, and when
I went out to play, I would take her with me. If I wanted to actively participate in
a game, I would carefully lay her on the coir mat at the doorstep of my girlfriend's home and join in the fun. On becoming a mother myself, I shuddered at
how blasé I was in so caring for my little sister. From the time that Julie was a
toddler, I enjoyed sewing dresses or knitting for her and giving her the love and
attention which had been denied to me by my mother. Fortunately, my father was
not so biased against girls as my mother and I recall fondly the many times that
he showed affection and pride in my school work, leaving me feeling that I had
at least one kind and loving parent.

I was seven when I met my elder brother for the first time. He had been cared for and indulged in by his paternal grandmother in the Chinese village of Ching Woo. Coming straight from China, he could not speak a word of English. I was ordered by my parents to teach him to speak English and I recall him sitting beside me at school for about a year. Jim was a quick learner and, before too long, he had progressed sufficiently to be promoted to an appropriate class for his age.

My memories of my early school years at the Catholic school are still strong. Each Monday morning, I had to admit when asked that I hadn't attended church the previous day. According to the nuns, I had "sinned" which meant a slap on the hand with the ruler. At the end of Year Three, my parents decided to take us from the Catholic school as we were then old enough to travel on public transport to attend the State (public) school. This had also been precipitated by an incident arising from our being non-Catholics at the Catholic school and not wanting to take our first Communion as all my classmates were doing. I recall numerous visits by the nuns to the market garden as they attempted to convert my parents, but without success as my parents fell back on the old line of "no understandee"! Once the nuns realized that we were not going to be converted to Catholicism, they treated my brothers and me as "second-class citizens," as they presumed that "our souls" were "beyond salvation" and assigned us unpleasant tasks like emptying garbage tins and cleaning up the schoolyard. I don't think that they were explicitly racist in their behavior towards us but were colored by their perception of us as "heathens."

When I did well at school, I gained the approval of both my father and my teachers at school. To this end, I was conscientious and applied myself diligently to my school work and won some scholastic awards. Moreover, I believed that by being a good student, I had an identity and would achieve greater acceptance by my Anglo-Australian school friends. I recall that I was the only Chinese student during those three years of high school and I tried determinedly to be accepted by the popular girls in my class and while I had several sound one-on-one relationships and didn't want more companionship at lunchtime, I was never part of the "inner circle." On leaving school, I cannot recall regarding any of my former classmates as my best friend. However, when I reflect as to why I was so determined to establish an identity by excelling at school and speaking well, I don't think I was motivated by feelings of being marginalized due to my ethnicity or gender but possibly by feelings of not wanting to be seen as being economically disadvantaged. I recall feeling ashamed to be always wearing school tunics or blouses that were "hand-me downs" and never new outfits. I couldn't wait to leave school following completion of the Intermediate Certificate as I knew that, by getting a job, I would become financially independent and escape the dependency for money on my mother, and would not feel disadvantaged by the clothes that I wore.

Photo taken at the parade when we wore the dresses which we had made during our last year of high school (1955).

Thus, once I commenced work, I reveled in being able to buy dress fabrics and, using the dressmaking skills I had learned at school, to sew a new wardrobe for myself. During my young adult years, I felt that "clothes maketh man" and reflected your social standing. It was only in my more mature years, with a lessening need to impress and to gain social status from "looking good," that my focus changed to accepting myself for what I had achieved in life and not getting anxious over matters which were out of my control.

My parents appeared to have changed their minds to return to China with their family following the defeat of the Nationalist Army by the Communists, as I think that they then believed that their Australian-born children would have better opportunities if they settled in Australia. Moreover, I think that the political instability and the Communist ideology in China resulted in a more compassionate treatment by the immigration authorities towards the relatively long-established Chinese families in Australia. The immigration requirements were relaxed for my parents and, soon thereafter, my elder brother, my half-brother and my mother's brother immigrated here. In the late 1950s, my parents and elder brother became Australian citizens.

The hard work and single-mindedness of my parents brought just rewards as, in 1956, the family moved into a newly-built, three-bedroom brick home adjacent to their market garden. A few years previously, the neighboring market garden was rezoned for residential housing. My parents, with sufficient savings, thought it appropriate that we move from the ramshackle house in which we had all lived since my mother's arrival in 1941. Thus, when the blocks of land went up for sale, they were the first to purchase one. At 15 years old, I was charged with the responsibility of identifying a builder (fortunately, a girlfriend's father was in the building trade and gave me valuable referrals), guiding my parents in the design of the home, getting the house built and choosing and purchasing the furniture. Being so inexperienced, my selection of the décor, paint work, etc., was strongly influenced by what I believed a modern Australian home should look like, with many ideas being based on my girl-friend's home. I loved the responsibility that I was given and I was so pleased that we had finally acquired another highly desirable Australian status symbol…a brand new home to which I could bring my friends, just as my Anglo-Australian counterparts did. Also about that time, the family purchased its first new car, a Ford Zephyr, as two of my brothers had obtained driving licenses. Finally, I felt that some of the shame of being different and being seen as "poor" was receding and we were "fitting into the norms" of a suburban Sydney life.

In early adolescence, my best friend was a girl who lived a few doors from me. Nancy and her family gave me the first intimate glimpse of Australian family life. Her parents were very caring and understanding and often allowed Nancy's friends to play in their home. On many occasions during my early teens, I would run to Nancy's mother, Dulcie, in tears after a "fight" with my mother. Dulcie would soothe and calm me down, often feed me, then send me home. To me, Dulcie was the mother that I believed I didn't have. She was the first person to show me what unconditional love for one's child was like. It was at their home that I was introduced to a baked lamb dinner. My very first smell of such a dinner baking is still so fresh in my mind. At home, we only ate Cantonese-styled food, so a baked roast dinner was so exotic by comparison. My mother did not like the strong smell and taste of lamb, preferring to use only beef or pork in her cooking. In our new home, I often baked a leg of lamb for Sunday lunch for my siblings and me. In addition, we also enjoyed the Saturday lunchtime ritual of a home-cooked spaghetti bolognaise meal. As we introduced Western dishes into the home, my mother's tastes adapted and she became a proficient cook of some Western style dishes such as Irish stew and braised rabbit.

When I was around 16 years old, my parents told me that I would be "disowned" and be "cut off" from my family if I continued to fraternize with my friends, a mixed group of Anglo-Australian boys and girls. My parents were very fearful that I would marry an Anglo-Australian. They were strongly racist, believing that the Chinese were a more superior race and were single-minded in only wanting their children to marry within their own racial group.

I was constantly reminded of the lot of my mixed-race great uncles (whom my mother kept referring to as "half-castes") and the shame that I would bring to the family if I also gave birth to "half-castes." The term "half-caste" is now rarely used or heard; however, it had currency during the 1950s and 1960s in both the Chinese and Anglo-Australian communities. It was a somewhat derogatory term and was not only used with the mixed-race children of Chinese and Anglo-Australians but also those of Anglo-Australian and Aboriginal descent. The views that my parents held during the 1950s may have been due to deep-seated roots in China's long history of seeing itself as the culturally rich Middle Kingdom and the rest of the world as "barbarians" or "gwei-loos," though I believe it was more likely to be based on a narrow view of maintaining racial purity. While my parents were so determined that I would only marry a Chinese boy, my brother who is 13 months younger than me, announced to my mother, about two years after I had married, that his Anglo-Australian girlfriend was expecting his child and he was going to marry her. No amount of angry ranting by my mother would change his mind. Within a relatively short time of my parents' requirement that I only marry a Chinese, a breach in their view of racial purity was made.

Until my younger brother married his Anglo-Australian girlfriend, my parents were also discriminating as to whom amongst the Chinese community they wanted their children to marry. I recall when I was about 15 years old, my father coming home from the markets and telling my mother and me that a Chinese fellow market gardener had a son whom he wanted to "marry off" to a Chinese girl and had offered a "dowry" of 500 pounds to my parents, if I would marry his son. As I knew the family, and the son, I flatly refused to be "sold off" in such a manner. My father was not too upset with my answer as he admitted that he thought the boy was "not good enough" for me as he would just end up becoming a market gardener, like his father.

In general, my parents' attitude to fellow Chinese was no different to universal views held by people of any ethnicity inasmuch they were cordial towards our relatives and small circle of Chinese friends if they held similar values and they could respect them. Nevertheless, their behavior towards relatives with whom they did not have a high regard was always masked by politeness upon meeting, even though they would speak more disparagingly of them in private.

Where his children were concerned, my father always believed that they were "well-behaved" and if there was any mischief or trouble when we were playing with Anglo-Australian friends my father would blame or rationalize that they had led his children astray. The Anglo-Australian neighbor, who was the playmate of my younger brothers, constantly bore the brunt of this very biased view of my father.

On reflection, my parents were intolerant towards Anglo-Australians. While they were grateful for the assistance and kindness shown by our Anglo-Australian neighbors, particularly when we were little children and did not have fluency of the English language, they did not fraternize with them. The only family social occasions at the time were spent with our Chinese relatives. My parents had no desire to move out of the security of their ethnic enclave or to assume Western ways and affiliate with Anglo-Australians. However, after my father passed away, my mother did form some friendships with her neighbors but was more comfortable with her family and Chinese friends.

The opportunities for young Chinese to fraternize during the 1950s and 1960s were limited as the Chinese in Sydney were a much smaller ethnic group with most of my Chinese contemporaries being first- or second-generation Australian-born Chinese. To meet other Chinese, you needed to attend either the Chinese dances, the annual Dragon Ball or were part of the Chinese Tennis Association, The Chinese Catholic Youth group or the Chinese Presbyterian Church Fellowship group. There were also some Chinese families living in Sydney who maintained contact with other families whose forebears had come from the same province in China. Back in the late 50s, and fortunately for the local Chinese girls, Sydney was awash with Asian men as the Colombo Plan was in full swing. And, unlike the latter half of the 19th century, there was no shortage of eligible Chinese girls for Chinese boys to marry once you circulated amongst the Chinese community.

Chinese Dragon Ball, Sydney, 1958

Presentation of Doreen Cheong (nee Lee) to Consul-General's wife (Mrs. J.L.)

Me being presented to the Chinese Consul-General and his wife at the Dragon Ball, 1958.

My sister when she made her debut at the Chinese Dragon Ball in 1968. The photo also includes my mother (next to my sister) and my uncle (her brother) and three of my siblings and their spouses. The brother on the left hand side is Tom, who married the Caucasian girl, Pat. Next to my mother is my sister-in-law, Millie and brother Jim (This was the arranged marriage in Hong Kong). Beside him is my youngest brother, Robert, who was a single man at the time and, on the right hand side, is my uncle.

In hindsight, the young Chinese in Sydney during the 1950s and 1960s had a different view of the connections that they were seeking. They were a very conservative group and most had a strong reluctance to marry outside their own race. My view on why the Chinese preferred to marry within their ethnic group is not so much a feeling of being either superior or inferior but, possibly, a combination of racial purity and the perceived stigma of giving birth to "half-caste" children. At that time, it was not unusual to hear comments that these children were neither Chinese nor Anglo-Australian, with difficulties arising because they would not be accepted into either world. This was a less tolerant society in Australia as there was still a strong identification with the "mother country"—England. The change towards a multi-cultural society in Australia did not occur until the 1970s.

At the behest of my mother, my male cousin escorted me to monthly Chinese dances so that I could meet and mix with Chinese people of my own age. Soon, I had a new group of friends. I became more involved with the Chinese community and held office with the Chinese Women's Association Younger Set for many years. Becoming so involved with the Chinese community meant that I was often asked to participate as a representative of my ethnic group. An example which I recall, were the occasions during the early 1960s when my Chinese girlfriends and I were invited to "man" the Chinese community float during Sydney's Waratah Spring Festival.

Chinese girls and Anglo-Australians. Photo taken at one of the Sydney's Springtime Waratah Parade 1960. The Chinese girls from the Chinese Women's Association Younger Set, left to right, are: Florence Wong, the late Diana Young, Doreen Cheong and Helen Ma.

Publicity shot for a theatre production: a Caucasian
actress (whose name I can't recall), my girlfriend, Diane,
and myself (with the Chinese head dress).

The Younger Set group organized regular dances, gala balls, fashion parades, etc.,
to not only provide an opportunity for the young Chinese to get together and have a
good time but also to do some worthy fund-raising. These Saturday night dances
were held in venues close to the city as not many Chinese boys had cars and public
transport was generally the means of getting out and about. There was a predictable
pattern to these dances, which included a live band playing a wide repertoire of
music encompassing ballroom, rock and roll and cha-cha tempos. There were
always light refreshments, and to quench one's thirst, there was cordial but never
anything alcoholic. Many marriages resulted from attendance at these Chinese
dances. Now, nearly 50 years on, some of this "old dance crowd" still meet for lunch
several times a year so that we can reminisce and laugh over shared memories from
those times. Many of the couples are still married and anticipate celebrating their
50th wedding anniversaries in the near future.

As well as the adoption of a multi-cultural policy in Australia in the 1970s, other
enormous social changes were also taking place in the community. During that
decade, "no fault" divorces were introduced. Moreover, women were becoming
more empowered by the wave of feminism sweeping the world and by the abolition
of university fees in Australia. Women, no longer beholden to their parents or

husbands, were attending universities in huge numbers where they learned to critically analyze and to question. With empowerment, women were no longer content to remain in unhappy marriages where they were not treated as an equal or their personal integrity was not respected. For Australian-born Chinese girls who perhaps had married within their race to meet parental expectations, this was the moment when tough decisions could be made and actions taken. Throughout the 1970s and 1980s, it was not unusual to see some of the Chinese couples divorcing and, as mixed marriages were no longer frowned upon, many of their subsequent remarriages were to Anglo-Australians.

It was at one of these Chinese dances that I met Lanny Cheong, another Australian-born Chinese, whom I married in February 1961. Lanny was the seventh child and had grown up in Townsville, coming to Sydney after completing his secondary schooling. His father, Philip Yuen Cheong, also had two wives with Lanny's mother being the second wife. Lanny's dialect was Loong Doo, which was very different to Cantonese. Thus, the common language in our household was English.

My parents were not totally enamored of Lanny as they viewed him as being disrespectful towards them with his "bold" ways and "back-answering." There was a period when I was prohibited from bringing him home. However, they finally saw that the more they tried to discourage me from seeing Lanny, the more determined I was to disobey them. Moreover, I perceived marriage to be a legitimate excuse for me to escape the "strong control" of my mother. Finally, they relented because my father said, "at least, she is marrying a Chinese!"

Our forthcoming marriage brought forth the strong views and superstitions of my mother in respect of the natural order of family life and its concomitant consequences. Although I am the second-born child, I could not be seen to be marrying before my elder brother, who at that stage had no prospective bride. When my mother learned that we had set a wedding date, she quickly arranged to travel to Hong Kong, taking my elder brother with her to find him a wife. Moreover, she felt that it would be inauspicious if two of her children married in the same year. Therefore, while my brother and I were married only a month apart, my mother was happy as, by careful management, my brother was not only the first to marry but he was married in the old year according to the Chinese Lunar Calendar, while my wedding in the following month was in the new Chinese year. Despite all of my mother's concerted efforts, my brother and his wife divorced in 1972 and I was divorced six years later. My mother's words on hearing that I was separating from Lanny were "Why? You have a comfortable life, have a nice home, rarely have money worries and always have nice clothes. You are more fortunate than a lot of women and should be content with your lot!" It never entered her head that my self-respect and personal integrity were more important to me.

Wedding photo of me and my bridal attendants dressed in western style dresses and my mother wearing a traditional Chinese outfit.

With married life and our home in the suburbs of Sydney and with a young family to care for, our contact with the Chinese community became less and less, even with our closest Chinese friends who also had similar busy lives. Moreover, there were lifestyle incompatibilities with those of our other close Chinese friends who were still single.

In January 1963, our son, Stephen, was born. On the maternal side, he was the first grandchild and, to my mother's delight, he was a male child. She had a special relationship with him for all of his life with the bonding possibly stemming from the two years that she regularly looked after him for a few hours while I attended the local technical college to undertake my Leaving Certificate studies.

Towards the end of Stephen's first year, I felt that I was "on top" of my motherhood duties and with the pending cessation of the Leaving Certificate, I returned to night school so that I could matriculate under the old system. While my exam results gave me entry, I postponed going to university due to pregnancy difficulties and the boys being so young. However, once Andrew commenced primary school, I enrolled in a Bachelor of Arts degree course at Sydney University. My end goal was to gain the necessary qualifications to become an Adult Student Counselor as, with two young children, I would have had the school vacation breaks with them and be working in a role which I felt would be both stimulating and rewarding.

As I had had an easy first pregnancy with Stephen and he was a thriving healthy child, the unexpected loss of two near-term baby girls over a two-year period was heart-breaking. The first little girl survived half an hour after a Caesarian Section was performed at 34 weeks of pregnancy, while the second little girl was stillborn at eight months. While numerous tests were done on both my first baby daughter and me after the loss, no causes were identified and I was advised to "try again." However, soon after our second loss, it was established that our babies had died because both my husband and I were Thalassemia Minor. This is a blood disorder which, in a minor form in an individual, is not serious. However, as both Lanny and I were carriers, our little girls were Thalassemia Major, a serious blood disease which causes a baby to become anemic and, generally, to not survive beyond pubescence. Joy returned to our lives when our adopted child, Andrew, came into our lives in October 1966. He was 10 days old when we brought him home and, two months later, the Supreme Court declared that he was officially our son. Finally, Stephen had a sibling.

However, after about 10 years, our marriage was in trouble. In 1977, Lanny and I separated and, subsequently, divorced. On reflection, Lanny and I had very different value systems and, with maturity, these differences became very evident. As a consequence, our lives were increasingly becoming tension-filled. It was an acrimonious divorce, although I was fortunate in being able to remain in the matrimonial home, thus giving my sons some semblance of stability. Despite the set-backs, I completed my studies at the end of 1979, gaining a BA, majoring in Psychology and Economics.

Me in my graduation gown as a Bachelor of Arts in 1980

The early years of our marriage were happy and motherhood was a wonderful experience. I enjoyed being a full-time wife and mother. The boys were very affectionate, loved cuddling up and having stories read to them. Nevertheless, when it was suggested that they attend Cantonese classes on Saturdays, neither of the children were interested. Unfortunately, as Lanny and I only spoke English at home due to our differing dialects, the only times our sons were exposed to the Chinese language was when we went to visit my mother. However, this wasn't an ideal learning opportunity because my mother and I spoke "chinglish," due to my poor fluency in Cantonese.

My children's western leanings were even more evident when they elected to undertake modern European languages, rather than Chinese, when they attended high school. We allowed our children to choose their own friends and, as young adults, their friends were a cross-section of the community. Yet when they began dating, all of their girlfriends were Anglo-Australians. It was no surprise when Andrew chose Elizabeth to be his wife, with Elizabeth becoming my Anglo-Australian daughter-in-law. The best man at their wedding was a Chinese.

My son Andrew and my daughter-in-law Elizabeth on their wedding day

Both of the boys were very natural sports people, excelling in soccer and tennis and they loved snow ski-ing. Coincidentally, they were each awarded an "All Round Sportsman's" trophy in their final year of Prep School. At around eight years of age, both of them started classical piano lessons, which they continued for about eight years. They also each played a second instrument: Stephen, the clarinet and Andrew, the guitar. The two boys had very different personalities. Stephen was more reserved and sensitive, while Andrew was more action-oriented and mischievous. Both were good students, although only Stephen wanted to attend university. Andrew's preference was to pursue a career in the hospitality industry, which culminated in his appointment as executive chef for a large American catering organization. Stephen completed degrees in commerce/law and was undertaking a Master of Laws degree when he was tragically killed in a car accident in October 1990, in his twenty-sixth year. I have some beautiful memories of the time that we had together but I still miss him so much.

Stephen as a member of the 10A cricket team, 1973.

Andrew as a member of the Under 8 ruby team, 1974.

Stephen with his parents as he graduated as a Bachelor of Laws, 1987.

Stephen and me as he was admitted to the NSW Bar,
1988.

During our seventeen years of marriage, Lanny and I completely assimilated into
our local community. Our closest friends were Anglo-Australian families with children of similar ages to our own. We felt accepted as we had readily adapted to their
culture and lifestyle. Lanny and I felt at ease with the open-minded and casual lifestyle of our new friends and the similar interests we shared through the children's
activities. If any comments were made about our ethnicity, it was in a jocular and
affectionate "Here comes the Yellow Peril!" manner. If anything, our ethnicity was
seen as something of a novelty and I never felt that we were being objectified.

As young parents in the suburbs, we readily assumed the mantle of the "modern
nuclear family." Our children were sent to the local pre-school and school and to
Sunday School (because that was the expected thing to do), the house was kept
tidy, the lawns were mowed and the flower garden tended. Dinner parties in one
another's homes were high points on the social calendar. My dinner parties were
always eight-or nine-course Chinese banquets, which meant that I was busy for
days preparing. If I were completely honest with myself, I would have to admit to
an element of "keeping up with the Joneses." During the day, I was kept busy with
the children's school activities, driving them to different sporting events and training sessions. In addition, I did fund-raising work for the local branch of the
Children's Medical Research Foundation, including holding office as President

Jocelyn Dufty and me as office bearers of the Children's Medical
Research Foundation—St. George Branch.

for several years. I satisfied my thirst for knowledge by attending fortnightly
meetings of a local "Discussion Group." Topics discussed were structured around
a series of lectures developed by the Adult Education Department at the University
of Sydney. I was the only non-Anglo-Australian within the group and I found the
mornings to be both interesting social occasions and a vehicle for some structured
learning.

When the children were young, my siblings' families and mine would return to
the family home every Saturday evening for dinner. The little cousins had a wonderful time playing together and getting into all kinds of mischief. My mother had
become a good cook over the years with most of her skills being self-taught although
there was some prompting from Dad in the early days. She was always eager to learn
about new dishes, mostly Chinese but also some Western. The dinner table was a
rowdy affair with everyone, in typical Cantonese style, talking at once and often rais-
ing a voice to get a point across. It was such a contrast to the dinner table behavior of
the dinner parties with my Anglo-Australian friends. After dinner at my mother's
home, the mah-jong table would be set up and there would be a jostle to be one of the
four "legs" required for a game. These family get-togethers continued until I became
too busy with my university studies and had to focus my priorities on another area of
my life. Moreover, I had separated from my husband and a new man had come into
my life, an Anglo-Australian. I knew that he would have difficulty accepting the

long hours that I would need to spend with my family playing mah-jong on such a regular basis and not giving priority and energy to developing our relationship.

By co-incidence or otherwise, I found that after my divorce, I was more attracted to Caucasian men because they respected me as a person and appreciated my need for independence. While there may have been an initial attraction on their part because I was Chinese, this novelty aspect would not have been sufficient to engage me for long without some evidence of the other qualities and values which I knew were fundamental to a healthy and loving relationship. The inter-racial aspects of such a relationship did not particularly worry me because I believed that Australians and, specifically, the social circle in which I moved, was and is much more progressive and liberal in thinking for that to be an issue. Generally, in my experience, Chinese men prefer their partners to be more "genteel," less flamboyant and not so independent-minded and I think that they would have found me too difficult to "manage" because of my high need for independence and my questioning approach.

After my divorce, I had expected to remarry and while I have had some substantial relationships with Caucasian men, I did not feel that I wanted to make a permanent commitment to any of them. I do not think I could ever have been described as the stereotypical submissive Chinese woman although I was possibly seen as "a trophy wife" by my husband.

The term "trophy wife" is still used today but the connotation has changed as it generally refers to older men who marry young attractive woman to enhance their egos. Generally, these older men are more urbane, have had successful careers, and are more likely to want their wives to be financially dependent on them. Often, these wives have very little power. However, many women's views of their lot in life changed with the rise of feminism in the 1970s, resulting in major social changes from a desire by these women to be treated as equals rather than just being seen as prized possessions. This other group of women are well-educated, are independent-minded, have generally forged successful careers and, frequently, have chosen to live on their own.

My first job in 1956 was with an insurance company. I became competent in my work as a book-keeping machine operator, learned a lot of social graces and enjoyed being treated as an adult although I was the most junior staff member. If there was any discrimination, it was more to do with gender than with race and this was not unusual as Australian workplaces in the 1950s were very hierarchical and male-dominated. For example, there was not one female manager, I always addressed my immediate superior as "Mr.", and I was always called "Miss Lee." It would never have occurred to me to be less formal. However, my overall memory of my time there is a happy one. More importantly, I was financially independent although I was still living at home. My parents would not have supported my moving out of the family home until I married.

After a few years, I was approached by a Chinese friend to work for Chequers Theatre Restaurant as their "day" Office Manager/Secretary. At that workplace, most of the kitchen and maintenance staff were Chinese and non-English speaking. I recall having to deal with them, needing to communicate in my poor Cantonese and getting frustrated because they could not understand me. At the time of my leaving, three years later, there was a noticeable improvement in my ability to communicate with them. Once the night staff arrived, however, another "mask" was donned as I was dealing with English-speaking staff who upheld western traditions and values and were worldly. I loved that job for its diversity, the glamour and the opportunity to meet some of the celebrities who performed at the club. These celebrities included Shirley Bassey, Della Reese and Jane Russell. The impending birth of my first child triggered my saying "good-bye" to an incredible three years or so of my life.

Between 1963 and my return to the work force in 1980, I was seen, primarily, as a wife and mother, although I had been a business partner in my former husband's business until we divorced. However, post-divorce and the need to establish a new life for myself gradually gave rise to a new identity that was independent of ethnicity or gender. I believe that my new identity evolved with my burgeoning self-confidence from earning the respect and being treated as a professional by my work colleagues and clients after joining Coopers & Lybrand (C&L).

In early 1980, after graduating and a 6-week holiday in Europe, my job search began in earnest as I knew that I was now the sole bread-winner in the household. My former husband had become very unreliable in making family support payments. A few weeks of job interviews followed and, in the end, I was fortunate to be offered two positions. One was the sought-after role of Adult Student Counselor with TAFE and the other as a Trainee with the Management Consulting Division of Coopers and Lybrand, a large international firm of chartered accountants. After discussions with an investment banker friend, I was advised to take the job with C&L as it was likely to offer better promotion prospects and salary in the longer term. How right my friend was. My undergraduate studies in economics and psychology would prove to be a boon to my human resources-oriented consulting work.

When I joined C&L in 1980, it was very male-dominated. At the time, there were only 30 professional staff in the consulting division in Sydney. By March 2000, when I retired, there were 5000 consultants in Australia as the firm had both grown organically and through a merger with Price Waterhouse, becoming PwC.

In 1980, I was only one of two female consultants in my division. While I cannot recall one instance of being discriminated against because of my gender or ethnicity or being involved in racial office politics, I strongly believed from my early days in the firm that I would have to work twice as hard as my male colleagues if I were to make an impact. My immersion in my work was total and the self-imposed working hours were long. I was ambitious to advance through the organization, and if I was competitive, it was only against myself. I attribute my acceptance of these work conditions and the determination to succeed to the strong values and examples shown by my parents.

It was through being totally committed and having a professional approach to my work, and my technical competence, that I believe I earned the respect of my colleagues. Moreover, I believe that my behavior and presentation adapted to the requirements of my somewhat prescribed professional work environment. However, I didn't completely allow my identity to be "watered down" by my generally conservative, "dark-suited" colleagues. This was achieved by having the faith and confidence that I could deliver the results expected as I progressed through each level of the organization and always seeking to look "the professional," albeit "doing my own thing" within limits, in terms of dress code.

Over the 20 years with the firm, I grew in self-belief and the knowledge that I was in control of my own destiny and that I could survive and live a very comfortable life on my own. In the first instance, I loved the challenge of attaining technical mastery in my specialist area and building on-going relationships with my key clients so as to be "top of mind" if they needed to use my type of consulting services. The exposure to a range of the firm's "blue chip" clients as well as to more experienced colleagues gave me an excellent grounding in the world of "big business." My clients were diverse and covered the range of medium- to large-sized corporations in both manufacturing and services industries and the public sector. My work provided the opportunity to travel within Australia and, on occasions, to areas within the Pacific region. Much satisfaction from my work came from training young members of the team, sharing my knowledge and experience, and seeing them develop into highly effective professionals. I thank my immediate manager for my contentment in my job as he gave me full autonomy. He had "read my measure," being aware that, although highly independent, I could be relied upon and would do my utmost to deliver and meet the overall goal(s) due to my focused and professional approach to my work.

If there were any disappointments during my time at C&L, it arose from what I believe was age discrimination. My immediate superior was the same age as myself, which meant that we would both be retiring about the same time. In 1990 I was appointed a Director. However, in line with good succession management principles, I was not made a partner of the firm, as I had expected. My superior and I had a close respectful relationship and it hurt when he told me that I wouldn't be appointed a partner and that another female colleague who was 25 years my junior was being "fast-tracked" so that an orderly succession could take place. But there was never a question that I would resign over this issue, as I loved what I was doing.

My retirement on my twentieth anniversary with the firm in March 2000 was due to health reasons. Seven years previously, I had been diagnosed with a chronic liver disease—Primary Biliary Cirrhosis. It is not known what causes the disease although informed opinion is that it is an auto-immune problem. The prognosis was that unless I had a liver transplant, it was likely that I would not survive ten years. The dilemma for my gastroenterologist was deciding when I should have the transplant. His decision was to postpone it for as long as possible while I was still relatively healthy yet not leave it too late in case my health worsened, as this may have jeopardized my survival from such a major surgical procedure. I felt well enough to continue working full time although, in the last few years, I eased off the pace a little.

In late 2000, my specialist believed that my condition had deteriorated and it was necessary for him to transfer my care to the Transplant Clinic at Royal Prince Alfred Hospital, Sydney. To be considered a possible candidate for transplant, I was required to undergo an extensive array of tests and it was a relief when I was told that I was on the waiting list. It was a nervous wait of nine months before I received the phone call on September 11, 2001. I was told that there was a possible donor liver available and was asked if I could go to the hospital immediately. After 16 hours on the operating table, I was given a new liver but had lost a spleen in the process. Naturally, I am eternally grateful to the organ donor family for giving me this gift of life as I had come through the procedure with "flying colors," experiencing only minor hiccups. The constant monitoring of my condition by the Liver Transplant Clinic has been very reassuring. I also enjoy being an active member of the Liver Support Group where I not only keep in touch with other liver transplant recipients but also contribute to the group's fundraising activities.

Unfortunately, with the medication required to prevent rejection of my new liver, the ageing process has accelerated, this manifesting, primarily, as osteo-arthritis. I endeavor to manage the decreasing mobility with my weekly group tai-chi and physiocise classes.

Other activities have also kept me busy in my retirement years. For about nine years, I have been working one day per week on a pro bono basis at the UNSW in their Department of Psychology. As my profession had given me so much, I felt it was time to give something back. Specifically, my work entails supervising second-year Master of Organizational Psychology students. These interns work in a specific place-ment program, with their "clients" being students on campus who are in need of degree course/career management advice. It was my experience in psychometric assessment and knowledge of the job market from my employment at PwC that has been found to be useful.

The six years that I attended weekly Cantonese conversation classes has allowed me to increase my vocabulary beyond my previous kindergarten level and to speak with better fluency. Since going to these classes, I have felt more confident convers-ing with my Cantonese-speaking friends when they visited from Hong Kong. Concurrently, I attended French conversation classes, again, so that I could improve my conversational ability. Sadly, I can't report a similar level of fluency there, how-ever, I have enjoyed the opportunity to have my mind stimulated. Another activity which I have enjoyed immensely since my retirement is my attendance at the weekly art appreciation/history lectures at the Art Gallery of NSW. In addition, the Art Gallery conducts a series of lectures as part of their "Learning Curve" program. Their range of topics is vast and includes philosophy, literature, comparative reli-gions, etc. These lectures are another excellent way of keeping the mind alert.

Other passions in my life are the theatre and overseas travel. I have visited every continent with one of my most memorable trips being to Antarctica in 2006. The pristine beauty of the place and its stillness are indelibly etched on my mind. I have also visited China on four occasions over the past eight years as I have been fascinated by the diversity of its natural beauty and its rich cultural history. However, I have yet to visit my father's family village but it is certainly on my list of places to visit.

My most fulfilling role over the past three years has come about with the birth of my first grandchild, Isabella, in November 2007. I spend at least one day a week caring for her and am delighted with the special bond that we have developed. Isabella is the little girl that I never had and she has certainly re-defined the word "joy" in my life. It's wonderful to see the world through her eyes and her innocence. Isabella is Eurasian and has the beauty that comes from taking the best physical features of both her parents' different racial backgrounds. My personal view of the multi-cultural milieu in which Isabella lives is that it is an exciting one as it will be populated with men and women of mixed heritage due to Australia's multi-cultural

Isabella, Andrew and myself depicting three generations
of my immediate family.

policy. I am confident that it will be a world with greater tolerance for race and
gender and will offer opportunities to all who are motivated to make the most of
what is offered to them and are willing to contribute to the community.

My mother, who suffered from advanced Alzheimer's, passed away last August in
her ninetieth year. One can only describe the last three years of life as being of poor
quality. It was sad to see this person who was so feisty (and controlling) in my adolescent years become baby-like, sleeping for most of the day and only waking so that she
could be fed. I have long forgiven her for the way she treated me during my childhood.
Her only model for bringing up a daughter was the one based on her own upbringing.

In retrospect, I see that the first two decades of my life were dictated by the
Confucian value system. It is no surprise that my mother and I were so different, not
only because of natural individual and educational differences but, primarily,
because we were exposed during our formative years to totally different cultural
environments. In her world, females were not given, and should not have expected,
the same status as males, whereas I had observed in my Western world that this did
not need to be the case. My world places a greater emphasis on the individual and
the need to develop independence and self-esteem and to question, while my mother
wanted me to be more submissive, to respect the words of my elders or authority,
and to show filial piety and propriety. The discrimination shown towards me by my

mother only caused me to try and prove myself to be worthy, not only to my parents but also to the broader community. In the process, I developed emotional resilience and a sense of survival and this has stood me in great stead when confronted with some heart-wrenching losses and other vicissitudes in life.

Generally, I see myself as an Australian-born Chinese because I cannot and do not want to reject my Chinese heritage. I am passionate to find out more of my father's and his forebears' histories and am frustrated by not having the language skills and thus ready access to the ancestral records to do further research. On the other hand, I value the opportunities that being an Australian citizen have given me, particularly as it has allowed me to appreciate and lay claim to "my personal space" as well as allowing me to achieve, as a woman.

Certainly, I would not describe myself as a "hybrid" as I believe that connotes some mutation while, genetically and "in spirit," I feel that I am Chinese. While it is obvious that there has been some cross-cultural symbiosis due to living in an environment which gives supremacy to a western lifestyle, when asked by either Chinese or Anglo-Australians what my ancestry is, I answer without hesitation. The need by others to question my ancestry may be due to my physical appearance being somewhat that of a Eurasian and my western-like behavior, on the surface.

Not since my childhood days can I honestly say that I have encountered racial discrimination in my personal or work life. However, on discussing this issue with my son recently, he admitted that throughout his school years, and at a school with a large percentage of Asian and Jewish children attending, he was subject to racism taunts from his Anglo-Australian schoolmates.

My Malaysian Chinese friend, Oi, and me

Most of my closest friends are Anglo-Australians, while one of my dearest and closest friends is a Malaysian-born Chinese. She has lived in Sydney for about 50 years and, recently, she told me of an incident to which she was exposed recently when a group of Anglo-Australians made a racist comment at her as they walked towards her. While this may be an isolated incident, one cannot deny that some residual racism must still "linger" in Sydney.

My cherished relationships with this small group of close friends are not based on the color of their skin but on how I value them as people who enrich my life. Admittedly, they are all as one (as I am) with the values, cultures and traditions of western society; yet, when necessity dictates, they can readily "don the mask" to make the socially desirable impression and facilitate a positive effect in the interactions in which they engage. I believe that we all "don masks" throughout life with the only distinction being that with maturity and experience, you become more adept at identifying the occasions where you feel the need to "don a mask" and the other instances where you feel there is no necessity to "play a game." Similarly, our self-perception and, thus, our identity generally change with each chapter as we progress through the book of life.

In summary, I have been very fortunate to live in a country, and an age, where females and those of different ethnicities are accepted as equals. I have taken from both of the cultures to which I have been exposed as I see them as complementary rather than mutually exclusive. Moreover, I believe it is that fusion of my Chinese ancestry and the freedom and egalitarian values that underpin life in Australia that has made my tapestry of life so rich and colorful. Maybe this has been due to my long-held belief in wanting to be valued as a person and the "tough" training course to which I was exposed due to my mother's Confucian-based value system. While it is with regret that this chapter of my life is not shared with a "soul mate," I can be truly thankful for the love and support which is so unstintingly and unquestioningly given by my family and small group of dear friends. Unequivocally I can say that "I am very happy in my skin" and have few regrets of the journey that I have taken, so far.

Chapter 4
The Voice of a Man: Reg Mu Sung

*As Gregor Samsa awoke one morning after disturbing dreams,
he found himself transformed in his bed into an enormous
insect.*

Franz Kafka, *Metamorphosis* (1916), quoted by Reg Mu Sung

Reg Mu Sung

L.L.-S. Ngan and K.-b. Chan, *The Chinese Face in Australia: Multi-generational
Ethnicity among Australian-born Chinese*, DOI 10.1007/978-1-4614-2131-3_4,
© Springer Science+Business Media, LLC 2012

In this chapter, we shall present a second autobiography, this time by a fifth-generation male Chinese settler in Australia—Reg Mu Sung—whose family has been in the country since the 1870s, almost one and a half centuries ago. In this chapter, he emphasizes quite a few times that he and the Chinese in Australia are assimilated. Assimilation could be a personal or social fact as process or consequence, a self-declaration, an intention, a desire. Sociologists and historians have long pointed out that assimilation is one thing, but approval and acceptance by the mainstream is quite another. Identity is socially bestowed and also socially approved. While growing up in Australia, Reg lamented the Chinese Australians' lack in numbers, possibly because size matters in terms of power, social capital, visibility, and acceptability, even assimilability. As it happens, there is a deep irony here: Chinese are instantly recognizable and visible because of skin color, the Chinese face, the Chinese body, their 'smallness,' but they are also at the same time invisible because of their lack of power and status. This irony of visible invisibility is the result of a strange but lethal mix of faciality/physicality and social deprivations. The Chinese face ironically renders the bearer of that face faceless, without a face, "having no face," or lost face, which is equivalent with shame in the Chinese parlance. You are how you are treated, especially by those whose opinions about you matter a lot to you—an important fact captured by the sociological concepts of the significant other or the reference group. In a way, my sense of selfworth depends on my worthiness in the eyes of others. The externals determine the internals.

Reg continues to claim to the "fact" that he and his Chinese coethnics are assimilated into Australian society. He says it as a fact, an intention, a desire, perhaps a pledge of loyalty and allegiance to his birthplace. When he was accused of being "un-Australian" for not letting a woman "jump the queue" in a local supermarket, he felt like "a stab to the heart," he wrote. This incident happened 20 years ago when he was 40 but Reg said, "I am still angry and upset to this day!" He continued, "The use of the word 'un-Australian' has become more common in current society and to me it is a code word for racism dressed up in acceptable language."

Is Reg assimilated, or is he not? Is Australia racist, or is it not? Reg, like almost a million other Chinese settlers in Australia, has long learned to cope with overt or blatant racism by avoidance, keeping a distance, not confronting, "walking off and away." Racism might have done underground, invisible or less visible than before, subtle, or, as Reg put it, presented in code words nicely dressed up. If victims of such subtle racism choose to ignore, avoid, and forget about it, then society can soothe its conscience and proudly say either there is no racism or it is a thing of the past; society has rehabilitated itself. Co-author Chan made this observation in his two monographs on Canada, *Smoke and Fire: The Chinese in Montreal (1991)* and *Coping with Racism: The Chinese Experience in Canada (1987)*. What (rape, fraud, theft, sexism, racism) was not reported did not happen. Do victims of racism collude with society by not reporting their victimization? Do racial minorities play a part in helping society to uphold the "great white lie" of no racism?

Growing up as a Chinese boy in Australia, Reg was acutely aware of his body and his look, the former more so because Chinese boys, as a racial minority, were eager to join society, to belong. One way to do that in school is to excel in sports, which would enable one to become part of the gang, the in-group, all in an attempt to struggle for social belongingness and acceptance—or to fight isolation, loneliness, the stigma, or spoiled identity of an unfortunate person bearing a Chinese face.

Perhaps, amidst the excitement and ecstasy of a football game, the Chinese face does not matter or at least it is temporarily forgotten—until he returns to the dressing room to remove his jersey, the group's uniform and symbol of "insidedness."

While failing up to the white men's hegemonic hold on masculinity and femininity, what one fails in the body, one tries to make it all up in the mind. Like Doreen in her autobiographical chapter before this one, Reg, like all Chinese boys and girls growing up in a white country, tried the hardest to gain respectability in academic pursuits. He was eager to reclaim an identity that was robbed of him. Reg became a professional, a librarian. But as he might have told us in this chapter, in others' eyes, he was a Chinese first, a man second, a librarian third, an Australian maybe a distant fourth or fifth. His Chinese look has sort of betrayed him, given him away, so to speak. Doing well in school didn't help much either as Chinese in specific or as Asians in general all over the world are stuck with stereotypes such as being diligent, nerdy, model minority, conformist, socially inept, and so on. Chinese girls, as Doreen told us in the earlier chapter, would need to cope with a completely different set of stereotypes altogether: they are exotic, petite, quiet, docile, weak, and charming, which make them into white men's objects of desire.

Reg shared with us many times rather disturbing anecdotes of him not feeling comfortable among the diverse groups of Chinese newcomers to Australia, the Chinese in Hong Kong, his village folks and kinsmen back "home" in China. Like co-author Ngan, Reg does not read nor write Chinese, neither does he speak Cantonese and other southern China dialects. Among the Chinese in Australia, Hong Kong, and China, he is as much a stranger, an outsider, as he is among the white Australians. His wife, an immigrant from Hong Kong, thinks he is pretending to be Chinese and considers him to be an Australian, trying "to take the best of both worlds." She thinks being Chinese is like a thing Reg puts on and takes off at ease, like a mask, or a "min larp,"—a Chinese coat filled with cotton to keep warm, to survive the winter. Or so Reg wishes. As it happens, Reg is a classic example of the American sociologist Robert Park's (1929) "marginal man," who is eager to belong to both worlds but accepted by none. A stranger, adrift and homeless. Park predicted some 80 years ago the single barrier to assimilation into white society is skin color.

What about his children—sixth-generation Australians? Reg wrote this, "They are *thoroughly westernized.* Australia *has changed* with the advent of the multicultural society and the growth of the Chinese population to 700,000 (2006 census). They consider themselves to be *Australian and not Chinese,* but their *appearance* will always *mark* them as Chinese and *how they will cope is unknown*" (emphases ours). If Australia has indeed been changed for the better by multiculturalism and his children are thoroughly westernized and consider themselves Australian, not Chinese, why did Reg say, "how they will cope is unknown?"

Reg said many times in this autobiographical chapter he is "thoroughly assimilated" but he also reminded us that racism itself has changed. His children have many code words to contend with.

Reg mentioned upward social mobility, wealth or business success might possibly compensate for the Chinese' lack because of race and skin color. He wrote, "social class and prestige trumped and overcame the problem of being Chinese and the aura of power... made being Chinese an irrelevancy." Reg thinks, or hopes, class matters. Does it? If it does, cash-rich immigrants from Hong Kong buying up property in Vancouver, Canada, and flashing fleets of multicolored BMWs, Lexuses, and Mercedes in their front yards would not have incurred such public rage. Sociologists writing in the field of social stratification have long pointed to the crucial difference between money and respectability. Though the two often go together, the fact that money is objective and respectability is subjective and therefore can be withheld by those who are in the position to give it goes a long way in reminding us all that, plain and simple, there are many things in life that "money cannot buy." So unfortunate, yet so very true.

Reg Mu Sung's Autobiography

My family has been in Australia since the 1870s and I am the fifth generation but since there has been only one instance of inter-racial marriage I am still Chinese in appearance. I was born and raised in Sydney and I am thoroughly assimilated with English as my main language and Australian culture the only one I have known. Yet in spite of this my Chinese appearance sparks a reaction in white Australians that I am different from them. How does a multi-generation Chinese resolve the dilemma that although I look different from the others I am the same as them in language and values? How do I cope with the many situations where I am treated because of the way I look?

My older brother and me

Growing up in Australia in the 1950s the factors which affected me were the White Australia Policy and the absence of other Chinese people. The White Australia Policy was a government-sanctioned policy of racism in both overt and subtle ways. The Official Year Book of the Commonwealth of Australia in 1968 stated the immigration policy as follows:

Admission of non-Europeans. Australia's immigration policy is based on the need to maintain a predominantly homogenous population. It is fundamental to the policy that people coming to Australia for residence should be capable, both economically and socially, of ready integration into the community.

There was no acceptance or tolerance of difference. When I was a child I remember our next-door neighbor coming into our shop and shouting at my father that our "foreign" cooking smells were ruining his clothes hanging on the line to dry. Subconsciously you were told that Chinese people were not allowed into Australia, that you were a non-person and that you were not wanted. The psychological effect of this was a sense of not belonging and not being accepted. Since the introduction of the White Australia Policy in 1901 and the virtual exclusion of Chinese this had resulted in the Chinese population gradually declining. By 1947 there were 12,000 Chinese in Australia and they formed 0.15% of the population. Being such a small number they did not pose a threat but on the other hand this made them feel powerless as they were a minority and helpless in dealing with casual bullying. On a broader scale China was in a state of self-imposed isolation from the West from its founding in 1949 until the loosening of diplomatic relations in 1973. During this period of the Cold War it was seen together with Russia as among the great communist adversaries. Therefore there was an added stigma of being identified as a communist at a time when this vitriolic term carried even greater denigration.

The depth of anxiety about racial purity and the overarching desire to produce a white homogenised society was shown in a newspaper report from 1954 discussing the White Australia policy:

The fact that Chinese in Australia have, to a great extent, retained their racial purity and not intermarried is held, by immigration authorities, to support the view that Asians are not easily assimilated. Immigration authorities do not criticise these Australians of Chinese origin as citizens, but they go against the grain of an established immigration policy which aims to produce a homogeneous population without national groups and colonies.

A watershed occurred in 1973 when the White Australia Policy was officially abolished by the Federal Government and this psychological Damocles sword hanging over our heads was removed. There was no overnight change but the sense of foreboding of being Chinese and looking different was no longer present. When slavery was legal and institutionalised in the United States, all African Americans were viewed the same, whether they were slaves or free men. Similarly the White Australia Policy was an official declaration that the Chinese were not wanted and that they were worthless. The policy of seventy years of restricting immigration meant that the numbers of Chinese in Australia had decreased to such an extent that they no longer posed an economic or social threat. Their numbers were so small and their assimilation into the multicultural melting pot so complete that they had become part of the homogenised white Australia.

Showing the prevalence of unconscious racism in Australia, there was a popular saying which was repeated recently by Peter Costello, the former Australian Treasurer, when talking about his childhood: Don't pick up anything in the street because it was touched by a Chinaman.

The stereotype of the Chinese in the written history of Australia was that they came in the gold rushes of the 1850s and provoked racial riots on the gold fields. At Lambing Flat in New South Wales in 1861, over 2000 European miners attacked the Chinese mining camp and 250 Chinese lost all of their belongings. This in turn led to the racial smearing by the *Bulletin* magazine in the 1890s, which depicted them with their vices of opium smoking, gambling and prostituting white women. The *Bulletin* persisted with their anti-Chinese campaign with their motto '*Australia for the white man*' printed under the title of the magazine until 1960. The Chinese disappeared from public view except for the occasional story of them being deported. I could find no mention of me as a Chinese person in Australian history until 1975 when C.Y. Choi published his pioneering work *Chinese Migration and Settlement in Australia*. For the first time the Chinese were significant enough to have their history recorded and I could see a part of me that had been hidden from the public view. With no public face I had avoided identifying as Chinese and now there was an alternative in being Chinese. I cannot count the number of times that I have been asked where I came from and I have always replied that I am Australian. This inevitably leads to the next question of where I originally came from and when I replied China the questioner is satisfied.

In his famous novel *Metamorphosis*, Kafka depicts an individual who changed overnight into a giant insect and how his family and society suddenly changed in their attitude toward him:

> As Gregor Samsa awoke one morning after disturbing dreams, he found himself transformed in his bed into an enormous insect.

They reacted only to his outward appearance even though he had not changed internally. The way that people see you is the way that they will treat you irrespective of who you are. Your face is paramount but your identity only becomes evident through experience, sharing and familiarity. So if you look Chinese then in a white Australia you will be treated as Chinese and being different.

My great-great-grandmother was an Irish woman who had co-habited with a Chinese miner and gave birth in 1872 in rural Queensland to a daughter.

My great-grandmother with her grandchild

My great-grandmother, in turn, married another Chinese miner and in 1895 a daughter, my grandmother, was born in the tin mining region in northern New South Wales. When aged sixteen she also married a Chinese miner who was aged forty-four and my father was born in 1918.

My grandfather   My grandmother

The family quickly returned to China to my grandfather's native village of Du Tou in Zhongshan and my father spent the majority of his childhood in China and grew up more Chinese than Australian. He returned to Australia in 1930 in the depths of the Great Depression and work was difficult to find. So, in 1932, he went to China for four years and then spent the rest of his life in Australia. As my father was Chinese and born in Australia, he was entitled to a 'Certificate Exempting from the Dictation Test,' which allowed him to re-enter Australia without taking the dictation test designed to exclude unsuitable immigrants.

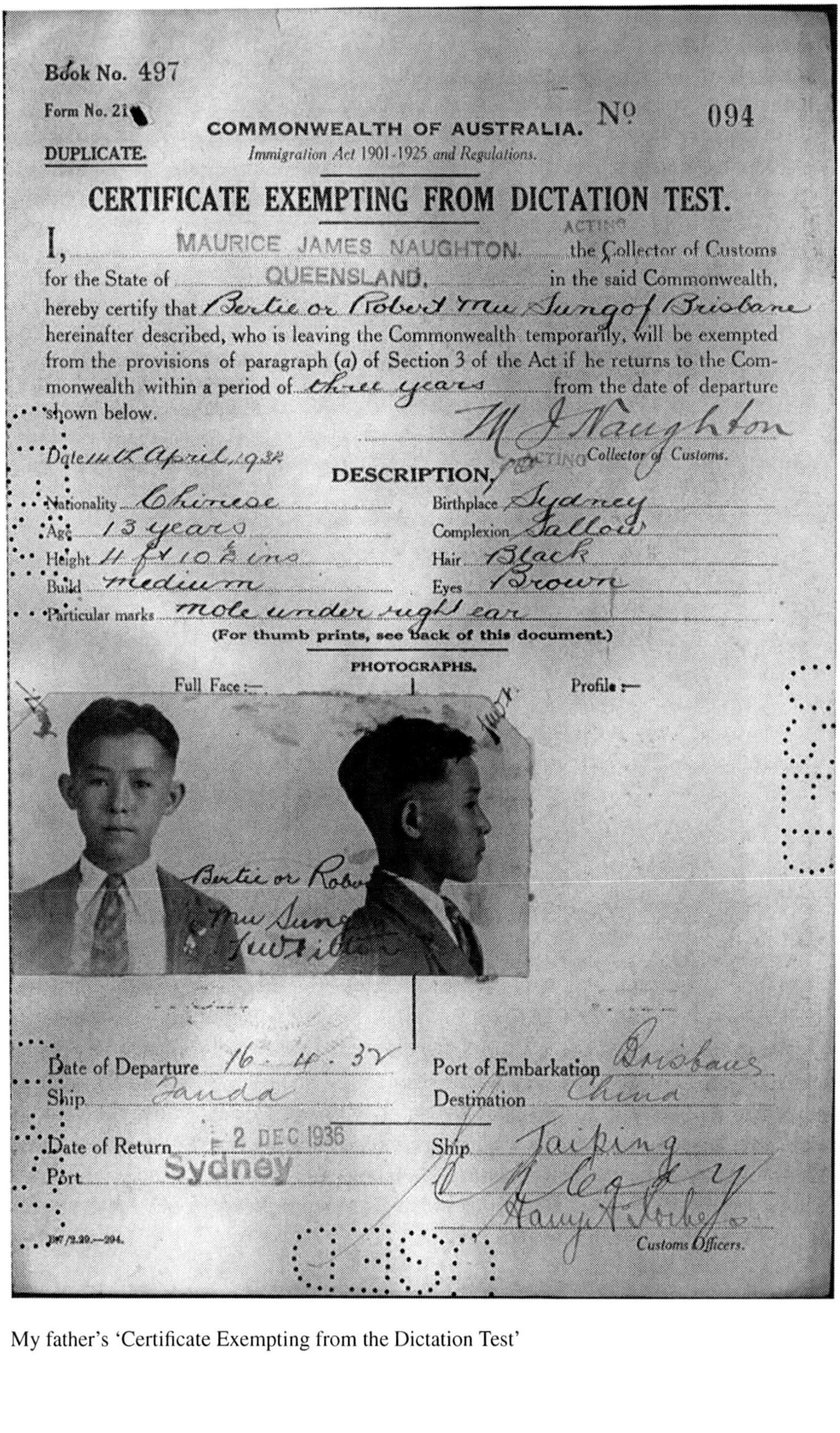

Book No. 497

Form No. 21.

COMMONWEALTH OF AUSTRALIA. № 094

DUPLICATE.   *Immigration Act 1901-1925 and Regulations.*

CERTIFICATE EXEMPTING FROM DICTATION TEST.

I, _____ MAURICE JAMES NAUGHTON. _____ the Collector of Customs
for the State of _____ QUEENSLAND, _____ in the said Commonwealth,
hereby certify that *Bertie or Robert Mu Sung of Brisbane*
hereinafter described, who is leaving the Commonwealth temporarily, will be exempted
from the provisions of paragraph (a) of Section 3 of the Act if he returns to the Commonwealth within a period of *three years* from the date of departure
shown below.

Date *11th April 1932*   *M. J. Naughton*
ACTING Collector of Customs.

DESCRIPTION.

Nationality *Chinese*   Birthplace *Sydney*
Age *13 years*   Complexion *Sallow*
Height *11 ft 10½ ins*   Hair *Black*
Build *medium*   Eyes *Brown*
Particular marks *mole under right ear*
(For thumb prints, see back of this document.)

PHOTOGRAPHS.

Full Face :—   Profile :—

Date of Departure *16 - 4 - 32*   Port of Embarkation *Brisbane*
Ship *Tanda*   Destination *China*
Date of Return *2 DEC 1936*   Ship *Taiping*
Port *Sydney*

Customs Officers.

My father's 'Certificate Exempting from the Dictation Test'

The Jesuits have a saying 'Give me the child until he is seven and I will show you the man' and my early upbringing in an Australian setting shaped the rest of my life. I was born in 1951 in Sydney in a working class suburb where my father owned a small corner grocery store. Our suburb had three Chinese families and two of them owned grocery stores. These stores were ubiquitous and in our street alone there were four such stores.

Our grocery store and home

The shop was open twelve hours a day during the week and six hours on Saturday and four hours on Sunday. My father opened the shop every day of the year and never had a holiday in forty years. As we grew up we worked in the shop from an early age, learning to serve the customers and performing many of the small duties. We would buy sugar in thirty-pound hessian bags and then repack them into smaller one-pound bags for sale. There was no self-service and we would get every item asked for by the customer off the shelf.

My brothers and sister

As owners of the store we were part of the local community but rarely socialised with them. As a family of six children we played primarily together and our family's social circle was our larger family network, other Chinese who were scattered around the suburbs, and perhaps informal linkages with clan and lineage members who were distant relatives anyway. Although both my parents had been born in Australia they had returned to China when quite young and had spent their childhood and adolescence in China. When they came to Australia as teenagers they felt like first-generation immigrants with Chinese as their first language and no experience of this new country. Subsequently speaking in Chinese remained their preferred means of communication and they felt uncomfortable conversing in English. Amongst the Chinese people language was another subtle marker to differentiate those from the different counties. In Guangdong the counties had different dialects of Cantonese and your language would identify your home area.

Like other first-generation immigrants they found support amongst their family and other Chinese-speaking people with whom they felt comfortable and shared the same values. One of our father's friends was a man named Chan who had a market garden near the airport and he would cycle over to visit us. When we went to visit his home in the market gardens, I remember it was a ramshackle building made of timber with a rough floor with a single light bulb hanging from the ceiling and I thought that this was how Australians saw Chinese. Another friend of the family was memorable to this young child because when we went to visit him in his suburban restaurant he would offer us a new experience and start up his deep fryer and cook us spring rolls. Over the years my parents' English language skills did not improve and they remained content to socialise with other Chinese-speaking people. As this was our family culture I did not find it strange that they socialised only with Chinese people. Yet they did not feel any affinity with recent immigrants from Hong Kong or China as they shared no common interests nor had an opportunity to mix with them socially.

A paternal aunt married a Chinese man who had come to Australia as a student and he subsequently became a successful businessman. This gave him entrée into the highest levels of society and his large house on the north shore became the centre of social activities. Australia in the 1950s was a class-conscious society and modeled itself on British society with distinct social classes based on wealth, upbringing and position. The upper classes appeared in the social pages and the middle class occupied the positions of authority such as doctors and bank managers. The working class had no visibility or power and toiled anonymously. The majority of Chinese were working class or self-employed and suffered the double disadvantage of class and race, disqualifying them from power.

Apart from the occasional activity my father maintained a social distance from his side of the family. On these social occasions they would bring out the mahjong[1] tables and the adults would break into male and female groups to play the sixteen rounds over the course of a long evening while the children would watch television. As he played mah-jong my father would smoke and drink—something that he did not do at home.

As one of four boys and two girls I did not notice any difference in the way that our parents treated us until adolescence when my older sister was scolded for not helping with washing the clothes while the boys were not asked to do this. My father was the head of the house and my mother never worked except as a housewife. Domestic duties were divided with my mother cooking the meal, my father washing up and the children helping with drying and putting away the dishes. We spent more time with our maternal grandparents who owned a corner grocery shop in a neighboring suburb. My mother ensured that we visited them regularly and one of my fondest memories is of my grandmother who was one of the sweetest people that you knew, with never a cross word. She had been born and raised in Sydney and she always spoke English with us. Due to the economic effects of the Great Depression and the lack of work in Australia, she had returned to China during the 1930s, where she had raised her four daughters in a village and, consequently, her English language was far better than theirs. In Australia my mother and her sisters attended the Chinese Presbyterian church and on one occasion when she took our family along to have afternoon tea with the minister, I remember him as an old fashioned minister with a loud voice and an accent I could not understand.

---

[1] A tile game of Chinese origin, usually played by four people.

I attended the local primary school and when we had to choose a scripture class I heard all the other children say "Church of England." So when it was my turn I also said "Church of England" and this was how my religion was chosen. This was the predominant religion and sectarianism was rampant with Catholics still being discriminated against and non-Christian religions such as Buddhism unheard of. I was one of the brightest in my class and was in constant competition with several others in examinations. When I came first in the exams in my final year I became dux of the school, which signaled that I was the best in the school academically and there was a great sense of achievement. My siblings were average in academic achievement and apart from my being a voracious reader it was a carefree time with no pressure to perform academically in order to gain admission into a selective school. Here is my school photograph from 1957 and there are three Chinese children. Do you notice them or do they blend in?

School photograph

In the 1960s I went to a selective boys' high school with two of my classmates while others went to local comprehensive high schools. I was placed in the top class and the other two boys were placed in lower classes and we drifted apart. There were only two Chinese boys in my whole year of 120. I had gone from being a big fish in a small pond to a very small fish in a big pond. Being one of the smallest boys in the school and not being very sporty did not make life easy. Schoolyards are extremely competitive and belonging to a social group made life more enjoyable. One of the easiest ways to forge social bonds with others was by joining a sports team. Sport was compulsory on a Wednesday afternoon and was divided into two streams. The inter-school competition was for the better sporting types and interest focused on the first-grade football team whose exploits were duly reported at the Monday morning school assembly. Those who could not qualify for the inter-school competitive teams played house sport—a term for pseudo-sporting activities looked down upon by everyone. I was a late physical maturer and finally in the fourth year of high school I qualified for a rugby union team in my age group and I was selected in the lowest team.

School football team

I had just scraped in but I was very happy. I was beginning to belong and I continued to play football in my subsequent years at school and also played cricket—a quintessentially Anglo sport with its uniform of white clothes.

Wearing my cricket uniform

Looking back at my school yearbooks, two thirds of the contents listed the achievements of the sporting teams and there was no mention of the boys in the school and so I could not even tell you how many classes or boys there were. No wonder I felt invisible at school. The school was ruthlessly competitive in promoting excellence and those who did not thrive were ignored. My best friend arrived in the later years of high school as a German exchange student with a poor grasp of English and he always carried a pocket dictionary, which he pulled out when he could not understand a word. I think that he carried the stigma of being German with the aftermath of World War 2 and the Nazis being still an object of hatred, felt like an outsider.

My father in the grocery store

My father worked long hours in the shop, seven days a week, and above all he wanted his children to have economic success and stability. Education was the pathway to success. During the 1960s it was becoming easier for working class children to attend university and we were encouraged to further our education. I then went on to University of Sydney where I gained a science degree in chemistry and psychology. The size of the university population made it easy to lose yourself in the anonymity of the crowds and the liberal and elitist values of the students made me feel as if I were no different. In the early 1970s the proportion of Asian students was probably higher than the proportion of Asians in the general population and this engendered a tolerant atmosphere as the visibility and presence of Asians was a sign that they shared the same values. The science faculty had huge general lectures of several hundred students in mathematics and chemistry and this placed a barrier in forming friendships. My friends coalesced around the chemistry laboratory where I spent most of my time and I would wear a white laboratory coat to psychology lectures as a mark of my youthful independence. By 1973 when I graduated, less than five per cent of my age group had a university degree which was an advantage in getting a sought-after job.

Graduation day with my father and sister

My friendships over the years have been predominantly with white Australians as I have felt myself to be Australian and they were the ones who shared my interests and values. At work we talked about sport and gossiped about what was happening in the office and laughed at the same jokes. For many years my passion was my children's sport and this was the main topic of interest that I shared with other fathers who were Australian. With three children playing sport this occupied the bulk of our weekends in terms of time and became the centre of my attention.

My parents spoke Chinese to each other at home but the children grew up speaking only English. We overheard Chinese conversations and could understand a smattering but could not speak or read Chinese as our parents believed that to succeed you needed the ability to speak English, in which they were not fluent. Our Australian family surname was given to my grandfather when he arrived in Australia and was made up by the immigration official. I did not learn my Chinese family name until my twenties and even then I did not take much notice. When I was married at twenty-eight we had a traditional Chinese wedding invitation printed in Hong Kong in both Chinese and English and I finally learned my full Chinese name. However it is something that I cannot remember or recognize when it is written down and my Chinese name is not used by anyone.

My parents had come out from China in the 1930s and 1940s from a rural village in Zhongshan near Guangzhou and their Chinese language reflected this time period of being both rural and slightly old-fashioned. Recent immigrants in the 1990s from the cosmopolitan cities of Hong Kong and Singapore found the Australian Chinese language to be old-fashioned and spoken with an Australian accent and a point of differentiation between the Australian-born Chinese and the recent arrivals. Within the Chinese community there are multiple levels of differentiation based on place of origin and language. The Australian-born Chinese initially were the majority and occupied positions of authority within the community and transactions were conducted in Cantonese. They have been overtaken by arrivals from Hong Kong, Malaysia and, most recently, mainland China and there has been a shift toward Mandarin as the predominant language which the ABCs cannot speak. The old guard have given way to the new arrivals who, by sheer weight of numbers and economic clout, now wield the power. The Mandarin Club was founded in the 1960s as the centre of Cantonese social activity with its dim sum[2] lunches and poker machines. As a sign of the declining influence of the Cantonese community the club has closed down and its premises in the city centre have been sold.

At home my mother cooked rice every night for dinner and the next morning we would eat leftover rice for breakfast. We quickly became adept at using chopsticks and this was a small indicator of our cultural heritage. Our school lunch was homemade sandwiches and once a week there was a treat from the tuckshop where we were allowed to buy a pie. At the weekends my father would cook a roast lamb dinner as a result of his days as a cook in the army during World War 2. He never spoke of his experiences in the army during the war apart from the fact that he was a reluctant conscript and only once alluded to the horrifying nature of warfare in Papua New Guinea. He did not participate in the Anzac Day marches and one small memento was a photograph of him in his uniform. Anzac Day was a glorification of the valor of war and like my father I shared the belief that war was a futile attempt to solve problems and should not be the cause of celebration. Public holidays were an occasion to escape from the rigors of opening the shop and an opportunity to have a family picnic in one of the many public parks in Sydney or to go to the beach. The only times that our family ate out for dinner would be a trip to Dixon Street for a meal at Lean Sun Low, one of three restaurants in this small enclave of Chinatown. We would squeeze into a booth or around a formica table and devour wonton[3] soup or fried rice noodles. At other times he would bring pots to the restaurant, which they would fill with the food and we would have our takeaway meal at home.

The Chinatown of the 1950s consisted of Dixon Street which formed its heart and was located near Paddy's Markets, the central produce markets. There were a small number of restaurants, Chinese grocery shops and boarding houses where

---

[2] A type of Chinese dish, similar to tapas where food is served in small individual portions, usually in a steamer basket.

[3] Chinese dumpling.

elderly Chinese would sleep in tiny cubicles. The grocery shops were the only places in Sydney where you could buy Chinese groceries and in Campbell Street on the other side of George Street there was a roast meat vendor where you could buy a treat of roast pork. These excursions into Chinatown were part of our routine but we did not feel that we belonged to the group who lived here.

Unusually for a fifth-generation Chinese immigrant family there has been only one instance of inter-racial marriage in the direct line of descent and we still maintained our Chinese look. During the period of Australian history from the late nineteenth to the early twentieth century the sex-ratio imbalance between Chinese men and women would imply that there would be a great deal of intermarriages with white women. Although this did occur, Chinese women as in the case of my ancestors tended to marry Chinese men due to cultural imperatives and their relative scarcity made them highly valued to the traditional males. My parents belonged to a generation that married within the Chinese community that was small and knew each other.

The Chinese community was scattered throughout Sydney but, like a spider's web, maintained ties with each other. My generation had more opportunities and contact with the wider society due to our Australian upbringing. As a result interracial marriages became more common and my parents accepted that two of their daughters-in-law were Australian.

One incident that stands out happened twenty years ago when I was forty. It was in a supermarket and a female of that indeterminate middle age approached me as I was standing in the queue with a full trolley and asked if she could push in as she only had a few items. I politely refused and then ignored her. She then raised her voice and began a speech to everyone how un-Australian it was not to allow anyone to go ahead. She continued ranting in this vein and repeating how un-Australian this was. I tried to ignore her but I was getting angrier and angrier and no one else in the supermarket queue made any response. Her aggressive behavior and her repeated use of the phrase un-Australian felt like a stab to the heart. I am still angry and upset to this day as I have always tried to avoid conflict as much as possible. Looking back I see that it was the use of the phrase 'un-Australian' which I was hearing used for the first time and also that it was a rare occurrence when I was involved in a public dispute with a stranger. The use of the phrase un-Australian has become more common in current society and to me it is a code word for racism dressed up in acceptable language.

Subtle racism occurs when you use the concept of race to signify your disapproval of a topic. *The Australian* is a national business newspaper which supports the conservative Liberal Party in Australian politics and consistently opposes the Australian Labor Party. They gloated about the recent national elections in which there was a swing to the Liberal Party and that the only people who voted Labor included those on social welfare and Middle Eastern people. This was the only ethnic group singled out and who coincidentally are the scapegoats for news on terrorism, crime and illegal immigration. Each generation of society has its racial scapegoats on which to hang social evils. Australian society in turn had Chinese, Italians, Vietnamese and Middle Eastern immigrants as the stereotypes.

Having seen how the Chinese were previously portrayed as the criminal outsiders with their gambling and opium smoking I can see how and why the Middle Eastern people now occupy this role.

As a young adult I would go to the movies on a Saturday night to the cinema strip on George Street. In the hurly burly of the crowds that jostled each other, groups of youths looking for excitement or danger would call you names such as 'chinaman' or 'commo' and I would ignore them and try and walk past as quickly as possible. Racist outbursts would occur in public places where you would be insulted by strangers. In Hobart on a holiday in the main street in the middle of the day, my family with young children was abused by a drunken homeless man and we walked on as quickly as possible. I later thought that this was due to the provinciality of Hobart where there were not many Chinese. With their distinctive look Chinese will stand out and be noticed in public places. In many parts of Australia where there are not many Chinese, the appearance of one in the street will be a noticeable event and bring to the surface any underlying attitudes. My brother mentioned that when he stayed in caravan parks which are not normally frequented by Chinese, he has encountered instances of racial abuse. In areas where there is a high concentration of Chinese they are not seen as different. The suburb of Chatswood in Sydney has long been an area where the Chinese have congregated and in 2006 they constituted sixteen per cent of the population. It has become a de facto suburban Chinatown providing a critical mass of services for the Chinese population such as grocery shops, restaurants and doctors. Similarly the suburb Richmond in Vancouver, Canada serves the same function of being a magnet for middle-class Chinese and their presence is the norm rather than the minority. However in the working-class suburb of Cabramatta in Sydney there has been a conflict between the older Anglo stores and the newer Asian stores which the former see as taking over their suburb and not having signs in English and which they feel will ultimately drive them out of business.

My twenty-year-old daughter recounted a story where only this year she had been in the Sutherland Shire, the scene of the Cronulla beach riots, with a group of white friends when another group of white youths began to taunt them racially in the street. Her friends decided to avoid an incident and moved on and my daughter said that she felt so angry that she had wanted to retaliate. On an opposite note she finds herself targeted by Caucasian males who find Chinese females to be exotic and she finds this equally distasteful.

When I was growing up, because there were so few other Chinese I did not think of myself as an Australian-born Chinese or ABC. I thought of myself as being Australian. I spoke and wrote English and had very little knowledge of the Chinese language. I was unfamiliar with Chinese customs and did not celebrate Chinese festivals. My parents thought that the only way for us to succeed in life was to assimilate and be the same as everyone else. There was no expectation that we would identify as Chinese. We celebrated birthday parties with soft drinks, party hats and a birthday cake and food such as frankfurts. At Christmas we eagerly awaited Christmas morning when we rushed downstairs to see what Santa had brought and we tore open the presents.

My brother's birthday party

With the abolition of the White Australia Policy and the gradual influx of Chinese from overseas I first heard the term ABC from one of these overseas Chinese who was more aware of these cultural differences than I was. The recent Chinese immigrants were professional or entrepreneurial types who were different from the local Chinese who tended to be on the lower socioeconomic scale. I felt that I had little in common with the newcomers whose language and interests did not coincide with mine.

My sister married into a well-off Hong Kong family who had immigrated to Australia. They had the trappings of success: a large house in a prestigious suburb, private schooling for the children and a Mercedes Benz. This entrée provided an insight into the world of the successful overseas Chinese and also the traditional Chinese culture that I had not experienced before. Her wedding was a large formal Chinese banquet where ten courses of food came flowing to your table. The formality and respect paid to the Chinese elders was another contrast and the rituals associated with Buddhism such as the burning of incense broadened my perspectives.

A turning point came in my life when I went overseas to Europe in 1975 and on the way home stopped off in Hong Kong. For the first time in my life I was no longer surrounded by white faces but was in a sea of Chinese faces. I was no longer the outsider like the hero of Albert Camus' novel *L'Étranger* and I felt that I belonged. This sense came as feeling of freedom and relief as I did not have to try to fit in. The problem had now changed. My face was the same as everyone else but underneath I was still different and could not understand the language. The local Chinese that

I came into contact with in restaurants were not sympathetic to my plight of not being able to speak Chinese. My Mandarin acquaintances have said that they experienced similar treatment from the Cantonese-speaking people in Hong Kong when they spoke Mandarin to them and that they found them to be arrogant and unfriendly.

My interest in Chineseness intensified when I married my wife who was born in Hong Kong. We met at my aunt's sixty-first birthday party which was a lavish social occasion which gave me the opportunity to meet other people. There is an old adage that you marry someone whom you are familiar with, someone you meet through work or family occasions and with whom you share common values.

When I learned that Lucille Ngan was conducting her research into the multi-generational Chinese in Australia I volunteered because I wanted to learn more about myself and my Chinese identity. This was an area specific to my situation which spoke to me for the first time about being born in Australia of Chinese descent. When I was being interviewed by her, I reflected on a conversation that I had with my wife:

> My wife still considers me to be Australian. She thinks I wear my Chineseness like something that I can put on and say "Oh I am Chinese I have a 'min naap' on" and then I take it off. She doesn't think I am Chinese at all … My wife says "You are pretending to be Chinese and you are talking about things you don't know anything about. You are trying to take the best of both worlds. You are trying to be Australian but you are trying to be Chinese at the same time."

My wife is my sternest critic and insists that I am not Chinese in my behavior or thought. Her parents had been raised in China in the traditional manner and she had grown up absorbing many of their values.

My father-in-law as a young man with his parents

In a later conversation my wife elaborated on how the older Chinese saw the 'native born' (*to saang* in Cantonese) who were the younger generation born in Australia. They were seen as lacking the traditional values of the Chinese because they were born here and also, as young people, they lacked the respect that should be shown to their elders. My aunt had complained that these *to saang* would greet her with an exaggerated version of hello by saying in a mock accent '*har lo*' which she interpreted in Cantonese as prawn person. In public I would address my aunts as *gu mou* and in private mix my Chinese and English by distinguishing them as big and little *gu mou*.

My wife further critiqued my Chineseness by discussing my attitude to our wedding. I had wanted the ceremony to be held in a church and then the reception held in a Chinese restaurant with a ten-course banquet for the three hundred and fifty guests. However my side of the family adopted only those Chinese wedding customs that suited us. In a traditional Chinese wedding the groom pays the bill but I insisted that we split the cost in the western manner and in the end I prevailed and we split the bill. Furthermore in the Chinese custom we offered my mother her choice of the wedding gifts from which she took four items but in return she never offered the jewelry, which was to be given to her new daughter-in-law. I followed the traditional customs when there was an advantage to me or did not require any great effort. I paid respect to the parents by ceremonially offering them tea at the wedding reception (*jam cha*) and gave her brothers a pair of trousers because she had married before them. At the reception my wife and I stood publicly in front of the guests and we would proffer tea (*jam cha*) to the older Chinese and they in turn would give us a red gift packet (*lai see*) in return.

My entry into her family's household led to a small cultural reversal on my part where I adopted a Chinese persona. At dinner time we would sit around the table and wait for her father to arrive and we could not begin to eat until he said *sik faan* (eat rice). However I did not adopt the habit of greeting her parents when I arrived at their house by saying *jou san* (good morning) which they excused by saying that I was only a *to saang*. When we stayed in Vancouver with her relatives she vigorously enforced this rule by ensuring that I greeted our hosts every morning. Her father was an artist and he painted the painting below for her, which she valued as a memento of her Chinese heritage.

Painting by my father-in-law

Another physical object which symbolized Chineseness to me was the camphor wood chest with its distinctive carvings and aroma and I lusted after one as if to prove and reinforce my Chineseness. We purchased one from Hong Kong and its arrival was another sign of my growing Chinese identity.

Chinese chest

I had gained a new interest in being Chinese which answered my questions of who I was and I began to learn and adopt the custom of my new role. I attended a Cantonese language community class for one year but dropped out at the end of the year as my Cantonese had not improved at all and I was not using or speaking Cantonese in regular situations. However by going to regular classes and having a Cantonese dictionary my understanding of hearing Cantonese spoken by my in-laws had improved and my vocabulary had also increased. My wife and brothers would mock me in what they saw as an affectation in trying to speak Cantonese. Attempts at speaking Cantonese to my in-laws would provoke mirth as my accent in pronouncing tonal Cantonese words would give them the wrong and usually inappropriate meaning. One time we were discussing the traditional Chinese custom of arranged marriage and I meant to say that I chose my wife (*gaan* in Cantonese) but with my accent apparently I said that I raped her (also *gaan* in Cantonese).

In high school I had studied French and Latin for three years and I felt comfortable with my schoolboy French so that when I went to Paris on holidays I could easily understand simple conversations with the French people. I would often be asked by waiters "Êtes vous chinois?" and I would reply in English "No, I am Australian" and this would lead to linguistic confusion as there would be uncertainty about which language to conduct the conversation in. Also the fact that I said that I was an Australian confused them more as they expected me to be Chinese and their visions of Australians would be different from what they saw before them.

On another occasion, sitting in a restaurant in Venice with my family, we were approached by an expatriate Australian living in Italy who had overheard our conversation and recognized our Australian accents. She came over to join us. We reminisced about life in Australia and she displayed a nostalgia to reconnect with her homeland that she had not seen for twenty years. Her homesickness mirrored my own feelings that Australia was my home and that I could connect with other Australians overseas with whom we shared a common bond.

In Hong Kong I never felt comfortable with the Chinese language as I found that I could not handle even simple conversations with the waiters. Attempting to speak Cantonese was even more trying as my level of fluency was so low that I could not say simple sentences because of the tonal pronunciation of words. I sensed that in Hong Kong many of the people outside of the tourist areas were monolingual and therefore indifferent to those who could not speak Cantonese. When I travel overseas I always feel like a tourist and I do not have a sense of belonging as I stay in these locations for only a short period. Language is the main impediment that prevents me from fitting in. My inability to converse in Italian in Venice or Cantonese in Hong Kong prevents me from feeling comfortable. I felt much more at home in England and Canada as the ability to conduct conversations in English simplified life. In Hong Kong they can identify you as overseas Chinese and make you feel different.

As a librarian in a university I often gave classes to students on finding information. Afterwards in a reference inquiry with another librarian they will mention that they have already attended an information class with the Chinese librarian. On the one hand as the only Chinese librarian giving information classes it is a quick way to identify me but on the other it emphasizes how your face becomes your primary means of identification. In another instance when I had a disagreement with another driver on the road he hurled a torrent of abuse and swear words at me calling me a **** Chinese so that identifying me as Chinese becomes my primary identity and also a mark of abuse.

When our work group goes out for a social lunch to celebrate birthdays I prefer going to yum cha[4] as the variety of dishes is more satisfying than a single dish. I tend to do the ordering of the dim sum from the trolleys as they pass but as the supervisor and with the group's unfamiliarity with yum cha this seems like the normal thing to do. Yum cha is a Chinese experience with the different food and the Chinese language spoken by the trolley ladies; it is an acceptable and enjoyable aspect of a different culture. I still encounter many older Australians who do not eat Chinese food and cling to their traditional eating patterns.

---

[4] A Chinese dining experience which involves drinking tea and having a variety of dishes and delicacies.

As a young man my experiences of dating were disastrous. As Caucasian Australian women were the only ones I met socially, I attributed my lack of success to my gaucheness rather than to my ethnicity. At that tender age there were not many opportunities for meeting people and I lacked the social skills and confidence to interact with females successfully. After my trip to Europe when I traveled around in a Kombi van for two months I learned a lot about dealing with people. I matured in my social skills and changed my mind about dating Chinese women. Previously I had unconsciously avoided them since that would emphasize my Chineseness. I realized that was an inappropriate response and I had the confidence to embark on blind dates with Chinese females whom relatives seemed to know. Match making was a favorite pasttime for older female relatives and acquaintances and nothing would delight them more if they were successful in matching young males and females who were both Chinese.

After marriage to my wife my cultural sensitivity increased as I realized that the plurality of cultures in Australia no longer meant that the mainstream Australian culture was the only choice and my wife would point out instances of my cultural ignorance. Chinese associate the color white with death and wearing white on inappropriate occasions such as births or weddings may cause offence. Similarly the number four, like the Australian number thirteen, had connotations of misfortune and death. Chinese would avoid any connection with this number and would not buy a house with a street address with the number four in it. For them the number eight was the lucky number and a motorcar license with the numbers 888 almost invariably indicated a Chinese owner.

In the 1990s when I took my children to Saturday morning soccer I entered this public sphere of strangers. As I looked around at the other families my children were the only Chinese on the field. When you arrived at a playing field and you were waiting for the game to begin you observed the players and nothing distinguished them except the way they looked. Once the game started this feeling dissipated as the action became the focus and all thoughts concentrated on the flow of the game. From my own experience I had absorbed the stereotype that Chinese were not good at sport and I was worried that my children would fit this image. Soccer is physically competitive and it quickly becomes obvious who the better players are and their skill is the important factor in being accepted. My son was one of the better players and had the vital role of midfield in generating the attack and then dropping back to help in defense. He graduated from local to representative soccer and as he played for the Ku-ring-gai and District Soccer Association against teams from the Sydney metropolitan area his playing ability ensured his acceptance by the others. At this level the only thing that mattered was how good you were and whether you could help the team achieve their goal of winning. Being involved in a team sport and working toward a shared goal facilitates your sense of belonging.

My son playing soccer

The Chinese festival of Ching Ming, where we go to the cemetery annually and pay respects to those who have passed away, has been one of those customs that I have adopted. My father, sister and son are buried here as well as my wife's parents. Sometimes the pain of grief can be overwhelming but the simple ceremony of *bai saan* (praying) provides a soothing balm and a sense of continuity that the grief felt at bereavement is a necessary adjunct of life and helps with the healing process. We would offer food, burn paper money and incense and bow. It is better to remember those who have passed away than to forget them. We have already purchased the plots for our family to be buried together and I hope that our children will continue to remember us.

Paying respects at the cemetery

My interest in family history grew very slowly as my father never talked about his parents and he only briefly mentioned that they had died when he was very young. A glimmer of interest was aroused when my aunt showed me the only photograph that existed of my grandfather and I had something tangible to look at. Then when I needed to have my wedding invitation printed in English and Chinese I learned my full Chinese name (Louie gam-yat) for the first time. My father then wrote the names of my siblings and I saw that we had the same generation name. Learning my family history has filled in the gaps that were previously blank. I began my family history project to discover who my ancestors were and the joy of unearthing previously unknown facts has been rewarding. The process of research and of going to archives to look at original documents widened to examine how our family history fitted into the wider context of Chinese Australian history, and how our story could illuminate and contextualize the experiences of Chinese in Australia.

I joined the Chinese Australian Historical Society, CAHS, to satisfy my curiosity about my family history and the Chinese in Australia. The members were a mixture of Chinese and Caucasians and the presentations were predominantly in English. The society tried to balance the needs of those interested in family history and academic researchers but favored the academic angle. Its highlight was the organization of an international conference in Sydney on Quong Tart, the Chinese businessman in early twentieth century Australia. As a result the members interested in family history drifted away to join another group, the Chinese Heritage Association of Australia, whose focus was on familiar topics and had less academic rigor.

Within the Society there is one elderly member, the Vice-President, who attempts to maintain the cultural values of the Chinese. He acts as the host at the meetings and will introduce members to each other. I am always introduced by name and then my ancestral district Zhongshan is mentioned, even my home village. The majority of Australian-born Chinese in Sydney originated from Guangdong and those from Zhongshan formed the largest sub-group. At one of these meetings I was introduced to another member from my home village and this coincidence was a great pleasure; I established a link with someone with our common surname Louie. Her family had a series of grocery stores in northern New South Wales and employed people from the same district of Zhongshan and my father may have worked for them. The Chungshan Society was formed in the early 1900s to assist immigrants from Zhongshan and it still remains active to this day though its membership has declined with the passage of time as members move into the wider community and find other means of social support.

Membership of the society has focused my interest on the importance of the home village or *heung ha* to the Chinese immigrants. Their district of origin in Guangdong provided their first means of social support in Australia through their district associations and shops. They supplied mutual support, economic assistance and channels of communication with their home villages. Within the Chinese community the first level of loyalty lay with their family and village, then the district and finally to the broader Chinese community. My interest lay in exploring the history of our district grouping of Zhongshan and an in-depth analysis of their role in nineteenth- and twentieth- century Australian history. An area of further research is the role that district associations played in the lives of the Chinese miners on the gold fields and tin mines. As an outsider on the border between the Chinese and Australian cultures I had the curiosity to understand both sides of the equation.

At a talk given at the CAHS, John Yu, the pediatrician and hospital administrator, reminisced about arriving in Sydney in 1937 as a two-year-old with his family. Earle Page, who was later to become Prime Minister of Australia, carried John Yu off the boat unchallenged and undocumented by Customs and Immigration. This came about as John Yu's grandfather had been a Presbyterian minister and his uncle was the first Chinese graduate in Medicine from Sydney University and Earle Page was a classmate. In this instance social class and prestige trumped and overcame the problem of being Chinese and the aura of power which surrounded John Yu made being Chinese an irrelevancy.

There is still a tenuous link with our home village in Zhongshan. My brothers have made fleeting visits to see the house where my father grew up but their stay was hampered by the fact that they could not speak Cantonese and thus could not converse with the villagers on such a short visit. The cultural industry of finding your roots is a growing phenomenon and represents an attempt to establish a link with your Chinese heritage. They did not feel an affinity for the village and felt more like tourists and outsiders who had come to observe but were not part of the life there.

Ancestral home in Zhongshan

In a similar example of cultural tourism I visited the town of Emmaville in northern New South Wales where my grandfather was a miner in the tin mines during the 1880s and 1890s. The surrounding district was the largest tin producing area in the world for a brief period in the 1870s and attracted over two thousand Chinese miners but is now a sleepy rural town of only a few hundred inhabitants. I walked along the streets and tried to imagine what it was like one hundred and forty years ago but most traces of the mining industry have disappeared and the only Chinese presence is the grocery store which was previously owned by Chinese.

My children

My children, the sixth generation, are thoroughly westernized. Australia has changed with the advent of the multicultural society and the growth of the Chinese population to 700,000 (2006 census). They consider themselves to be Australian and not Chinese but their appearance will always mark them as Chinese and how they will cope is unknown. At their age my goal was to assimilate and I believe that will be their fate. There is a current debate in Australia about multiculturalism sparked by the rise of Islamic fundamentalism and the wearing of the niqab, the enveloping outer garment, by women in public places. This challenges the principle of assimilation and asserts the right of ethnic groups to be culturally distinct. This presages the debate about how much tolerance there will be for a society to function harmoniously if a minority attempts to assert their cultural beliefs. Two examples are the orthodox Jews saying that in their beliefs the Sabbath is a holy day and that they cannot work and the other is a day set aside in the public swimming pool for Islamic women so that they do not appear immodestly in public in front of strange men.

So finally how did a multi-generation Chinese resolve the dilemma that although I looked different from the others I was the same in language and values? How did I cope with the situations where I was treated because of the way I looked? You learn to accept this by attempting to assimilate and become like them but as I grow older I accept that looking Chinese is part of my identity. It has been a long journey but my identity as an Australian-born Chinese has been validated: someone who looks Chinese but feels Australian but can put on Chineseness like a *min naap* which is only a superficial covering. My wife who is traditional Chinese has strengthened my identity by providing this Chinese part of the jigsaw puzzle. Fate and chance will decide your destiny but I believe that marrying a Chinese has been a positive choice.

Chapter 5
Authenticity and Physicality: Chineseness in Cultural and Racial Discourses

Cultural authentication of race is manifested by physicality or faciality; it is there, like a tattoo or a birthmark, an inescapable "reality" that long-settled ABCs are compelled to confront in their daily lives. Their "Chinese" face is the source of objectivity, expectations, and constraints, precluding the bearers of its acceptance into Australian society—as "real" Australians. The ABCs are also subjected to differential treatment by both overseas and local Chinese communities who see them as outsiders. The two ends don't meet. This "configuration of power" based on essentialized racial attributes consolidates a racial hierarchy that stratifies, even stigmatizes, long-settled ABCs within and outside of Australia. Despite Chineseness (or any racial identity) being frequently criticized as a construct of essentialism, it remains an inerasable attribute for ethnic Chinese in defining and asserting their identities, thus providing normative accounts of social reality and values.

Who is Chinese and who is not Chinese? To be or not to be Chinese? While answering these questions we unknowingly engage in a process of authentication, often by imposing order and fixing the notion of Chineseness as natural, given. However, defining Chineseness as natural and inherent is a common essentialist fallacy—one that is taken for granted, whereby identity is seen as a static structure and persistent over time. The diasporic paradigm we have reviewed thus far argues that Chineseness is not a fixed entity; as Ang (1998: 225) puts it, "be it racial, cultural, or geographical—but operated as an open indeterminate signifier whose meanings are constantly negotiated and rearticulated in different sections of the Chinese diasporas." The notion of "being Chinese" varies in different localities as people are influenced by local contexts and construct new ways of being, doing, living. One informant, Rodney, illustrated the diversity of diasporic Chinese communities around the world this way:

There is no such thing as *a* Chinese person anymore unless you define exactly what you mean by Chinese. Are we talking about Chinese from China, Chinese from Hong Kong,

L.L.-S. Ngan and K.-b. Chan, *The Chinese Face in Australia: Multi-generational Ethnicity among Australian-born Chinese*, DOI 10.1007/978-1-4614-2131-3_5,
© Springer Science+Business Media, LLC 2012

Chinese from Australia, Chinese from the States or Chinese from Singapore? I think everybody has different identities and those are sub-cultures of a larger Chinese identity.

Within Australia, cultural diversity exists within Chinese communities, as Sean, our informant and a fourth-generation ABC, observed:

When I am referring to Chinese I don't really distinguish them on whether they were born overseas or born in Australia. When I think about Chinese I tend to think of ones who can speak Chinese reasonably well and associate with other Chinese. I don't really think of ones who can't speak English. I guess they don't enter my sphere of interaction because I can't interact with them. So they are mainly students here and those who were born here. But those who have forsaken their Chinese identity, I tend to stay away from them. And then there is the group who speaks Mandarin, I can't communicate with them at all.

These propositions entail a criticism of Chinese essentialism, a departure from the usual mode of defining Chineseness in terms of binary oppositions of authentic and inauthentic, real and unreal, pure and impure. Nevertheless, while critiques of essentialism are necessary, such orientations have resulted in a reductionist presumption, characteristic of the postmodernist perspective of identity formation. We are never going to locate a definite or definitive identity and only versions of it, as we argued in Chap. 2.

The existence of "Chineseness" does not need to be disputed—there would be millions of people around the world who would identify themselves as Chinese in one way or another, either voluntarily or being impinged upon by others. The key question then is no longer about whether someone is Chinese or not. The more relevant question is: How and where is Chineseness evoked and invoked? Moreover, the theorization of Chineseness would be incomplete without a concurrent problematization of its configuration of power that stratifies the hierarchical positions of the diasporic Chinese in differing social situations. As Mohanty (2000) reminds us, an enriching theory of identities does more than simply celebrate or dismiss the various uses of identity; rather it provides an explanation of how and why identities are problematic and where and why they are empowering or disabling.

In examining Chineseness through the prevailing discourse of authenticity, this chapter focuses on the physicality of racial attributes and language that serve to consolidate subdivisions through essentialized boundaries. These attributes act as modes of identification by others and the self which could or would become a centering device for hierarchical categorization and segregation between the long-settled ABCs and mainstream "Anglo" community and across diasporic Chinese communities.

Authenticating Chineseness Through Phenotypical Attributes

Racial notions serve to consolidate not only the subdivisions intrinsic to the heterogeneous nature of humankind but also a racial hierarchy, established through racial boundaries. "Race" has commonly been perceived as visible physical divisions among humans that are hereditary, and reflected in a morphology which is fundamental to the creation of racial boundaries. The general tendency is to view phenotypic characteristics as the defining marker of cultural identities, thus automatically, unquestionably, and permanently determining one's membership in a particular racial group. Park (1928: 890) argues, "the chief obstacle to cultural assimilation of races is not their different mental but rather their divergent physical traits." Physical attributes in this way provide the preeminent basis on which an individual is ethnically or racially assigned and categorized (Gilroy, 2004: 25).

However, there has also been much debate on the limitations of the biological traits as a source of authentication of identity (Ang, 2001; Balibar, 1991; Gilroy, 1987, 2000, 2004; Kibria, 1998). The experiences of our informants point to this: a number of them "look" Chinese but do not necessarily consider themselves as "real" Chinese due to the large cultural differences among Chinese communities in Australia. Moreover, there are children of mixed descent whose physical appearances are located in a zone of "in-betweenness."

While the variations among Chinese communities are obvious, the fixity of perceptions based on essentialist characteristics often demarcates Chineseness into an absolute oppositioning of authentic and inauthentic, real and fake. The fact is that many people still naturalize the "other" according to perceptions of fixed essential differences and as such while physical traits are socially constructed, they still function as tools for collective identification. Our purpose in this book is to examine how physicality, which is so often downplayed in the scholarly literature, is an important mode of identification that has a fundamental impact on the negotiation of Chineseness among the long-settled ABCs. All our informants are Han Chinese, whose families originated from Guangdong Province, the southern part of mainland China. Out of 43 participants, 28 claimed there had not been intermarriage with a Westerner in their line of the family. Of the 15 where intermarriages had occurred, only two participants had intermarriages in their family in more than one generation. In short, most of our informants "look" Chinese in appearance.

Phenotypic characteristic is an existential condition for long-settled ABCs, and one which has been hegemonically constructed as an initial sign of identity regardless of the particularities of personal history. Even for those whose families have inhabited Australia since the mid-nineteenth century, their Chinese appearance is still the immediate source of racial identification. This is particularly significant in the Australian context as it is largely a Western society where the mainstream is dominated by Anglo-Celtic Australians. A brief discussion of the changing social context in Australia is important in understanding the construction of difference and identification for "Chinese-looking" Australians.

Immigration was a major focus of class struggle in nineteenth-century Australia as employers called for the recruitment of non-British labor to restrict the power of trade unions. By the later part of the century there was an emerging sense of Australian nationalism through the notion of racial purity. Macqueen (1970) explains that there was an intimate link between racism and the emerging feeling of Australian identity and nationhood, creating a new egalitarian society while maintaining British culture and heritage. By the time of Federation in 1901, the White Australia Policy was seen by most Australians as fundamental to national survival. One of the initial pieces of legislation passed by the new Federal Parliament was the Immigration Restriction Act, enacted in 1901, which restricted the migration of non-Europeans, particularly Chinese, with the intention of creating a culturally homogenous and cohesive "white" society. The restrictions included passing a written dictation test, which could be in English or any European language (e.g., French or Italian). Cultural practices based on stereotypes of the "yellow peril"—the fear of an Asian invasion into the sparsely populated continent—also contributed to racial discrimination against Chinese migrants. According to Fitzgerald (2007: 28), because Chinese were nonwhite, no matter how well behaved they were or seen to embrace different national values, they were portrayed as "hierarchical and not egalitarian, cruel rather than fair, [ones who] put profit before friendship, demonstrate slavish adherence in place of sturdy independence and prefer Oriental despotism to Australian democracy."

However, as it became apparent that insufficient British immigrants wanted to enter, recruitment was broadened to other parts of Europe, including Italy, Greece, and Spain, as immigrants from these places were considered relatively easy to be culturally and socially absorbed and able, because of their European background and appearance, to rapidly become indistinguishable from the existing Anglo-Australian stock—compared to Asian migrants (Vasta, 2005). As a result of having to provide the much needed labor and population growth particularly after World War II, there was progressive relaxation of the immigration policy. In 1958 the government introduced a simpler system of entry permits and abolished the controversial dictation test. References to race were avoided in the revised Immigration Act.

While there was progressive development, overt racial segregation was still apparent in the 1950s. This is demonstrated by our informant, Jerry, who returned from Papua New Guinea to Sydney after deportation. Jerry's parents had been born in Papua New Guinea and, because of the breakout of war, were deported as refugees to Sydney in 1941 where he was born in 1942. Due to their refugee status the family was reluctantly sent back to Papua New Guinea in 1949. However, through continuous appeals they were later allowed to return to Australia. Jerry recalled the discriminatory treatment at the Sydney airport on his return from Papua New Guinea:

> It was apartheid then. I remember going to the education office to sit the exam to come to Australia. You had to pass an English test. I remember I was in the office of this white education officer. I must have stood there for an hour while he sat behind this desk. There was another thing. When I arrived in Australia at Kingsford Smith Airport, coloreds were separated from whites.

The perpetuation of such an essentialist ideology of racial boundaries can be highlighted by informant Sunny's sense of difference experienced during his childhood in the 1960s:

> I was always aware that I was different because in primary school I was picked out all the time. You got all these Italians. They were migrants themselves… You know little kids, they are very cruel, they call you "Ching Chong," slant eyes and so on. You look very different. But Italians don't look all that different from Aussies. The Chinese were very different straight away and you got segregated. So I knew I was different from primary school onward.

While it is not possible to conclude that Italians or other Australians of European descent are exempt from the "prism of otherness" in White Australian society, the intensity of differential treatment by the mainstream society is greater for those of non-European appearance. This is largely due to the effect of racial sentiments in the period of the White Australia Policy. Although there was a subsequent change to the ethnic composition of the Australian population that led to the alteration of government settlement policy from one of open racism, through the White Australia Policy, to an official policy of pluralism and the multicultural policy in a short period of around 30 years, the perpetuation of the earlier racial discourse that defined the nation and ethnic boundaries continues to impact on the experience of long-settled ABCs today.

Western Hierarchical Stratification

The fixity of social perceptions often leads to the pigeonholing of identities into predefined boxes, which does not reflect reality (Pickering, 2001). Jerry, a third-generation ABC, expressed his frustration at the evaluative forms of labeling impinged upon him by others:

> I noticed that whenever I go to parties, dinners, theater with a group of people and tell my Western friends about the event, they would all ask, "Were they Chinese?" and that's a very strange question. I don't see the relevance of the background of what company I keep. Then when I told them that my parents had moved to Chatswood into the nursing home, the first thing they asked was "Oh, are they all Chinese?" and that really puzzles me. That means they put me into a box, C for Chinese or whatever. It's very weird... I also organized this old boy's reunion for ten of us plus their wives at a French restaurant in Balmain. So out of twenty people there were only three Asians—me, my cousin and her husband. I told my other Western friends about the night with my high school friends but they still said to me, "How are your Chinese friends?" It wasn't a Chinese night, it was an old boys' night but their emphasis was on your "Chinese" friends...

Common to our informants' experience is that no matter how "Australian" or "Westernized" they may feel, their physical Chinese appearance is always a definite racial marker. The stereotypical identification involves a process of distancing the designated through the construction of difference. In this way, Chineseness is often forced upon them by the wider Western society. Dianne, a fourth-generation ABC, stressed the impossibility of being a "real" Australian because of the way she looks:

> Being Australian means being able to go out into society and not to be judged by your looks, which is difficult because you can't change the way you look. I can go out there and be an Australian. I can act like an Australian, I can talk like an Australian, and I know all the traditions of Australians, but when you look at it from an Australian's perspective, I guess I'm not an Australian because of the way I look.

Even a fifth-generation ABC similarly experienced the difficulty of full integration:

> My identity is basically Australian. I see myself as Australian and I think like an Australian. But unfortunately, I look Chinese, which makes it difficult... Well, people treat you with a sense of Otherness. To them I will always be Chinese... People will treat you the way you look. And so because I am Chinese they will always treat me in a certain way. You will always be Chinese to them. That is the first thing (Rob).

It is important to understand that cultural identity attains its significance by relational positioning such that a person's identity will vary depending on the context and the questions posed to his/her identity (Hawkes, 1992). As such, although our informants' families have resided in Australia for over three to four generations and they may perceive themselves as Australian, they are still continually viewed through a prism of otherness which reinforces their Chinese ethnicity. The importance of such reinforcement by others was articulated by Rob's explanation of his preference for a Chinese person as his children's marriage partner:

…even though I wouldn't mind my children marrying whoever, it would be nice if they could maintain their Chinese looks. Their cousins already look Australian, they are *looking that look* so people won't treat them as Chinese. If no one is going to *treat you as Chinese*, then you won't feel you are Chinese!

Although physical characteristics as a source of identification are problematic as well argued by postmodernist theorists, the point is that the negotiation of Chineseness is unavoidably associated with "looks." Furthermore, it is important to point out that individuals themselves are caught within the authentication process. This internalization of difference—a self-fulfilling prophecy, through physicality— was highlighted by Dianne:

See, if I say, I'm Chinese, I'm not really Chinese because I was born in Australia, so I'm embracing more of the Australian qualities like the culture and whatever. So if I say I'm Australian then I think to myself I'm not Australian because I don't look like your typical Australian!

Ethnic identity thus is often reinforced by appearance, as cross-cultural borders cannot be easily transgressed because of the underlying process of othering through difference and sameness.

To further illustrate the immutability of racial constructs, all of our informants expressed the view that when questioned by others about their origin, "Australia" never seems to be an acceptable answer. Sean's encounter was typical of our informants' experiences:

When people ask, "Where are you from?" if I say, "I am from Australia" they will say "no, no, no," then I say "Oh you mean I am Chinese 'coz I look different?'" Oh okay then "I am actually Chinese but was born in Australia."

Sean's agitation about the label placed on him highlights the intensity of the hegemonic construction of racial imageries by the wider society. Such dismissal of one's proclaimed identity by others reveals the anxieties that motivate identity politics. Often the rejection reveals that the question is not about origins but, as Ang (2001: 29) describes, "disturbing signals for the impossibility of complete integration." Moreover, as Pickering (2001) maintains, those who stand out as being different from the majority because of skin color are turned into a spectacle, an exhibit, even a source of entertainment. The continuous racial encounters faced by Vera who is a third-generation ABC point to this:

You know people would just yell out at you the usual things about your physical appearance or tell you to "go back to where you came from" and that sort of stuff. It always stuck to my mind. It was very upsetting. Although it didn't happen that often, it was more than enough!

Racialized collectivities are stratified within a broader social spectrum in which stereotypes are often imposed on others by the dominant groups.

In-group Hierarchical Stratification

While Ang (2001: 30) maintains the collectivized notion of "Chineseness" has been continually reconstructed as a result of the lingering dominant hegemony of the Western culture, the process of authentication which inevitably impacts on the hierarchical stratification of identity is also shaped by the action, collusion, or cooperation of in-group members. For a number of informants who identify with being Chinese, the continual inquiries into their origin by in-group members, particularly when traveling in China, highlight that an essentialist paradigm based on physicality is deeply embedded within the Chinese diasporic world. The continuous questioning of Mary's identity by Chinese in Hong Kong highlights such phenomena:

> I knew that I was different from other people because people would ask me, "Where are you from? What nationality are you?" and all that sort of thing. And I just used to take it for granted that I was Chinese, but when they used to ask me—they couldn't tell what I was sometimes! I thought that was a bit queer, because I just automatically thought I was Chinese, but even last week somebody said, "You don't look Chinese!" and I said "Oh, don't I?" She was a lady from Beijing... When I went to Hong Kong in 1958 a Chinese man on the plane walked by and he said, "Are you Filipino?" He went through a lot of other nationalities because he didn't know what I was and in the end I just said, "Sydney"... So, I think the best answer is to say you're Australian with Chinese roots.

Under the Western hegemonic construction of Chineseness, subsequent generations who have stereotypical oriental features would be generically labeled as "Chinese" by Western observers. As Mary explained, in Sydney, she just took for granted that she was Chinese. However, as illustrated, the physical marker of Chineseness invariably changes for diasporic Chinese living in different localities. Those like Mary who are of mixed descent—whose "looks" are located in a zone of "in-betweenness"—become a source of spectacle. As Gilroy (2004: 106) explains, "to have mixed is to have been party to a great betrayal. Any unsettling traces of hybridity must be exercised from the tidy, bleached-out zones of impossibly pure culture." Ethnic identity is thus reinforced by the external appearance, as crosscultural borders cannot be easily transgressed. Mary's experience reveals that the underlying process of otherness perpetuates not only within the Western discourse as the perspectives of in-group members also shape their own social hierarchy.

Jerry's experience in Beijing further shows this process of othering by in-group members. Similar to Work's (2001: 19) cultural encounter in her autobiographical essay on her inability to speak Chinese, Jerry felt stupefied because he was unable to meet the cultural expectation that a Chinese-looking person must be able to speak the Chinese language:

> Living in Beijing made me ashamed. More ashamed and inadequate because sometimes I'd go to the restaurant or the coffee shop with a few white people, say some colleagues from work. The waiter would come straight to me with the menu and then the white person, the

egg[1] who is so fluent that the waiter takes a double look at me because I can't speak Mandarin properly. So this is the *banana*[2] and that's the egg. So embarrassing… I felt I was in a no man's land. Similarly last night I went to the Chinese restaurant in Kensington, I was trying to bullshit my way through the menu. There was something on the menu (everything was in Chinese) but I didn't know what's in it. I asked, "How is it done?" He says something in Chinese. I know what's in it but I can't express it in Chinese. All these kinds of things plus not having the vocabulary really cut me.

From this excerpt, it is evident that to a "white" person, competence in Chinese is an index to the existential value of Chineseness. Such construction of Chineseness is established through a system of values that arises with Westernized ascriptions— but is also framed by in-group members as well. In this way, in-group members also play an important role in establishing their own categorization of identities.

Moreover, individuals associated with a particular minority group may attach evaluative labels to themselves to enable a better understanding of the social world they inhabit (Alcoff & Mohanty, 2006: 6). For example, Daisy, a fourth-generation ABC, and the descendant of a prominent Chinese merchant who migrated to Australia in the 1850s, was raised in a Westernized family where intermarriage continued through the generations. Although she is identified as only one-eighth Chinese and does not have stereotypical Oriental features, she still has a very strong connection with her Chinese heritage:

First and foremost I think of myself as Australian. I have a strong interest in the Chinese side of my family. I get on well with most Chinese people I meet. I'd say probably eighty percent of me thinks of myself foremost as Australian but the rest of me acknowledges and welcomes the Chinese element of my being.

Daisy explained that at times she feels that she is a "fake" Chinese, especially when she is among "full-blooded Chinese" who look and speak Chinese. Self-ethnicization in this case serves as the trigger of a prescribed otherness whereby one is situated in a state of liminality, between the "real" and "fake." As Ang (2001: 30) contends, discourses of ethnicity begin to proliferate as ethnic minorities assert themselves in their stated desire to maintain their cultural identity. The accumulative impact of the impossibility of total integration into the Chinese or Western community and of being a continuous spectacle often results in profoundly ambivalent experiences for those caught in between.

---

[1] "Egg" is a metaphor for Westerners who are knowledgeable about the Chinese culture, which includes the ability to speak and write Chinese. The metaphor is based on the stereotypical color of racial groupings. The white egg shell on the outside and the yellow yolk inside refer to Westerners who are "white" and Chinese (yellow) internally.

[2] "Banana" is a metaphor for Asians who speak and write English fluently and live a Western way of life. The metaphor is based on the stereotypical color of racial groupings; yellow skin of the banana on the outside and white flesh of the banana inside imply Chinese who are identified as "yellow" are actually Westernized (white) internally.

Complex Negotiations of Belonging

In the Australian context, which is predominately "white," Chinese appearance is often the source of involuntary segregation. The seeming impossibility of attaining a sense of sameness is expressed by Pete, a fourth-generation ABC, whose feelings are typical of most informants: "It's always there, on the level that this is what you look like. People will always ask you where you come from. You never have an entire sense of being the norm." There is always a physical sign of difference that interferes with ethnic minorities' attempts at integration. The consequence of this sense of difference and stigmatism led to our informants' deliberate disconnection from the Chinese heritage and culture.

Lilly, who identified herself as being one-eighth Irish, displayed defiance, almost a renunciation of her Chinese background during our interview. She deliberately emphasized the Irish component of her ancestry and showed much fondness of the natural blond strips in her hair:

> My cousin's hair is darker than mine. Because mine sort of has this blonde through it, which I think possibly came from my great-grandmother! Mum's not pure black, obviously, with a Eurasian father...but I'm the one with the lightest... I like keeping it with the grey and stuff, because you can tell that it's still got the blonde through it. I really like the color of the hair. Yeah. It's great!

Lily also claimed that she has no interest in Chinese men, dislikes the loudness in the way Chinese people speak, and sees herself as a "real Australian" except for her yellow skin, an inescapable Chinese phenotypic identifier. Her emphasis on her western physical features, Irish background and her effort to differentiate herself from other Chinese ironically suggest her intense self-consciousness of her identity.

While desperately attempting to dissociate herself from things Chinese to merge with the mainstream white society she contradictorily has genuine interest in Chinese history and associates with people of Chinese heritage. Co-author Ngan met Lily several times at meetings organized by a Chinese Australia community association before conducting the interview with her. This peculiar love–hate relationship with her Chinese background is characteristic of those who are living a hybrid existence.

While yearning for sameness with the majority may lead to negative association with being Chinese, class and status are also important factors segregating the long-settled ABCs from other Chinese communities in Australia. Lily expressed the differences between different Chinese groups based on wealth:

> Well, I'd have to say I'm an Australian-born Chinese. But I'd say I'm different from other Chinese—because obviously now there's the wealthy who live in these high-class suburbs—well, even like my friend Henri, who's now working in Sweden, and Linda—they're wealthy, they were born here but they were from wealthy families. We were from a poor family and have lived here for generations. So there are the rich recent migrants and the poor Australian-born Chinese. There's a difference...a different lifestyle... Well, most of the Chinese people went to university and things like that. I didn't go to university. I suppose that's in every nationality, though. I just had my education in a different way! Instead of going to university I just learnt it in life, really.

Lilly's remark about wealth and education suggests social dimensions of identity—middle-aged single woman, relatively minimal education, low wage earner—intersect with ethnicity to produce a profound impact on the conception of cultural boundaries. It seems possible that her cultural disassociation from her Chinese heritage would uplift her social status, giving her a sense of superiority in terms of class and culture. This feeling may have emanated from the racist notion, as maintained by Robb (2003), that being Chinese meant that you were of a lower status in society in colonial Australia although, as Lilly stated, the status of Chinese nowadays has improved. In the same manner, Rob also expressed the difference between different categories of Chinese in Australia:

> It is the pecking order. It depends if you are the ABCs who put themselves at the top or recent migrants who put themselves at the top and think that the ABCs are at the bottom. The reason they think that is because the recent migrants are financially successful, that's how they get in whereas most ABCs are just average Australians. There is no way you can consider me to be financially successful.

Furthermore, the adoption of colloquial terms such as "FOBs" (fresh-off-the-boat) and "bananas" in the speech of some participants is evidence of an enduring sense of difference that segregates themselves from other Chinese/Asian groups. A clear example of disassociation from other recent Asian migrants can be illustrated by Bill, a young man in his 20s:

> Do you know the term FOBs? Fresh-off-the-boat. I hate them, to be honest with you, sorry to say this to you, but I mean all my Asian friends hate them. It's, for example, the way they drive, they think they are still in Asia, double parking all over the place, driving all over the place, crossing lanes! When I go to Cabramatta, for example, I see people spitting on the ground and especially the way that they talk to you, the rudeness! I hate "foby" cab drivers, the ones that can't speak the language and don't know where they are going...

Although there is acknowledgment of an "Asian" identity that is shared among his Asian friends, it is clear that there are tensions and differences between groups within the so-called Asian-Australian community.

However, being identified as Chinese is not necessarily all negative. Some informants indicated that their Chinese identity can be positive and enriching and that "being Chinese" is fundamental to a sense of group belonging. The substance of identity is based on the notion that individual security can be attained in a social setting in which the sense of belongingness of one individual depends on his or her association with others. As Kuah-Pearce (2006: 224) points out, individuals look to the socialization process during which the self enculturates the norms of the particular group that they belong to. Thus as children, when the home is the most dominant environment, looking similar to siblings becomes an important aspect of gaining a sense of place. This is highlighted by Sarah, who is of mixed heritage[3]:

> [When young,] my siblings looked more Chinese and I looked less Chinese than everybody from my real or my adopted family. I am the only one who doesn't look Chinese. They all looked more Chinese. So as a matter of fact I wouldn't mind if I looked more Chinese at all. I have always wanted to look more Chinese because I looked different from my siblings.

---

[3] Eurasian.

As Chambers (1994) articulates, the need for a sense of belonging is often created by a fantasy and an imagination of a homogeneous physical reality. Children always like to dress in a way that is similar to their sisters, mothers, and best friends. It is the awareness of a self-sameness with others that enforces a sense of group membership, conformity, and security. For Sarah, during her childhood, to look more Chinese implied a stronger sense of belonging and connections with her family.

While physicality is an important factor for developing a sense of group membership, commonality or differences in cultural life and traditions also define how long-settled ABCs position themselves. Janice, a fourth-generation ABC, explained that the intensity of her sense of difference in relation to the dominant Anglo-Australians gradually led her to "gravitate back" to those who share a similar background:

> I think our upbringing was very Asian-based. When I was at school there were hardly any Asians in my class, there were probably none! So all my friends were Australians. I have always realized that I ate different food, I looked different but more importantly I had a different lifestyle. I have always moved towards an Asian lifestyle. Maybe they always like the beaches, sports, swimming and stuff like that—we weren't that style of people. Maybe we always had that problem because we looked Asian, there was a lot of name calling when we were growing up as there were not many Asians around. Basically we just stuck to ourselves, we just didn't mix very well. I found that even with my school friends, their way of thinking was different from the way I thought, so when I got older I gravitated back to Asian people or even with Australia-born Chinese people who think similar.

For Dean, rather than a gradual gravitation to the Chinese community, difference from the dominant group was comfortably accepted as an advantage in the socialization process:

> It's not an issue now… It gives me, when among my Anglo friends, a slant of difference on things…they would always ask me about Chinese food or places to go in China, this and that. It's not negative or anything. And the Chinese community in Sydney is not a marginalized community like some others, like Lebanese, for example, who are really battling along.

A contributing factor also associated with one's sense of difference or sameness is located in complex notions of recognition and belonging, where the central question arises as to how individuals interpret, construct, and reconstruct themselves in the culture of which they are a part (Anderson, 1999). As such, for our informants, the experience of group membership is located in the very definition of Chineseness (and Australianess) since the significance of any identity depends on one's association with others, as identity construction is a relational process. The formation of identity involves entering a state of hybridity, such that their sense of identity is often situated in a liminal space as they negotiate and display who they are or how they want to be seen in different contexts—or, we might say, one face, many masks (Chan 2005a). While hybridity through the combination of cultures and the cross-cultural influences can produce a positive outlook for the hybrid actor who can glide between cultures, those who find it difficult to concretely locate their identities and their social placement can also feel a heavy burden which leads to estrangement and disillusion from society.

Chineseness as a racialized collectivity is stratified within a broad social spectrum through the dialectic of sameness and difference. Certainly, particular stereotypical physical attributes (e.g., black hair, slanty eyes) imposed by the dominant group (which, within the Australian context, is Anglo-Australian) subsequently become an important source of reinforcement of Chineseness. However, it is also important to understand that essentialist ideologies are also the basis on which in-group members make sense of their identity. Concisely, the construction of difference and sameness is a mode of identification by others *and* the self. Identifying with a particular group brings with it security and acceptance; consequently, long-settled ABCs' sense of belongingness within the Australian context has led to differential associations with being Chinese.

Authenticating Chineseness Through Language

Ethnic identity is often authenticated by language competency and, under the Western hegemonic discourse, it is an ideological demand and cultural expectation that one naturally speaks the ethnic language if one is to belong to an ethnic community. Because ethnic membership is widely believed to be a cultural and also biological matter, the presumed cultural trait of language is often seen as a natural part of an "imagined community" as it has always been a tradition of thought in the West (Anderson, 1983).

Interestingly, while Chinese competency varies, the Chinese language continues to be used by members within the families of long-settled ABCs, though not necessarily by our informants themselves. It needs to be noted that articulating precise language competency levels for participants in our study is difficult as, first, interviews were conducted in English and as such, it was not possible to assess the fluency of their verbal Chinese skills directly; and second, individuals' assessments of their language skills were often vague, with claims such as being able to speak "a little," "broken bits and pieces," "pigeon Chinese," and "just enough to get by". While competency cannot be clearly demonstrated and judged, approximately 14 out of our 43 informants indicated that they regularly communicated in Chinese with particular members of their immediate family, 8 claimed they had no knowledge at all, and none could read or write more than a handful of characters in Chinese. Moreover, there are different dialects of Chinese—Mandarin, Cantonese, Hakka, and Seeyup—which are spoken by older members of their families. However, for our discussion here, all references to the Chinese language in this book denote a broad categorization of the different Chinese dialects, not privileging Mandarin or Cantonese in particular unless otherwise specified.

The language competency of informants shows a distinct shift from the minority language (in the Australian context, Chinese) to the dominant daily language, English. Even for those who can speak Chinese, it is spoken only as a secondary language and in rare circumstances, although such a condition supports Clyne's (1991: 54) argument that ethnic minorities tend to lose their ethnic tongue over the generations (see also Breton, Isajie, Kalbach, & Reitz, 1990; Castonguay, 1998;

O'Bryan, Reitz, & Kuplowska, 1976). However, Chinese literacy should not be a sole criterion of the evaluation of Chineseness as a variety of factors both promote and inhibit the maintenance of language. In the case of our informants, language transition does not necessarily lead to declined ethnic identification with their Chinese heritage. Jean could only "speak a few words" of Chinese, yet she felt that she was "genuinely Chinese" and despised people who judged her Chineseness based solely on language competency:

> I definitely am Chinese. I don't like people stereotyping Chinese saying that you can't be Chinese because you can't speak Chinese! That is ignorance in my opinion. From the fact that we have been brought up by my grandparents, we have a generational link. In that way we are very traditional. It's quite an insult!

Jean's experience demonstrates that a lack of language competency does not necessarily equate with the lessening of one's sense of Chineseness. Perhaps a more vivid example can be found among members of the Chinese Heritage Association of Australia. The association's overall aim is to promote a better understanding of the Chinese community in Australia, and its current focus is on Chinese Australian family history. The majority of its members are people of Chinese descent and have a long family history in Australia. While a few are competent in various Chinese dialects, the mode of conversation is in English. Nevertheless, there is certainly a shared sense of Chineseness through common interest in their Chinese roots and migrant history.

While it is not always possible to evaluate how Chinese individuals are or how much they are in touch with their Chinese heritage based on their language competency, nevertheless language continues to be seen as a pertinent factor of cultural linkage with individuals' heritage. Such a perception can be illustrated by Don's mother, who insisted on him speaking Cantonese during his childhood, even though he was the fourth generation in Australia:

> We generally spoke English at home. They would speak English between them but some-times they would also speak Cantonese. Dad would speak to me in English fully. Mum would deliberately speak Cantonese even though she could converse with me in English because mum wanted me to learn, understand and use Cantonese. That was why mum sent my brother, sister and me to Cantonese languages classes that our church conducted. This was when I was eight or ten years old. I asked 'Why do we have to do this?' Coz at school, my friends, they were not Chinese and I didn't speak Chinese. And learning how to write was just a burden because I was never going to use it. But mum was saying that when I travel overseas I can use my knowledge of the Chinese language. When you are ten years old it is very hard for you to think ten years ahead. She wanted us to learn and understand our background.

Not only is language perceived as a linkage with the Chinese people and culture, but it is also seen as a key to ethnic membership and belonging. For example, Sarah, who does not have any Chinese skills, states, "I think if I know how to speak Chinese, I will feel much closer to the Chinese culture. It is sad that I haven't learned it when I could have." The intimacy between language and culture was similarly felt by Pete:

> In a lot of ways I was evading my Chinese background. It is quite a daunting thing. You feel it is a vast separation if you don't have the language… I would like to be able to do it. I think in some ways it is harder. If it was a completely new language you don't have a psychological barrier.

While the status of Chineseness is a discursive construct rather than something natural, it is in fact a matter of subjective experience and not just a question of theory in real life. The point is not to argue about the adequacy of language as a condition of Chineseness, as individuals are bound to have different opinions, but to investigate its functional significance in relation to the changing social contexts.

Marriage Patterns and Changing Contexts

Our findings cast doubt on theories of assimilation that often overexaggerate the absorptive powers of the dominant group and its culture and oversimplify the progress of social change in terms of directionality and dimensionality. The transition from Chinese to English as the primary language is not a gradual process over the generations as changes are affected by the social context of a particular period and also by individual family situations. For the generations of the early 1900s, the ability to speak Chinese was an important mode of communication to members of the family who were often dispersed in both China and Australia. Wang (2000: 44) highlights that Chinese who went overseas in this period were expected to return home with the social expectation that if they were "good sons who were filial and loved their homes, they would always return," or if they "failed to return home to die, would have tried wherever possible to ensure that their children would still consider themselves Chinese." With such a normative approach of duty and loyalty, Wang argues that early overseas Chinese never stopped being Chinese and if they abandoned their Chinese loyalties and gained upward mobility, these were done consciously. Certainly language retention is associated with the notion of Chineseness; however, it is important to understand the contributing factors of practicality and necessity related to the social context in the early part of the twentieth century.

As discussed earlier, Federation imposed a White Australia Policy in 1901 and transformed Chinese residents into "domiciles" with restricted rights. During the years of the "white" policy, Chinese families were excluded from the political, social, and economic life of mainstream Australia due to immigration restrictions, economic regulations, and racial discrimination within broader society (Choi, 1975; Fitzgerald, 1997). The result was a steady decline in the numbers of Chinese people in Australia (Williams, 1999). Furthermore, due to immigration restrictions, the Chinese female population was extremely small—consequently, many Chinese men returned to China to find a bride (Choi, 1975). To endure being on the margins of mainstream Australian society, Tan (2001: 2) explains, "Chinese families relied on the cohesion of the family as a tightly-knit unit for social and economic survival." As such, the retention of Chinese was largely a necessity in daily living.

In the families of multi-generational ABCs, it is certainly evident that a number of the first- and second-generation migrants did return to China/Hong Kong and "got married." Furthermore, if families had the opportunity, many tried to send their children back to China for a period of time to get some Chinese education so as to learn the Chinese language and the Chinese way of life. This behavior can best be illustrated in the previous generations of Andrew's family. Although his great-grandfather represented the first generation to come to Australia from Canton in the 1880s, there were continuous returns to China throughout the generations. The pattern of movement and marriage was similar for his great-grandfather, grandfather, and father—all born and educated in China, migrated to Australia to work in later years, returned to China to get married, then back again to Australia to work. Andrew explained that because there were very few Chinese women in Australia during the early period and the mentality of Chinese was to only marry people of the "same kind," they had to go back to their ancestral village to find a bride. Andrew, aged 65, was the first in his line of the family to be born and married with a first-generation Hong Kong-born migrant in Australia. He still communicates in Chinese with certain members of his family. This glimpse into his family highlights that the persistence of the Chinese language lies in the perception of its usefulness, particularly in the earlier period.

Overseas marriage patterns also have impacted on the language retention of subsequent generations. George's father, who was born in Queensland around the 1920s, lived in Hong Kong for 10 years because his grandfather sent his father back "to look for a wife." George's father married his Hong Kong-born mother in Hong Kong and later moved to Sydney around the early 1940s to escape the Japanese invasion[4] of Hong Kong. Although his mother could only converse in Chinese, his father and siblings communicated mainly in English. George's mother taught him Chinese at an early age. Unfortunately, due to mental illness, she lived most of her life in an institution and since she could not speak in English she was not able to properly communicate with others. As such, George had to take on the responsibility of a carer (which usually occurs during adulthood) at an early age in his adolescent years. While he has a number of siblings, he is not married as he is gay (we will discuss the impact of sexuality on Chineseness in greater detail in Chap. 6), and because of this he was entrusted with full filial responsibility to take care of his mother. Due to his familial circumstances he had to retain Chinese language skills to communicate with her:

> I retained my Chinese by necessity, because my mother was a typical migrant wife. She came from Hong Kong and then to Sydney with her husband and her three children. Typical of female migrants, my mum never learned English because she was domesticated at home and never needed to learn everyday English. The point is that because she didn't speak English, I had to retain certain amount of Chinese to communicate with my mum about day-to-day things. The reason why I retained some measure of the Chinese language was because of necessity, to communicate with my mum who didn't speak English.

Since language maintenance is often influenced by intergenerational communication with parents and other family members, children of overseas-born mothers in multi-generational Chinese families continued to speak the Chinese language.

---

[4] The Japanese invaded Hong Kong during the Pacific campaign of World War II. It began on 8 December 1941 and ended on 25 December 1941 with Hong Kong, then a British colony, surrendering to the control of Imperial Japan. The Japanese occupation of Hong Kong lasted for 3 years and 8 months.

While return marriage and Chinese education were part of a normative mentality among migrants of the early part of the 1900s, with the increasing growth of Chinese migrants in Australia because of the influx of refugees due to Japanese aggression in China and the Pacific in the 1930s and 1940s, the generations of this period were able to engage in relationships with overseas-born Chinese. As a result, Williams (1999: 2) explains, there was "a new generation of Australian-born people of Chinese origin." This "new generation" is exhibited in the marriage/relationship pattern of our informants and their parents. Thirty out of 43 of our informants had one or both parents born overseas, with the majority born in Mainland China and Hong Kong, and 16 out of 26 non-single[5] informants had a partner who is first- or second-generation ABC. These partners brought with them their own network of relatives, friends, siblings, parents, etc., which consequently led to their continued engagement with the Chinese-speaking community. Although our informants' families have resided in Australia for over three generations, due to continued social interaction with the overseas-born Chinese-speaking community, the Chinese language still largely remains an important means of communication in familial networks. Thus, the ability to carry out verbal communication in Chinese has a particular function in maintaining relations between members of the family. As such, often parents (particularly the overseas-born ones) of long-settled ABCs make a conscious effort to teach their children Chinese in their childhood years. For example, because his grandfather married a Hong Kong-born wife in Australia who could not speak English, Rodney learned Chinese by necessity to communicate with his grandmother and other relatives:

> Since my grandmother didn't speak English, I must speak in Chinese otherwise she would have no idea of what I was talking about. There was also this concern that I would never be able to communicate with my relatives if I didn't keep my Chinese.

Language retention or transition is often conducted in a conscious manner which is largely affected by events taking place in the private domain. For long-settled ABCs, the pivotal reason for language maintenance is the perception of usefulness and need in relation to usage of the Chinese language within the family. Although subsequent generations may not be totally competent in speaking Chinese, the Chinese language is a part of their social life, and, for some, it continues to function as an important means of communication. This is largely related to the pursuit of Chinese education in China among the early generations and marriages with overseas-born Chinese-speaking partners.

Intergenerational Influence

While the retention of Chinese has been necessary because of the functional utility of language in social settings for some of our respondents, there are also cases of deliberate transition to English, particularly during childhood. This can be illustrated

---

[5] It includes current partners of married, and de facto marital status, and ex-partners of divorced and widowed status.

in the way the parents of our informants responded to the pressure of the changing social circumstances which determined the opportunities or limitations of their access to mainstream Australian life. During the mid-1900s, demographers like Price (1956) and Borrie (1949) promoted the dispersal of immigrants to prevent ethnic segregation as well as to encourage the quick learning of English, thus discouraging the use of ethnic languages. Immigrants and their families strongly supported the notion of becoming fully assimilated Australian citizens. Schooling was seen to have a pivotal role in ensuring that the second generation and certainly the later descendants would reflect only the culture of Anglo Australia (Vasta, 2005).

Such an assimilationist atmosphere certainly impacted on the language development of long-settled ABCs. As Tan (2001: 3) explains, the family has significant influence as "gatekeepers" who monitor the border-crossing activities of individual family members between the home and the outside world. One interesting practice which arose from the assimilationist ideology was the way in which parents monitored the language development of their children. For our informant Dianne, because of the perceived benefit of English fluency for her children's future, she deliberately changed the primary language spoken at home from Cantonese to English:

> I used to speak Cantonese to my children when they were little, but as they were growing up and started to go to school we made English the primary language because we thought it was better for the children's education. As a consequence they've grown up not speaking Chinese, although my eldest daughter does now. My husband tried to teach the children as they were growing up, but my eldest daughter is the only one that's actually retained any competency in Chinese.

However, for Rodney, while his parents encouraged him to socialize in English outside, at home they communicated only in Chinese to maintain and cultivate Chinese culture as well as to manage familial relationships:

> My family was very interesting. My father always had Western friends, but family is family and friends are very different. We were never allowed to speak English at home, but when we had visitors we were never allowed to speak Chinese. They stressed that you must integrate but you must also maintain that respect and culture at home.

Similarly for Sunny, during his childhood he was encouraged to speak in English to integrate in Australian society. However, unlike Rodney and Dianne, his family was relatively more relaxed with the choice of language he spoke at home:

> I spoke Cantonese and English at home. Spoke Cantonese to parents and English to brothers. I can only write selected Chinese characters… My parents didn't ask us to go to Chinese school only because we were living in Australia—they thought it would be better for us to learn English and to make friends with Australian kids.

While the assimilationist ideology is pertinent, it is evident that there were various patterns in the way parents monitored the use of Chinese and English within and outside of the home. It was in this role as "gatekeepers" that parents influenced the language development of their children.

It is important to stress that while our informants' families have resided in Australia for over three generations, it was only in the last few decades that a large emphasis on English occurred. Wang's (2000: 43) discussion on the mentality of early migrants explains this phenomenon. He maintains that early migrants saw the host country as only a "temporary residence at a new place of abode" and they had strong intentions of return. For example, although Sunny's great-grandfather came to Australia in the late 1800s and his grandfather and mother were both born in Moree, there were frequent journeys back and forth between the two places, suggesting a strong link with China. Furthermore, when his mother was five years old, she was sent back to China by her family for Chinese education. She lived there for 20 years until she got married and returned to Australia in the early 1950s because of the political upheaval during the Communist takeover in China.[6] As such, until the political circumstances deteriorated in China—which meant the possibility of return was unlikely—the family base had always been China. While Sunny's parents placed much emphasis on learning English and on integration, at the same time they continued to speak to him in Chinese. Moreover, Chinese festivals were an important part of his childhood; he had "rice three times a day, seven days a week" and his "family friends were pretty much all Chinese." His experience highlights that retention or transition of language is often a conscious and deliberate decision effected by necessity and functional utility as perceived by the parents. Certainly the shift from one language to another indicates a possible intention of integration; however, it does not necessarily indicate an overall propensity toward shredding or losing an ethnic identity.

In Gerard's family, the transition into English only occurred in his generation— something that was a deliberate decision by his father. His great-grandfather had migrated to Australia in 1856 and even though their family has resided in Australia for over 150 years, it was only in his generation that English became the primary language. This was because his great-grandfather, grandfather, and father were all educated in China in the early part of their lives. In the case of his father who was born in Australia, he was sent to China by his grandfather at age seven to receive a Chinese education. When he came back to Australia at 17 years of age he "could not speak a word of English" and therefore could not enter the workforce. Due to this experience, his father always encouraged them to learn English and integrate to gain an easier life. Gerald explained his father's attitude toward the learning of Chinese this way:

> Before I went to school I was taught Chinese, but once I went to school that stopped. My father explained to me he had ten years of experience in China and that was of no use to him when he returned to Australia. He couldn't even speak a word of English when he returned to Australia so that was very hard on him in his work life. He had to become independent. In other words he couldn't work for anyone because he didn't have a piece of paper, right, so it was a conscious decision that once we went to school we were to learn as much as we could and the Chinese side was just taught socially. It wasn't important for us to speak Chinese if we wanted to live in Australia and our intentions were to live in Australia and earn an income here. In other words, why did we need the Chinese language if we weren't going to work for a Chinese business?

---

[6] Mao Zedong, the leader of the Communist Party, proclaimed the Republic of China on 1 October 1949. The political changes after the communist takeover caused immense social changes, particularly as a result of the propaganda that much of the previous ruling class was rightist. Such social changes led to a large number of Chinese civilians being discontented with China's economic and political transformation. In addition, the struggle for power within the Communist Party of China, which grew to include large sections of Chinese society, eventually brought China to the brink of civil war.

While assimilation strategies discouraged the use of ethnic languages in the early twentieth century, changes in the social attitudes of the Australian society in the later part of the century because of market demand on bilingual skills also revitalized the interest of informants to relearn their own heritage language. All of our informants indicated a wish to have better Chinese proficiency, particularly Mandarin, because of the advantages of bilingual skills. Certainly Mandarin is viewed—first and foremost—as an index to the existential value of Chineseness and many choose to learn Mandarin among many other dialects (see, for example, Chow, 1998; Tan, 2004b). The ability to speak the official language of China brings with it clear advantages, such as increased work opportunities. Sean shared his experience in a suburb of Sydney which is largely populated with Mandarin-speaking Chinese:

> I am comfortable with Ashfield.[7] When I walk around I just blend in with the crowd, Asian faces you know! But in terms of language I sort of feel *left out*. I sort of feel a bit *sad* that I don't speak Mandarin coz [sic] everyone speaks that now. Now that it is the official language and it is spoken widely, I wish my family spoke Mandarin rather than Cantonese so that I will be able to communicate with millions of people including those overseas.

Some informants perceived speaking Mandarin as resource that would allow them to be more in touch with their Chinese heritage. However, what is echoed by most of our informants is that with the economic growth in China and increasing migration of Chinese to Australia, competency in Chinese language is important as it is seen as an asset in terms of work and everyday exchange.

While the proposition about the tendency of an ethnic minority to lose their ethnic tongue over the generations is plausible, the transition from Chinese to English does not happen gradually but is rather directly impacted by social circumstances, family life, and intergenerational influences. In particular, the private domain has a great impact on the extent of intrusion of the host language as well as retention of the heritage language (Finocchiaro, 1995). Parental influence plays a significant part in the development of language of children. Often the decision to focus on mastering the ethnic or the host language is based on the perceived necessity and functionality of usage on the part of parents. This is clearly exemplified by contrasting behaviors of early and later generations within the same family because of the changing social context. We are not disputing language as a mode of collective identity; rather we want to argue that the retention of language is often impacted by practicalities in particular contexts and thus should not be used as a sole measurement of Chineseness.

Language as Basis of Hierarchical Stratification

The literature on diasporas maintains that the collectivized notion of "Chinese" is continually constructed and reconstructed in response to the enduring hegemony of the Western culture (see Ang, 2001; Chow, 1998). Being Chinese is tied up with

---

[7] A suburb in Sydney.

knowledge of the Chinese spoken language (at the least), traditions, and other cultural forms under the prevailing Western discourse of authenticity. As Kibria (1998) highlights, the distinguishing role of racial markers such as language is that they reflect relations of power—in particular, the ability of the dominant group to construct and impose identities upon others. As such, for ethnic minorities in the West, their identities are often subjected to the mainstream imposition of non-Western representations such as poor English-language competency.

Don, whose family has resided in Australia since the late 1800s, pointed out, "when people meet me at the church I go to, which is mainly Anglo-based, they may not say it straight away but after a while they always say 'I expected a different accent.'" Most people, including both Anglo-Australians and Chinese, usually do not expect him, a person with a Chinese face, to speak in fluent English, with Australian accent, because of his physical appearance. Jerry, an elderly, third-generation ABC, similarly experienced such racial encounters where his identity is forced upon him based on his Chinese looks:

> I did at one stage identify myself as Australian but I don't anymore because there's never that full acceptance. I don't know whether you've come across this before but sometimes you're in the street and you meet some people and they say "Oh, you speak very good English, where did you learn it?" Or "Where did you come from?" I'm sick and tired of that. Yes, I now don't bother with it anymore. A recent example, about a year ago, when I was living in my other apartment at Randwick,[8] the door knocked and there was this young guy with a clipboard selling Optus cable television. He was only about 21 or 22 but when he saw me I could see his gears change, "Ah! An Asian!" Before I could speak he said, "Hello, I'm here from Optus and all of your neighbors are signing on, they've all got cable TV," and blah blah blah but I could see that he was treating me as a dumb Asian "that-no-speak-the-English" … I said to him "Oh sorry, no speak English, I only been here three months. I learn English, I like your country very much." I realize that I shouldn't have done it to him but at that moment I just saw red. Even walking down the street, I think it was down Elizabeth Bay[9] somewhere. Just walking past the postman and I just said, "Good morning, how are you?" and then he turned around and said "Oh, you speak good English, where did you learn it?" I just ignored him. You get a lot of that!

Such evaluative forms of labeling and cultural expectations are the result of the lingering dominant hegemony of the Western culture. Chow (1998) highlights that Western imposition of identity often affirms its moral supremacy by way of stereotypical ethnic and national labels. Even when access into the mainstream society is achieved, the conventional simplification and stereotyping of ethnic subjects linger. The tendency to posit a single dimension of identity such as physicality as the sole determinant of one's cultural identity makes it impossible for long-settled ABCs to feel fully accepted as integral members of mainstream Australian society. The pervasiveness of the Western imagination of being Chinese was further illuminated in Vera's experiences in Europe:

> You get more problems over there because obviously they look at your face. I remember when I studied French for a year there was an Italian student asking me where I came from and I said I'm from Australia. And she's like "You can't be from Australia, what's wrong

---

[8] A suburb in Sydney.

[9] A suburb in Sydney.

with you?" and I said I was born in Australia. And I guess they can't understand why I would be calling myself Australian. This was about ten years ago. I have been back to Europe last year and things are not so bad now. And I had the same thing in England too with these white South Africans, they were just crazy. They would be surprised that I could use a knife and fork! And it's like, "what are you talking about!" So people in other parts of the world find it very difficult to understand me. So they sort of label you. Even in Sydney, they immediately make a judgment like that. Unless they hear me speak, they think I'm a recent migrant. But once they hear you talk, they just speak to you normally. So it's quite funny!

Yet it is also important to emphasize that in-group members internalize Western-imposed labels, which can be clearly illustrated by Jerry's remark toward his Australian-born cousins who speak fluent English with an Australian accent:

I look at my nephews, nieces and some of my grandnieces now. They all speak with Australian accent so in a way there's a slight incursion of negativity when I hear that. I think, when you speak in that broad Australian accent, that accent only belongs to whites, not to coloreds.

Through a system of values that arises with Western ascriptions, the existential index of authenticating Chineseness of a Chinese-looking person is often based on his/her competency in English. To this extent, illiteracy in English has also been fixated as a "Chinese" characteristic.

While the hegemony of Western ascriptions is intimately felt by the diasporic Chinese living in the West, the intensity of in-group ascriptions should not be underestimated. Ethnic language retention is often seen as an authentication of ethnicity, and being Chinese in the West is often tied to an authentication process such that one must possess qualities that originated from China. Thus, one's ability to speak the Chinese language often becomes an external indicator of one's Chineseness. Within the Chinese diasporic universe, those who are able to speak and write Chinese are differentiated from those who can only speak; those who can only speak fluent Chinese are differentiated from those who speak with English-accented Chinese; those who speak with English-accented Chinese are differentiated with those who cannot speak Chinese at all; those who speak Mandarin are differentiated from those who speak other dialects; and so on. In this sense, the lingering pervasive hegemony of authenticity based on language per se functions as a mode of collective identity which has substantial impact on the hierarchical categorization of diasporic Chinese.

The Chinese migrant population of Australia has undergone major transformations in recent decades due to reforms in migration policies and economic developments in the country. In particular, the increased intake of skilled Chinese immigrants from Hong Kong and China in the last 20 years has led to an increase in first-generation overseas-born migrants who have grown up in culturally different societies and are Chinese literate. Their arrival has created greater in-group diversity among Chinese communities in Australia. This can be clearly highlighted by Ada, a fifth-generation ABC, who can speak *Zhongshan*—a Chinese dialect. Because she speaks a minority form of the Chinese language, she is segregated from the main "Chinese" community made up of recent migrants from Hong Kong and China. When she married a "wealthy" Hong Kong-born migrant in Australia, her husband constantly reminded her not to speak in "that country-style language" and to learn "proper Cantonese."

He said that in a well-educated Hong Kong family it was considered lowly to speak a rural language. To be Chinese but unable to speak Cantonese or Mandarin is a contradiction to the social ideal of Chineseness which the Chinese community shares, and the hierarchical system through the discourse of language highlights the significant role of in-group ascriptions.

In-group ascriptions can often be clearly felt when our informants visited Chinese-dominated places. Most felt stigmatized because they were not able to speak fluent Chinese. Although language is not the only existential index of their Chineseness, it is certainly a physicality that is hard to hide or pass. Jenny, a sixth-generation ABC, related her experience in Hong Kong:

> In Hong Kong they are quiet racist. I find a lot of people are quite rude to me because I can't speak Chinese. I think they can tell just from looking at the way you dress that you are not from Hong Kong. You go into shops and stuff and they don't treat you very well. I feel I am being looked down upon. I guess most of that is language.

Such a sense of difference is often escalated when one steps foot onto the soil of China which, under the hegemonic discourse of authenticity, *is* the source of real Chineseness. Debra recalled her experience in China:

> There is this small part of me who is Chinese coz [sic] I can't deny my heritage. But I didn't have the language and didn't have any experience of it because it has been removed by two generations. If my parents had some experience of living in China and speaking Chinese, there would be a lot more connection. We were in fact *looked down* upon when we were in China because we didn't speak any Chinese, so I just didn't feel I was part of them.

Such a sense of marginalization was similarly felt by Jane when she visited China:

> We felt *left out*, coz [sic] people would look at you and say, "How come you don't speak Chinese. You look Chinese"… It made me feel inadequate, that I didn't speak Chinese very well.

Language is socially accepted as an important system of signs for identifying the uniqueness of any culture—and one which is crucial to cultural belonging. Within the social context of the Chinese diaspora, individuals who cannot speak the Chinese language—an existential index—are fraught with feelings of guilt and inadequacy. Jenny stated:

> I would like to go to China for tourist purposes. I would like to go back to where my parents' families were from but then I don't speak Chinese so I'd feel funny going back. I'd feel like I don't belong there coz [sic] I don't speak the language. It is not really undeserving or ungrateful but I would feel like I wasn't fully appreciating it if I didn't know the language and a whole lot of history about it. It would be a wasted opportunity.

The persistence of the perception that being Chinese must entail all things that originated from China certainly has cultural as well as political relevance to the negotiation of Chineseness in the world. The lingering pervasive hegemony of authenticity creates a hierarchical classification that stratifies the position of diasporic Chinese. Even within subsequent generational groups, authentication is also linked to the ability of speaking and writing Chinese. Sean recalled his feeling of superiority over other Chinese Australians when he traveled to China on a heritage tour which aimed to promote cultural awareness among Chinese Australians:

> Actually my Chinese was one of the best out of all those who went on the tour. Some of them couldn't speak at all! I felt that was shocking! I felt it was a shame that they couldn't speak it. Normally I am very proud and want to be the best. But I didn't feel proud, I felt sadness really, for the ABCs who couldn't speak the language. I felt I was lucky that I was raised to have this level of proficiency to at least get by.

Those who are recognized as Chinese but cannot speak the language are treated with shame and disappointment—not only by dominant groups of the West but also by the in-group members. Subsequent generations often experience a sense of humiliation and ambivalence because of their presumed inability to connect with the Chinese culture.

Conclusion

This chapter examines the complex idea of "Chineseness" through the disjunctures of essentialist and postmodern approaches to identity by engaging in a discourse of authenticity and recognition. Certainly, Chineseness is a negotiated, unstable assemblage of perceptions and the meaning and practice of "being and doing Chinese" varies in different social contexts and locations. Yet the idea of Chineseness—however one may define it—is still crucial to making sense of the daily life of long-settled ABCs. The different perceptions of Chineseness provide the criteria to ascertain the "authenticity" of diasporic Chinese.

We have explored physical appearance and language as physical markers of Chineseness. Through the dialectic of sameness and difference, we have teased out the relationship of power and sense of belongingness. We have demonstrated that regardless of their personal history, or how strongly their cultural identities may be grounded in Australia, they are continually seen as an outsider because of the racial and cultural discourse. While characteristics based on physical and language attributes are often imposed by Western ascriptions which subsequently become an important source of reinforcement of their Chineseness, at the same time the hierarchical stratification of identity is also shaped by the action of in-group members of the Chinese community. Because subsequent generations physically "look" Chinese they are subject to the cultural expectation of being able to "speak" Chinese, and those who don't meet the expectations often are made to feel ashamed. The rigid structure of identity means that people are either classified as a part of a social group because of sameness or singled out as a stranger. The cumulative impact of the impossibility of total integration into the Chinese or Western community and of being a continuous spectacle often leads to an ambivalent sense of belonging. The practice and politics of ethnicity are thus one of maintenance and resistance as much as of negotiation and construction.

While the salience of language as a marker of "authentic" Chinese culture is well acknowledged, we have pointed out that the retention of language is impacted by practicality and functionality in social contexts and thus should not be used as a singular measurement of Chineseness. Of import is that the transition from Chinese to English does not happen gradually through the passing of time or across the generations, but rather is directly impacted by the social circumstances of the family. In particular, parental influence plays a significant part in the development of language of children. Parents monitor, in a strategic way, the extent of intrusion of the host language as well as of retention of the heritage language. This is exemplified by contrasting behaviors of early and later generations within the same family. Because the mentality of Chinese migrants in the early 1900s was that of temporary residence in Australia, those who were born in Australia were often sent to China to receive a Chinese education, and English was not keenly pursued. Contrastingly, the later generations often had a mindset to settle in Australia and as such encouraged their children to learn English for their future well-being. A contributing factor was the unlikelihood of return because of the political upheavals in China during the mid-1900s. In recent years, bilingual language ability has come to be considered an added advantage, particularly with the economic boom in China, and so there is an increasing demand to master both English and Chinese.

Through the postmodernist discourse, contradictions and ambivalences in "being Chinese" have been critically significant in delegitimizing the notion of Chineseness as a collectivized racial or cultural category. However, as we have argued, homogenous notions of identity are still fundamental in determining the boundaries between out-group and in-group members. This is revealed in the way in which our informants position themselves relative to specific collectivities such as Chinese, Chinese Australians, ABCs, and Eurasians. Through relative positioning of oneself in relation to other categories, long-settled ABCs designate their sense of Chineseness and develop a sense of who they are. This "configuration of power" consolidates a racial hierarchy of Chineseness that stratifies the positionality of those who claim to be Chinese. As such, rather than simply celebrate or dismiss the various uses of the collective Chinese identity, this chapter has examined Chineseness through the discourse of authenticity and recognition. This provides an explanation of how and why identities are problematic and where and why they are empowering, thus pointing out the validity of Chineseness as an important category of identification and analysis. Let us make it clear that we are not disputing the critiques of the problematics of bounded and mutually exclusive identities—it is only its reductionism which we contest. The ways in which individuals negotiate and construct identities within preset boundaries need to be fully acknowledged, retained, and explored in their ramifications. Only in this way, collectivist discourses will not to be underestimated

Chapter 6
Chineseness Through the Life Course

> *The construction of identity involves a twin process whereby one's sense of ethnicity (such as Chineseness or Australianess) impacts on how one comprehends the world and, at the same time, an individual's social location (such as at a particular life stage) also determines the kinds of ethnic experiences they are likely to encounter. In this sense, Chineseness is constantly being negotiated and renegotiated, contingent on different age-related social identities as one passes through the course of life. While social constructs such as age-based identities and racial identities have been increasingly challenged as being unable to capture the fluidity of consciousness, they are nevertheless significant resources individuals use to locate themselves in society and to make sense of their positionality; thus the wisdom of them should not be casually dismissed.*

Age-based transitions are fundamental processes for the production of identity, as individuals continually reconstruct their biographical narratives when they move into different age identities through the life course. Aging, as Hockey and James (2003) point out, legitimates access to certain social experiences, while denying access to others, and also prescribes sets of expectations about behavior in relation to aged identities. For example, the elderly are assumed to have less engagement with social and economic life because of their decreasing physical and mental capabilities. To migrate at the age of 90 is a rather different experience than at 20 years old. It underscores the plight of venturing into a new lifestyle and experiencing a new culture at the end of one's life rather than staying settled in one country. In everyday life there is a "natural" tendency to recourse to the stereotypes of aging through which we place and locate people's identities because of the internalization of social norms, or in Bourdieu's words, *habitus*.

More importantly, age-based identities (e.g., during childhood, old age) also intersect with other dimensions such as race, gender, and class which imply social and moral obligations and have a powerful effect on what is expected of an

L.L.-S. Ngan and K.-b. Chan, *The Chinese Face in Australia: Multi-generational Ethnicity among Australian-born Chinese*, DOI 10.1007/978-1-4614-2131-3_6, © Springer Science+Business Media, LLC 2012 individual in different social contexts through the life course. Hockey and James (2003: 11) note that, "different individuals will draw on a diversity of resources to negotiate one among any number of later life social identities." For example, the extent to which individuals make choices about the way they express themselves and their identities as gendered or sexualized beings is not to be identified with only sexual or biological differences, but also with social conventions, cultural norms, racial ideologies, learned behavior, attitudes, and expectations attached to gendered and racialized bodies that take on different meanings at varying points across the life course. Beliefs about manhood and womanhood that individuals draw upon are forged in early childhood and are anchored within cultural ideologies. In this way, the multiple intersections of age-based identities with identifications of gender, race, and age produce profound and complex effects on an individual's sense of identity throughout the life course.

The intersection of race and age-based identities can be clearly illustrated by Jean's example, when she talked about how her sense of Chineseness transformed from when she transited from being a young girl in adolescence to becoming a young woman in adulthood:

> I am less Chinese than ever at the moment. I don't have that connection now. I don't have my grandfather giving conversations to me. I am presently more focused in my own life, working and all that. At certain points in my life I was more connected but that had got to do with priorities; in adolescence you were thinking about yourself, you are reflecting. I did deal with more of being parts of a Chinese group—it influences you.

Age-based identities which are continuously negotiated with other socially constructed imperatives, including race and gender, are fundamental not only to one's orientation to the world (what is noticed, what is absorbed, and what is not), but also to how one is seen by and interacts with others (Alcoff, 2006: 90). In this way, socially constructed identities are markers of one's social location and positionality, and identities are always subject to individuals interpretation of their meaningfulness in their own life.

Nevertheless, despite the aging process being one of the key bases for the production of identity, there has been relatively little research about how ethnic identities are, in practice, made sense of by individuals, in reference to the wider social and cultural norms of aging. Previous Chinese diasporic studies have focused on the social experiences of individuals at particular stages of life, while the complex social processes and hybrid experiences involved in "being Chinese" in relation to the life course have remained largely uncharted and certainly undertheorized. The few studies that have examined the relationship between life course and ethnicity include Rivas and Torres-Gil (1992), Levitt (2002), and Smith (2002).

Similar to the recent postmodern notion of identity, which has come to be seen to be changing and emerging through social relationships between individuals, the concept of "life course" has been adopted as "a way of envisaging the passage of a lifetime, less as the mechanical turning of a wheel, and more as the unpredictable flow of a river" (Hockey & James, 2003: 5–6). The life course approach reflects the temporal nature of lives by dwelling on the diversity of experiences within and across the varying stages of people's lives (see, for example, Alwin & McCammon, 2003; Elder, Johnson, & Crosnoe, 2003; Hareven, 1996; Hockey & James, 2003).

This orientation is situated against the earlier static life cycle approach, which sees life as a series of repetitive stages that all people go through.

The early model explained the life course in terms of transitions through a series of rites of passage which allowed every person to enter into clearly differentiated roles as statuses (e.g., Erikson, 1950; Hertz, 1960; Levinson, 1978; Van-Gennep, 1960). Because age transitions were perceived as a series of fixed states which implied social and moral obligations with a pattern that was to be repeated and to remain unchanged across the generations, the pattern of transitions was often represented as the "life cycle" (Hockey & James, 2003: 11). Erikson's (1950) theory of the life cycle is presented in eight stages of life—infancy, early childhood, play age, school age, adolescence, young adulthood, adulthood and old age—through which individuals in Western society pass as they age. He argues that each state represents a challenging task that must be accomplished to advance further in normal development. Each task must be dealt with, within a particular pattern, and these tasks confront the individuals at different age levels that reflect societal expectations (Clausen, 1986: 64–84). The eight stages, spanning from infancy to old age, are split into age ranges.

In Levinson's (1978) book, *The Seasons of a Man's Life*, he argues that the evolution of an individual's life course occurs through an orderly sequence of developmental stages and these stages are closely linked to chronological age. However, due to the varying trajectories of individuals' lives, discrepancies between the Levinson's sequences and the timing of life stages by age can be observed (Clausen, 1986). For example, a transition may involve becoming a parent or grandparent with the birth of a new generation in adulthood at a particular age, but the transition for individuals may occur at varied ages and the experience of parenthood would differ between gender and culture, leading to a diversity of trajectories. A girl who gives birth at 15 may experience motherhood and adulthood before she is legally an adult. Social time may not necessarily correspond with fixed chronological age, as life experiences will vary considerably from one milieu to another.

Although the theoretical framework of the life cycle has provided a guideline by which progress along the life course may be accessed in particular social milieus, it has increasingly come under scrutiny because of its inability to account for variation and diversity of movement through biography and historical time. If the postmodern concept of identity is characterized as "becoming" rather than "being" and as a social process which can never be fixed in place, this means that childhood, adulthood, and old age cannot be easily identified as static times and spaces between which individuals make transitions.

Nevertheless, while the life course paradigm adequately challenges the problematic notion of fixed states and the isolated and repetitive nature of the life-cycle approach, Alcoff (2006) contends that visible manifestations of life stage and race are, consequently, unavoidable features of the present-day operations of social identities. For those living between cultures, not only is life's movement always varied, vague and dynamic, movements through historical and biographical time further lead to a diversity of life trajectories. With such variations, how can one conduct any meaningful analysis of the temporal nature of lives? Life stages are signifiers and triggers which do play on people's lives. As Moya (2000b) reminds us, one's sense of identity in relations to their age identities also determines the experiences an individual is likely to have—circumstances in life create identity to the same degree as identity creates circumstances. It is common that individuals in the Western world identify themselves and others through the visible manifestation of life stages in one way or another, either voluntarily or being impinged upon by others. The notion of the Chinese identity, for example, is socially constructed and fluid in nature but there is something we call "Chinese." In the same manner, while the timing of transition into different socially constructed stages varies for each individual, we can still speak of continuity–there is something that we call adulthood or old age. As such, if we totally dismiss the social construct of "life stages" which provide a significant feature of the developing path of life, it makes it rather difficult to obtain any conclusive account of the meaning of variability of individual lives.

Life stages similar to racial categories share at least two features: both are fundamental rather than peripheral to the self and are relational to the other as they operate through socially constructed visual markers on the body. Parenthood, as a life stage, is fundamental to the self and is also relational, unlike one's identity, say, as a Chinese history teacher, which can change as one changes occupation. In most contexts, being a parent is fundamental not only to one's everyday life but also to an individual's relationship with a community, orientation toward the world, potential life choices, and cultural and political values. In turn, these properties can profoundly affect how we are seen and treated by others. Learning that someone is a mother produces unconscious or conscious reactions in people, often involving socially constructed presumptions. Furthermore, when racial identity is complicated with age-based identities, it often engenders unconscious assumptions about one's past experience or one's moral values (e.g., suspicion toward the intentions of a young Asian woman who has children with an elderly man).

Similarly, childhood as a stage of life is a theoretical construct, but it involves the kind of social theory that is pivotal to making sense of a central feature of our world. The theoretical notion of childhood refers not just to the experiences of children but also to a particular social arrangement of intergenerational relations and age hierarchies. The experience of children in this society is not self-evidently deduced from the lived experience of individual children, rather it is based on children's lives to the extent that it articulates an individual's social location. Such location is discovered by an explanatory account of the nature of generational stratification, how it is recreated and regulated, and the particular social groups and culture it legitimates. Therefore, while childhood is socially constructed, the constructedness does not make it illegitimate in advance. As Mohanty (2000: 38) explains, "experiences are crucial indexes of our relationship with our world…and to stress their cognitive nature is to argue that they can be susceptible to varying degrees of socially constructed truth or error and can serve as source of objective knowledge or socially produced mystification."

While postmodernists emphasize the importance of fluidity and fragmentation for understanding how identity is negotiated, socially constructed homogenous concepts which form identity-based narratives can be understood in terms of "real" political insights, as specific social identities are often stamped onto the malleable individual. As such, rather than dismissing life stages altogether, in understanding the experience of long-settled ABCs, we analyze the construction and operation of identity as Chinese through dynamic transitions across the life course by utilizing life stages as guiding markers. The aging process is a significant resource through which they negotiate their ethnicity; therefore age transitions provide a primary vehicle for understanding the changing contexts of lives. This chapter brings together the narratives of long-settled ABCs and examines how they make sense of Chineseness through specific age-based social identities from childhood through to old age. Gendered issues will be discussed in various stages of the life course where they are relevant to understanding the formation of Chineseness.

Childhood and Parenting

Within the family, each generation experiences life differently—each encounters vastly different problems from those confronted by other family members due to their varied social experiences. However, the parental generation is often held to be responsible by society for mediating the influences of social change on their children (Alwin & McCammon, 2003: 28). Intergenerational studies have brought to attention that the (re)construction of identity between generations takes place as part of an on-going process in which certain aspects of the traditional culture are preserved while others are reinvented, submerged, or discarded due to the impact of changing social environment (Alba & Nee, 1999; Nagel, 1994).

In Chap. 5 we discussed the importance of parents in monitoring the language development of their children between the home and the outside by either facilitating and/or hindering this process. Other than language development, parents also instill Chinese culture in their children through the everyday life cultural practices in family life. For example, eating rice daily, using chopsticks, having Chinese stir-fries with soya sauce, and celebrating Chinese festivals were daily practices within the family which engendered a sense of "being Chinese." These habits and routine events in their childhood became the "habitus" of daily living for the later years of life. Sandy, a fourth-generation ABC, recalled her childhood in the 1940s: "I remember you will get a smack if you play with chopsticks because it was bad luck and you were not allowed." Along similar lines, Ralph, an elderly informant, remembered the practices of Chinese celebrations during his childhood in the 1930s:

> We used to go to the joss house and all those processions. Every year they moved the three main josses to different families. If you got the main joss in your house you got good luck, good health and everything. Everyone wanted it. So every year they changed it around and people competed for it. You paid red packets when they delivered it and fire crackers and all that. When we were young, Chinese boys used to go around to different Chinese families to get red packets. In 1936–37 two pounds was more than a week's wage. It was big money! It didn't take much for a boy to get that.

Similar to their parents' effort in cultivating Chineseness in their daily lives during their own childhood, upon reaching parenthood our informants also engaged in monitoring their children's cultural development. As parents, they consciously rearticulated their identity to instill a sense of "being Chinese" in their children who were growing up in the white-dominated society of Australia. Bruce, who married an Anglo-Australian woman and was a soon-to-be father, expressed that he would like his child to appreciate Chinese heritage. For this very reason, he would give his child a Chinese name:

> I want to bring up my children as Australian but they should be proud of their Chinese heritage as well. I would want them to have a Chinese name and know that their dad is Asian. But they should be proud of their Anglo descent as well. I think they should have an opportunity to learn Chinese. To have multiple language skills is good for work and social life.

The importance of establishing a sense of ethnic belonging for the younger generations through teaching them Chinese heritage and culture was similarly felt by Ralph, who was a grandfather to a number of young children:

> When I started looking back at my grandparents' lives, I tried to find out how they came about. This was when I was in my 30s. Prior to that I was not interested because it was no big deal. But when you start telling your children and grandchildren about their Chinese heritage, if you don't know nothing [sic], you can tell them nothing! So you kind of dig it up a little bit. You want to tell them what you did, what they did. When you get older you start boasting a little bit! You are telling all these stories. It is a bit silly if you don't know nothing [sic].

In the same manner, Bill, a 28-year-old unmarried man with no children, identified more with being Australian when he suggested: "I am more Australian than I am Chinese." Despite this he believed that learning about the Chinese heritage would be fundamental in the upbringing of his children in the future:

> The reason I want to learn more about my Chinese heritage is because I want to know who I am and what makes me. Because when my kids grow up I will be able to show them a little bit about what their family is, where they came from, I suppose, who they are.

Parental and familial teachings of Chinese customs to children were viewed as an important part of building cultural and family heritage in multi-generational Chinese Australian families.

In this sense, childhood as a life stage is an essential point in the life course where different generations of the family are actively participating together in the negotiation of Chineseness. By consciously instilling Chineseness in their children, parents and grandparents are at the same time engaged in the process of rearticulation of their own identity. On the "receiving side," children simultaneously renegotiate Chineseness due to the influences of the dynamic external social context. These cultural practices and ideologies, which were firmly established by the older generations, work to either empower or restrict children's choices later on in the life course when children grow into adulthood. In this way Chineseness is forever undergoing transformation through the generations. For example, during Donna's childhood, she always yearned for the affection that she saw in other western families. Her mother was being traditional in the sense that she favored sons over daughters which meant that she, as a daughter, did not receive the same amount of love and attention as her male siblings did. As a result, toward her own children,

Donna deliberately discarded what she regarded as negative aspects of traditional Chinese parenting practices and ensured that her children received the kind of affection that was characteristic of western families:

> Donna: I think I was really a rebellious child, because my mother tried to constrict me to being "like Chinese," not going out to play and that kind of thing…every time I was naughty I was punished. So she was the one who punished me all the time. I think I was considered to be uncontrollable because I kept running off all the time! I could see that Australian homes were very loving. I'd go up to my friend's home and we'd be lying on the lounge room floor listening to the radio. There was a much warmer feeling in their family. My mother—it was a hard life for her. She was working in the market garden. There wasn't any affection, because Chinese weren't inclined that way.
>
> Co-author Ngan: Do you think your mother's upbringing has affected the way you brought up your children?
>
> Donna: It's more important to be a happy family unit. My classmates' mothers were involved in a lot of their children's activities and we'd go and watch them play sport, whereas my mother never ever came to anything I went to. It was a very different way of looking at children. You see how other Australian families behave, and you use some of that to model your behavior as well.

The life transitions of the younger generations are thus intertwined with those of the older generations. As such, no cultural values and practices can be totally repeated or recreated across the generations.

Certainly, the family was an important site for the engendering of Chineseness during our informants' childhood; however, the awareness of the children's ethnic identity only became apparent when they began socializing with peers at school and in the wider mainstream "white" community. Clausen explains (1986: 52) that during childhood a child comes to have a sense of self and others through relational differences that permit and demand complex accommodation. Such processes of identity development through relational positioning during childhood can be illustrated by our informants who were both mixed and full-blooded Chinese and who grew up in different social eras in Australia.

Tanya, a third-generation ABC of mixed race, remembered her first racial incident as a child in the 1920s when she was playing with her German friend in her backyard and the subsequent conversation with her Australian-born Chinese father that led to her conscious awareness of her racial identity:

> I remember an incident when I was young when I was playing with a young German boy, Red Apple, around the swimming pool. When I came in for dinner my father asked me what I had been doing and if I had a happy day. I said I went swimming by the pool and that boy, Red Apple, said to me, "Come on, you half-cast sausage machine!" I can remember the first time, my father had a slight change to his very calm Chinese face. He said to me "You know that there are some people who come from other parts of the world who come from other religions. The Jews who are being persecuted by the Germans have been made to feel they are from an inferior race. I hope you will never suffer from that kind of discrimination in Australia." And that was how he would talk to an eleven-year-old… I thought it was terribly funny to be called a "half-cast sausage machine." I probably showed it off more! It never hit home. But on thinking about it afterwards, using the word half-caste, was the first time I consciously thought of myself as "that." That was a name which was given to me by a German refugee in 1931 when he escaped Germany before the worst part of Nazism.

Similarly, for Sarah, a third-generation ABC of mixed race who grew up in the 1940–1950s, because of her physical differences from Anglo-Australian friends she was often racially stigmatized during her childhood, and these incidents made her conscious of her identity:

> Sarah: Probably in my late primary school people used to say you are half-Chinese and you are, what did you call it? I forgot the name for it. Mind you this was the Italians doing it to me. (Laughing) Yes, half-caste or some silly name. I remember some taunting going on. You know kids are cruel.
>
> Co-author Ngan: Were you upset by these incidents? Did you deny your Chinese heritage in anyway?
>
> Sarah: No, I have always been proud of being Chinese. I would say you are just jealous because you don't have a swimming pool, you know those silly things that kids will say.

George, a fourth-generation full-blooded ABC, similarly experienced an otherness that separated himself from his Anglo-Australian peers during his childhood in the 1940s:

> Apart from the usual "Chinaman" name calling, I never encountered racial discrimination. I think in my childhood I always fitted in really well. Academically, I wasn't a brain, but I always did well. And I was never anything else, I was always a Chinese living in Australia, and just getting on with life, never really conscious of my difference from the others… I suppose I felt a sense of being Chinese then by participating in a skit about *mah-jong*[1] playing, but the rest of the time I had always been just like any kids in high school and primary school, and was never really conscious of the fact that I was Chinese.

As children, multi-generational ABCs, of both genders, racially mixed and full blooded, were often stigmatized on the basis of their face—a fate that they could not and still cannot escape in Australia's white-dominated society. The identity forced upon them reveals the significance of physicality in determining one's experience of ethnicity.

A yearning for uniformity often emerged out of a dialectical process of sameness and difference. May, a third-generation ABC, recalled: "I can still remember when we were four or five, my little aboriginal friend and I would have showers together and she would be scrubbing trying to get white, so cute!" With the manifestation of physicality, strategic adaptations were necessary for multi-generational ABCs to manage their everyday lives in Australia. To cope with the inescapable racial vision and prejudices of others, subsequent generations learned to perform and self-regulate their behaviors and emotions to gain the acceptance and respect of peers. For example, for Dean, it was the avoidance of bringing "Chinese" food to school, which enabled him to blend in with white Australian peers. For Sarah, it was interpreting racially induced teasing as jealousy toward their family's wealth.

It was evident that regardless of the social era in which our informants grew up, or the length of time their families may have resided in Australia, visible manifestations and cultural practices during childhood were fundamental to the construction

---

[1] Mah-jong is a game with tiles that originated from China. It involves skills, calculation, and luck. Mah-jong is still popular as a gambling or recreational game in China today and among Chinese overseas.

of difference, creating cultural boundaries of inclusion and exclusion that were vital to the construction of Chineseness, all of which took on additional significance in adolescence.

Adolescence to Adulthood

Adolescence in western society is a time of self-exploration and expression, yet it is also a period when social and cultural influences play a major role in shaping an individual's identity (Clausen, 1986: 85). The accommodation of difference is fundamental in ensuring a sense of sameness and belonging. For most informants, the most effective method in safeguarding sameness and the continuity of one's identity in adolescence was through a denial of their Chinese background. Rob, a middle-aged fifth-generation ABC, described such feelings of denial and dissociation with "anything Chinese" that he and his daughters went through during their adolescent years:

> When you are young you try to compete. I wanted to be like everyone else because I couldn't be. Chinese are always smaller than Australians. So I was always the smallest boy in my year. It was not only being Chinese and being short, I wasn't good at sport as well... Like my children now, to them getting a partner is very important, and how do you do that? By doing all these things. But being Chinese I naturally didn't have these attributes. So being Chinese was a negative attribute when I was young... I just thought of myself as being Australian. And that was it. I didn't even consider myself as being Chinese. I didn't want this sense of being an outsider. That is what all people want, we want to belong... When I went to Hong Kong when I was older, I suddenly had this sense that it is ok to be Chinese. That is not what my daughters are doing; they are denying to be Chinese.

During adolescence, where social and cultural influences are most significant, being a part of not just any group, but the dominant group, Anglo-Celtic Australian per se, becomes pivotal in ensuring a sense of security. The interactions with peers provide an understanding of what is expected and what features and behaviors are desirable and that lead to successful group belonging. In addition, forming an intimate tie with a person of the opposite (or same) sex is a critical developmental accomplishment for many adolescents as it is a key to establishing a strong sense of individual identity (Clausen, 1986: 132). These factors often led our informants to resist and even discard their Chinese roots during their adolescence. Certainly sociocultural contexts change through time; however, as each generation goes through adolescence, most experience a similar need for a sense of sameness and belonging, subsequently leading to their unique ways of accommodation.

While Clausen (1986: 85) argues that social sorting processes that go on in adolescence tend to determine potentialities for the rest of one's life, life events can bring major transitions to the reclamation of an identity. As Rob noted, the turning point for him was a trip to Hong Kong when he was 25; it was the first time he had seen so many Chinese and he suddenly felt, "it was ok to be Chinese." For Jenny, a sixth-generation ABC in her twenties, accommodating differences was an important part of her transition into adulthood. She explained that the gradual attachment to her Chinese roots was due to maturity and the growing confidence in herself:

> I don't think about it in everyday life, but I think that probably as I got older I appreciated it a bit more and am more proud of it than when I was younger. I think when I went to school, it was very middle class, very white, no ethnic. You know when you are young you don't want to be different. Since then I have been working in the public service, there is a big cross-section of people, I feel more comfortable in expressing any differences, much more so than when I was at school. Now I am quite ok to do things and say things differently. I feel more comfortable and confident and not caring about what other people think as much. So it is okay to be different!

While long-settled ABCs have learned to accommodate ethnic differences through transitions from adolescence into adulthood, this process was not necessarily a smooth transgression. For Daisy, a fourth-generation ABC Eurasian who grew up in rural NSW in the 1950s, "being Chinese" or perhaps just simply *identifying* with her own Chinese heritage was a difficult and deliberate process. From her great-grandparents' generation onward, her family intentionally departed from "doing" anything Chinese because of the intense racism in Australia during the early 1900s. Although Daisy was always asked by others about her origin because she had an identifiable Chinese surname, within her family, their Chinese ancestry or their family migration history were never talked about. The intensity of denial by her family can be demonstrated by the incident where her auntie became furious with Daisy when she decided to research the family's Chinese history as she moved away from her home in rural town, to the city to attend university. Daisy explained that meeting Chinese people in university had significant implications for the development of her identity:

> For a young girl who has been brought up in the country, a single girl, very pure Anglo Saxon upbringing, it was fascinating to meet all these Chinese people in university! It fascinated me how I developed this interest in how I connected with them… I had no Chinese upbringing at all.

Daisy's statement, "It *fascinated* me how I developed this interest in how I *connected* with them…," highlights a paradoxical sense of identification. On the one hand, "fascination" suggested a delightful sense of difference that distinguished the self from the other—the out-group. On the other hand, "connection" suggested her sense of commonality and bonding, almost loyalty with or allegiance to other Chinese—the in-group.

It was evident that our informants continued to have feelings of ambiguity, ambivalence, contradictions, and uncertainty about their identity as they progressed from childhood and adolescence to adulthood. The ambiguous overlapping of identities can be clearly illuminated by Debra, a young woman in her 20s, who was feeling stranded between being Australian and Chinese, even in adulthood:

> When I was in primary school I didn't feel different at that stage. It's funny because now I feel different, because I'm older. I don't know why. Probably because you didn't have that thinking pattern when you're young, and the fact that I was actually born here. But at the moment my sense of identity—I don't feel that I'm Chinese and I don't feel I'm an Australian either.

The hybrid processes of identity formation that subsequent generations experience will be discussed in detail in Chap. 7. The point to emphasize here, however, is that the negotiation of identity concerns fluid and fragmented processes as conveyed in the notion of hybridity. It is a dynamic process that changes across the entire course of life and that entails discontinuity and change, particularly in adult life, as individuals go through marriage, divorce, parenthood, and, eventually, death.

Marriage

The conception of family life that is largely molded by one's parents tends to define for the individuals the expectations and requirements that they must meet in marriages, as they progress along their own life courses. There are important questions related to linkages between family contexts and outcomes of identity for subsequent generations of early Chinese migrants. What aspects of cultural–familial ideologies have genuine implications for particular outcomes? What are the implications of these values in one generation for the lives of those in other generations? Since long-settled ABCs have been socialized in the western world, their conception of Chineseness invariably differs from that of Chinese communities in Asia and elsewhere. Yet traditional Confucian ideologies still continue to shape and mold much of their contemporary life.

In a Chinese family, parents traditionally have high expectations for their children's academic achievement, career, and, most importantly, their marriage. Thus, while marriage is a personal matter between two individuals, to a large extent, it is also a cultural issue connected to Chineseness. Marriage, especially to an in-group member, is a filial obligation of children to their parents. The familial pressure for Jerry to marry a Chinese woman points to the importance of marriage in a Chinese family:

> My father always wanted me to be an accountant so when I went to UNSW[2] I did commerce. I went for a commerce degree but my heart wasn't in it so I had to repeat the first year. I passed all of the wrong subjects. I passed the easy subjects, what I thought was easy for me was modern history, which was useless to anybody, and psychology, so then I quit and I went to art school down at The Rocks[3] here. So I went there for three years but then they decided to get me married after that, so it was helter skelter you know, really crazy. So I was more inclined towards the arts but my father with his emotional blackmail…my parents are very good at emotional blackmail—they don't verbalize it, it's their body language. For example, if you could do this for me I'd be happy… That old-fashioned Confucianism. The guilt trip… They wanted me to marry a Chinese girl and that was because of the pressure from my aunties, big aunties and big uncles! They sent me to Brisbane where I met up with the wrong girl. Then they took me to Hong Kong. I was not interested. By the time they tried matchmaking, it was enough!… After my attempted suicide, they stepped down a bit but the silent pressure was still there. They loaded a lot of guilt onto me, which I still carry. Guilt for being a failure. A failure as the number one son because you haven't fulfilled your obligation. Guilt is a terrible thing.

---

[2] University of New South Wales.

[3] A location in Sydney.

Jerry believed that it was the "son's filial duty" to follow his father's wishes in life. Despite his genuine interest in the arts, he studied commerce in university; despite being gay, he went to Hong Kong for matchmaking. To him, these actions marked a solemn obligation dutifully discharged for the sake of the parents. However, he was unable to wholly fulfill his duty as a son because his sexuality led him to live an unmarried life and his eventual career in performing arts meant he was not able to become a "commercial success" as his father had wanted. Although he placed much effort in trying to obey his parents by going to Hong Kong for matchmaking, as well as taking on the dutiful role of looking after his younger siblings as he was the eldest brother, he was considered by his parents a failure as a son. His life was tragically burdened with guilt.

For Sarah, although her father, a second-generation ABC, was in an interracial marriage with a Caucasian woman, he still wished his Eurasian daughter would marry a full-Chinese man. When Sarah was a teenager, her father persuaded her to date with an overseas-born Chinese boy from China, who was literate in Chinese (thus bona fide by definition):

> Probably when I was 14 or 15, Dad tried to get me to go out with this Chinese boy, Ning, from China whose father had a fruit shop next door. Dad tried to push me to go out with Ning and got him to teach me Chinese. He got me the cheung-sam and just really wanted to push me into this. I didn't like him and just didn't want to be with him, not because he was Chinese, but just because I didn't like him. He was really quiet and I just wanted my dancing because I have been a dancer my whole life. My friends went dancing so I didn't want to go out with boys. I was about fifteen when my dad tried to make me go but I didn't.

Her father's request for her to wear the cheung-sam, a traditional Chinese dress, when she went out with Ning, was a way of pretending, passing, or cheating on her Chineseness—a physical mask to disguise her interracial hybrid identity.

Traditional familial ideologies have continued to influence the marriage patterns of subsequent generations. According to Ryan (2003: 63), there is evidence on mixed marriages in Australia to suggest that Asian women are more likely than Asian men to marry Anglo-Celtic Australians. The marriage figures of this study follow this pattern. Six out of 43 informants are or have been interracially married[4] and only one of the six married informants is male. Due to the sample size of this study, figures on interracial marriage cannot be conclusive of general trends of successive generations; however, individual narratives do suggest that the traditional Chinese expectation of marriage with in-group members is more a concern for male informants (whether married or unmarried) than female ones, suggesting the continued influence on Chinese males to marry Chinese women for lineage. Sean, a young man, who was recently married to a Chinese Indonesian, said this:

> Relationship with whites in terms of lust is ok... But ultimately for the sake of my children I would want to marry someone who is Chinese so that they have the reinforcement from both parents of who they are. Ideally I would want to marry someone who could read and write Chinese so that she can pass it onto my kids because I can't do that, but I must have forgotten at the time I married a woman who can't write Chinese!!!

---

[4] Including divorced and widowed.

It is clear that the cultural values of lineage are strongly embedded in the minds of male informants, consequently affecting the choice of marriage partners; nevertheless, other factors such as romance and love also play an influential role in one's marriage decision. Although Sean wished to marry a woman who is literate in Chinese, he did not marry one, suggesting that embedded notions can and do shift in accordance with varying life circumstances.

Our gay informants also expressed the cultural benefits of finding an Asian partner. George, an elderly informant, who recently broke up from a gay relationship with a Caucasian man that lasted 30 years, expressed the benefits of being with someone of the same culture:

> If I would like to have another relationship, I would like to explore having a relationship with an Asian, whether it is going to be long-term or not because we will have so much in common in terms of race, thinking, food habits and upbringing. I think I would get along better with another Asian person than with a Caucasian.

While sharing a common cultural background was often seen as an important factor for the choice of marriage partner, other aspects such as social class and economic prospects were perceived to be influential factors on the success of a marriage. The significance of these specific factors was expressed by Jane, who was divorced from an overseas-born Hong Kong Chinese man:

> When my marriage broke up I realized that we didn't suit each other because he came from a different background… I was brought up here and we thought differently. Maybe he was more middle class and I was below middle class… I think I would have been better off if I married an Australian-born Chinese. Chinese but born in Australia. It would have been easier.

Thus, while in-group marriage is a deeply embedded ideology for the continuation of Chinese lineage, other factors such as social hierarchy and class within the Chinese community (see discussion in Chap. 5), romance and love between two individuals, and cultural norms are important factors affecting the choice of marriage partners.

It is also important to note that Chinese cultural values of marriage are not static, but change through the course of life. This can be clearly demonstrated by the alteration in marriage expectations by Nelson's grandfather who was born in Papua New Guinea and has lived in Australia most of his entire life:

> My grandfather is quite nationalistic. Attached to the old ways, he still wishes his sons and daughter and grandchildren to maintain their heritage and to marry Chinese. But he is progressively becoming more liberal. My parents are quite liberal about the situation. They are changing with the times.

Interracial Marriages Through the Family's Gaze

For long-settled ABCs, their sense of Chineseness was often constructed and embodied within the parental family. The social norms of a culture and ideas of a family laid the foundation for marriage and ideals for children. While marriage was considered a consequence of courtship and personal choice on the part of the couple, the pressure to marry within one's ethnic group to a large extent determined the marriage pool, which strengthened ethnic and racial boundaries. As cultural customs forbade interracial marriages or attached a high cost to them, most of our informants' parents expressed negativity in varying intensity toward their children's engagement in mixed relationships. The common understanding among our informants was that, in the past, marrying "outside" was a shame to the family and marrying a Chinese was more important for a male than female as the former carried the family name. In the excerpt below, Donna clearly captured the opposition toward interracial marriage within Chinese families in 1950s Australia:

> My mother probably thought that I was going to elope with an Australian, and that would bring dishonor to my father's name. She always had a thing about carrying my father's name, all this kind of thing. So I think when she thought I was of marriageable age she just nagged and nagged about the fact that she would never accept an Australian person as an in-law… But the funny part about my family is that my brother immediately below me married an Australian girl. He just told my mother that there was an Australian girl that was pregnant with his baby and he had to marry her, so she couldn't do anything about it. She was extremely angry but didn't disown him because he is a boy. Well, it should have mattered because he carries the father's name… So, I think it was the fear of being disowned that really changed the whole way of looking at it. I think that was a real fear because I'd grown up in this fairly close family where the whole family, ten of us, sitting around the table every night, and I just couldn't imagine how I could just be cast adrift… I got engaged to a Chinese boy and even though my parents didn't really like him, my mother told me later my father said to her, "Maybe he back-answers us and even if we don't like him as a person, at least we should be grateful he's full-blooded Chinese."

The image of the "family" is often perceived as a site of homely domestic harmony, yet the family can also be the place for abusive social relationships where identities and life decisions can be manipulated or shattered. Regarding interracial marriage, since being involved in such partnerships is a "shame" and "dishonor" to the family, parental pressure to the highest intensity could lead to the children being disowned by their parents. This was particularly relevant to the experience of those living in the earlier part of the twentieth century (Ryan, 2003). As highlighted in the excerpt, although Donna's parents were not fond of her partner, in the end they accepted the marriage because he was a "full-blooded Chinese," a "pure" Chinese—which was, for her parents, the most important characteristic for a son-in-law. Donna's choice of partner was greatly affected by her parents' cultural expectations, as intimate relationship with a westerner would mean a loss of familial trust, love, and security.

While some experienced overt pressures from parents, others chose Chinese partners because of the unconscious need to conform with their siblings. Mary expressed the impact of familial influence on her choice of finding a Chinese partner when she was around marriageable age in the 1950s:

> When my brother married an Australian girl, I think my father never said "no," but I'm sure underneath it, he would have liked his second son to have married a Chinese girl. That was just Chinese thinking in those days, because in those days Chinese married Chinese, and that was the way of thinking… I didn't think "I have to marry a Chinese" but I just wasn't interested in Australian boys! (laughs)… I just seemed to be interested in Chinese boys! It's

funny, isn't it… Why would that be? I wasn't told ever who to mix with, you know, but I think you just follow the family. Like, you see your eldest sister married a Chinese, you see your second sister married a Chinese, you see your third sister married a Chinese, you see your fourth sister married a Chinese, you see your fifth sister married a Chinese, and then you see your sixth brother married a Chinese—you just automatically felt that was the way of life. Yeah. I suppose if I had maybe fallen in love with an Australian I might have thought differently then, but I didn't think like that.

In this manner, the values held by the family and the community significantly affect the way subsequent generations construct and do Chineseness through marriage.

However, with societal changes, negative feelings toward interracial marriages have eased through the generations. As highlighted by Khoo's (2004) study on the intermarriage pattern in Australia, the proportion of second-generation Chinese Australians with spouses of Anglo-Celtic ancestry is approximately 21% and for third generation it is 68%. Yet our informants still acknowledged the benefits of marrying a person of Chinese background because of the presumption of a greater understanding of each other through a shared cultural background. To this point, Rob argued, "My marriage is relatively happier than those of my siblings who married Westerners because my wife and I are both Chinese."

Interracial Marriages and Adoption

Another factor leading to the persistence of in-group marriage concerns issues of identity of mixed-raced children. Rob wanted his children to marry a Chinese person because he felt that "being mixed blood means you don't belong to either culture and that would lead to much pain… I don't want my children to go through such trauma." The difficulty of mixed-race issues led Donna to purposefully adopt a "Chinese" child:

> We already had to deal with the issue of adoption. So we thought it was probably less complicated to bring in a child from a full-blooded Chinese family into another full-blooded Chinese family. We thought we were very blessed in having that luck come our way. At that stage, I was really quite racist in the way I thought. I thought—my husband and I both thought—that we would prefer to have a full- blooded Chinese than a mixed Chinese child, and we didn't even think about adopting any other race…all through my life I'd grown up thinking that the Chinese were a pure race, that we had to keep the line pure and what not. And it was only later, when I matured in my mid-twenties or so, that I got to thinking, well, it doesn't matter what color skin and what not. But it's very hard when you had parents who are holding on to the Chinese side of things… My former husband and I were married for 17 years. After we broke up he married an Australian girl, so his views had also changed… Ours was supposedly a love match, but then we ended up divorcing!

The couple especially wanted a Chinese baby because they both were Chinese and as Donna explained, it was "less complicated" and socially desirable as they were a Chinese family with Chinese relatives and friends. The homogenizing idea of Chineseness had perpetuated through Donna's family where, with the exception of her younger brother who married an Anglo-Australian, all the other siblings married Chinese Australians. Consequently, to overcome the fear of disharmony and ambiguity of identity that would arise from having a non-Chinese child, the prerequisite for the adoption was to be a "full-blooded Chinese baby."

Similarly, Sarah was adopted by her Australian-born Chinese father and Caucasian mother because of her "mixed blood." Because her parents were not able to bear children due to health reasons, they decided to adopt a child and this decision was supported by the whole family. Her parents, however, had concerns about the possible social pressure and social stigmatization toward the family as a consequence of the adoption so they deliberately chose a mixed-race child whose physicality as a Eurasian would "match" with the couple's ethnicity. Sarah rationalized her parents' choice for a mix-raced child this way: "they have to have a half-Chinese baby. If not, how could you explain my dad's case? He is a full-Chinese."

The selectiveness of the adoption highlights that "being Chinese" is, to a certain extent, a matter of choice. Mathews' (2000) notion of a "cultural supermarket" or smorgasbord echoes Bourdieu's concept of "habitus" or Chan's (2011) concept of "identity options on offer," suggesting people can pick and choose their identity in accordance with fundamental factors such as age and gender as well as their personal molding, but also in negotiation with and in performance for others. In this way, Chineseness, to a certain extent, can be argued as a consumed affair as subsequent generations make choices according to the ways in which identity is constructed. Clearly, despite the postmodernist insistence on deconstructing the conceptually flawed and politically pernicious essentialist conceptions of identity, Donna's reasons for the adoption of a "full-blooded Chinese child" reiterated the notion that Chineseness is still informed by an ideology that is based on biology and physicality.

Within the context of the family, individuals may accept or reject the values and expectations of the older generations (Alba & Nee, 1999; Nagel, 1994; Thompson, 1995). Thus, while in the past Donna had grown up thinking that, "the Chinese were a pure race," and that it was her obligation to "keep the line pure," since adulthood she had learned that even by discarding certain traditional social practices she can still be Chinese as there are many different ways of "being Chinese." Donna expressed the view that, unlike her parents, she did not have any cultural expectation on the ethnicity of her daughter-in-law as she felt it was the personality of a person that was the most important. Such a change in cultural values was linked to the dramatic events in her life—marriage, parenthood, divorce, sickness, and death in the family. The experience of divorce tends to mark distinctive changes in the psyche, leading to alteration of deeply instilled values of life (Bohannan, 1979). Donna's life trajectory had progressively altered her cultural values toward interracial marriage.

Interracial Relationships Through the Gendered Gaze

As discussed above, age-related transitions such as marriage have considerable implications for the ways in which identities unfold across the life course. The customs against interracial relationships and marriage, which are deeply ingrained in the Chinese culture, are intricately intertwined with western sexual ascription, perpetuation of traditional gender ideology, and racial sexual stereotypes. For Jenny, the link between her Chinese background and the associated Western ascriptions of a Chinese woman was represented in all her interracial relationships:

> I find that most of the guys that I dated had a thing for Asian women. But what can I do? I guess in a way it is an advantage but it also makes you think, would it have been the same if I wasn't Asian? I know that initially it is always because of the way I look.

Jocelyn expressed a similar sense of ambivalence when she discussed the fact that her Chinese physique such as small oriental eyes and small stature and the stereotypical qualities of submissiveness and docility attached to Asian women was an initial source of allure for most of the white men she encountered. While it could be said that her race, skin color, complexion, shape, and height that made up her "Chinese look" was a value-added marker in terms of courtship, at the same time this maker belittled her sense of self-worth.

The literature, in the main, on the study of the Other underscores this point—the colonial subject seen through the exoticizing gaze of Orientalism (Appadurai, 1993; Said, 1978). Said's work on orientalism argues that the imperial West has legitimized its superiority over the subaltern based on romanticized notions of an exoticized Other. Western representations of Asian women frequently focus on their exotic and sexual characteristics, yet other stereotypes portray Chinese women as passive, submissive, and docile—attributes of the oppressed subject of traditional Chinese patriarchal practices (Ryan, 2003: 73). What is underlined in the plots of The World of Suzie Wong, Memoirs of the Geisha, Miss Saigon, Madam Butterfly, and endless western novels, movies, and operas about the orient is the emasculation of both Asian men and women, where they are portrayed to be in a position of inferiority compared to the powerful, masculine West. Such stereotypical portrayals of Chinese women and men have provoked gender tensions, as our informant Martin argued:

> I think the stereotypical perception of Asian women is better compared to that of Asian men. For example, the movie *Joy Luck Club*—from the women's perspective the movie is just about mother-and-daughter relationships. But a lot of Asian men are frustrated about that movie—it portrays that when Asian women are with their Chinese husbands or boyfriends they live a very sad life. But later on in the film when they leave their Chinese husband, and go out with Americans, they live a very happy life. So it gives a very bad portrayal of Chinese men…but in the end women just want to be looked after. They don't care what race it is.

Western hegemonic representations of Asian men have been traditionally portrayed as servile and effeminate while modern Western representations of Asian men paint them as hyperintellectual, geeks, patriarchal, chauvinistic, and asexual. In contemporary society where the body and the face are commodified as a marketing tool, the physicality of a man plays a significant role in the construction of masculine identity. The western hegemonic constructed images of Asian men make them less than manly compared to the image of Western men who are portrayed as strongly built, romantic, and liberal. While Martin's statement that "women just want to be looked after" is likely to provoke debates; the point to emphasize here is that physicality is an integral part of socialization for ethnic minorities, and both Chinese men and women are affected by the hegemony of western ascriptions.

In particular is the experience of Asian gay males. They have been identified as presenting a greater risk of body image disturbance than heterosexual males because of the aesthetically driven gay culture. Murry's (2005) study on Asian gay males in South Australia shows Asian gay men struggle with the notion of portraying themselves with a masculine presence in a white, heterosexual, Anglo-Australian environment because of their Asian physical appearance. Our informant, Leon, a young gay man in his 20s, likewise acknowledges similar body identity concerns attached to being an Asian gay male:

> When I was starting dating, I started having different perceptions of myself because I became aware that I was physically different from Australians. Being Chinese, I am not physically attractive. I sort of always had this feeling when I was growing up. The media was Caucasian. Chinese were unattractive and it is always the case when Chinese appear in all western media.

The constructions of Oriental Others, according to Said (1978), sustain the manipulation of Western hegemony, as in the case of the hyperfeminine Asian woman and the asexual Asian man. To this, Ang (2001: 144) expresses her experience of being on the receiving end of such ambivalence: "(The fact that) one cannot prove any 'hard' racism here while still feeling objectified, subjected to scrutiny and othered."

While it is necessary to highlight the experience of Chinese women as objectified subjects, it is also important to examine the ambivalent moments of male subjects whose experiences are largely invisible. For long-settled ABCs, the orientation for a partner based on ethnicity seems to be far more problematic for men than women, as females generally seemed more relaxed toward interracial marriage. Our informant, Sean, suggested that the flexibility of women toward interracial relations is because "guys have more pride in their heritage than girls. The predisposition of girls to communicate more freely makes the difference...." His claim brings to light the existence of structural ambivalence created by western hegemonic stereotypes of Asian men and women. This tension has manifested itself in difficult gender and sexual relations created by cultural incommensurabilities.

The common feelings of discomfort and anxiety of a number of male informants toward interracial relationships between a western man and a Chinese woman can be illustrated by Rob's one-line statement: "I get that awful feeling when I see a Chinese girl with an Australian man." The "gaze" of Chinese men often becomes the confronting end of what Ang (2001: 144) describes as, "not direct racial assault or straightforward discrimination...but something much less tangible than that." It is important to note that there are varying kinds of responses, behaviors, and attitudes toward mixed-race couples. In the case of Asian women partnered with Western men, there is a sense of begrudging acceptance, as Martin argued:

> I am not trying to be racist but this interracial thing does bug me. I have had a lot of experiences, I have liked Asian girls and they have gone off with Australian guys... When you see Asian girls with Western men I feel a sense of betrayal. If she went out with an Asian guy I didn't feel as jealous. There are certain girls that I know who have said that they only go out with white guys. They give their reasons as they are taller and funnier. There is the perception that we Asian guys are geeky and we have no sex appeal at all. That gets me angry sometimes.

However, in the case of Asian men partnered with Western women, ambivalence is converted into a sense of victory. Sean articulated such opposing feelings:

> When I see mixed couples, if I see an Asian girl going out with a Western man, I look and see if she is pretty. If she is I think it is a waste, if she is ugly someone has got to take her. If an Asian guy is going out with a Western girl, I say good on ya! It is like a sense of conquest!

Highlighted in the above are the significantly opposing responses towards the two variants of interracial partnerships, Asian women with western men and Asian men with western women—most studies have been confined almost exclusively to the Asian women as the objectified subject through the western hegemonic gaze. The source of such opposing gendered attitudes can be understood in terms of Said's (1978) claim that the Occident has always seen Orientals as degenerate and uncivilized.

Furthermore, it is also related to issues of stereotypes and notions of hegemonic, subordinated, and marginalized masculinities that allude to the complex relations between sex, gender, sexuality, and race. However, the point of the above narratives is that the articulation of Chineseness goes hand-in-hand with the articulation of sexism. While the experience of the objectified is crucial, to adequately encapsulate the entirety of the self/other relations, the perceptions of the "gazer" are also necessary. Interracial relation is a site for struggle among proliferating identity options and provides important ways of understanding the management of dynamic racial boundaries across the life course.

Later Years

To a large extent changes in roles and lifestyle in the later years, as noted by Clausen (1986), were experienced by a number of our elderly informants. In particular, such changes had an impact on their construal of Chineseness. For our elderly informants, Chineseness came increasingly into the consciousness when primary family roles diminished through retirement and widowhood. Where time was always an issue for the younger cohorts as they engaged in the rush of daily living, from career development to parenting, our elderly informants commonly expressed they had more time and freedom in their later years, which afforded them space for self-reflection. The elderly female informants explained that the cultural expectations of a Chinese mother assumed much responsibility such as rearing of children, household chores, taking care of the in-laws—making the middle years of life rather busy. For Mary, because of the many duties of motherhood in the middle stages of life, she could not pursue her own interest in Chinese culture. Only in her later years as a widow did she have time to reflect on her Chinese heritage and develop Chinese language skills:

> As I get older and I'm learning more of the Chinese language and reading more about Chinese, I get more interested in their way of tradition, I suppose, and culture... I think that happens to all Chinese people that I know of. As they get older, they've got more time to get interested in things Chinese... You didn't think about that. Now we've got more time to think about it, and you've got more time to learn about it. When you're young you're just bringing up the children, getting meals...you don't have time.

Thus self-identification as Chinese is closely linked with gender and changes in the life course. For Mary, her Chinese identity became a matter of lifestyle in the "habitus" of daily living—only in the later years of her life was she able to reclaim her Chinese identity.

Another point highlighting the relationship between aging and Chineseness was our informants' increasing interest in their family heritage and family history. As noted in Chap. 1, community organizations including the Chinese Heritage Association of Australia and Chinese Australian Historical Society were initial points of contact for co-author Ngan to recruit participants for her research. Both of these organizations promoted discussion of the history of Chinese community in Australia and, among their many shared objectives, one was to assist members in the recording of family and community histories. Through participant observation at their periodic meetings, Ngan noticed that a majority of the attendees were made up of elderly retired Chinese Australians, although both organizations were also keenly interested in the recruitment of younger members. A number of older informants who were part of either one or both organizations expressed that these community groups are a safe place for socialization with those of a similar cultural background. For example, Sandy, aged 64, was conducting a research project on her family history. She became interested after attending an exhibition of old Chinatown where she saw much written about the long-settled Chinese families, but nothing about her. She wanted to honor her father, so she began her family research. While honoring the family was a major reason for her research, her pride in being a Chinese in Australia was also an important reason for doing the project. It is important to note here that such ethnic pride was not so much associated with China, but with the culture and the history of the Chinese presence in Australia.

Gendered Duty for the Aged

A major myth about the Chinese communities is that members of the older generations are secure in receiving support from their family members. The myth arises from the Confucian tradition, which maintains that respect for and taking good care of one's aged parents, as the moral duty, known as *Xiao* (filial piety), is considered a distinctive Chinese family cultural value that is part of the moral life of long-settled ABCs. While ethnic values of premigration culture represent a dependence on filial and kin assistance, among the majority of our informants, duty for the aged is still noted as distinctive of Chinese values. Donna explained that the care for her elderly mother was an obligation which was not shared with her Western friends who, if they decided to take on the responsibility of care, would do it because of love rather than duty:

> My mother and I don't have a strong bond, because she has this thing about daughters being second-class citizens, and that's what I grew up with. She's now 84 and she may have mellowed in that way, but before, daughters really were of no value because they didn't carry the family name and all that kind of thing. And I sort of think, well, that wasn't the right way to bring up children, they should all be treated the same...but I still feel duty-bound to her.

> There isn't the unconditional love that one should have for a mother that I see some of my
> Australian friends have, but it's more an obligation, a duty.

While long-settled ABCs are influenced by Western values, they still see their commitment to the aged as a duty. Seeking assistance from social welfare for aged parents was seen by many as shameful.

Related to the designation of children as carers is the issue of the respective roles of adult children and other kin in carrying such responsibility for the aged. Hareven (1996: 9) raises an important question: When adult children serve as the primary carer, how is their assistance augmented by that of other kin? For the long-settled Chinese community, the elderly were more likely to receive assistance from their children rather than from other siblings. Moreover, the perpetuation of the traditional gender ideology often resulted in sons being the main carers for their elder parents. Ryan (2003: 65) notes that in Legge and Westbrook's (1991) study on home care and nursing home experience for aged Chinese-, Greek-, and Anglo-Australians, it was found that the main carers for the aged Chinese were the sons and daughters-in-law, whereas for the aged Greek the carers were the daughters.

Sons as the main carers can be explained by the perpetuation of the traditional gender ideology. Donna's remark about daughters often being seen as "second class citizens" illustrates this continued influence of traditional gender norms. Similarly, gender inequality was also experienced by Jean. When Ngan asked her whether there were differences between how sons and daughters were treated in the family, she sobbingly answered "absolutely!" Full of sadness, and crying, she could not bear to talk about the issue and discontinued the interview. The intensity of her emotions indicates the extent of gender tensions in her family. In another interview her brother confirmed the unequal treatment of males and females in their family:

> My younger sister didn't have the same Chinese influence from my grandparents. The fact
> that she was a girl—my grandparents didn't pay much attention to girls which is unfortu-
> nate. Aside from that she didn't pick up the Chinese language as well.

The preference for males was also evidenced in Janice's family where her in-laws put pressure on her to give birth to a son "to carry the family name":

> It was my husband's family. They all said I should try for a boy. His mother wanted another
> grandson, I suppose. There is a ten-year age gap between him and his next brother, I being
> the youngest one of the whole lot of them. They all depended on me to try for a son to carry
> the family name.

Hareven (1996: 5) explains that generational relations in later life are interconnected with experience and transition from earlier life—thus old age is part of an overall process of generational interaction rather than an isolated stage. As the older generations transit into old age, obligations of family continuity through the birth of a son are brought to bear on the younger generations. This is precisely where generations are interdependent. The narratives of this study suggest that traditional Chinese gender ideology and family cultural values of duty and obligation to the aged still have relevance for understanding the Chineseness of long-settled Chinese communities in Australia. Gender has specific relevance for the way in which generational relations are acted out.

Being Gay and Duty for the Aged

An intriguing condition concerns the interplay of homosexuality and filial duty for the aged. Elderly homosexual male informants explained that their sexuality was a major factor that result in them taking on the dominant role of a carer for their elderly parents and other family members. Being a son, one is assumed to take on the traditional responsibility of caring for the parents. Being gay, which means an unmarried life and no children, is an additional reason for carrying the main responsibility for the aged parents. Often siblings will be married and have their own children to look after; as such, the unmarried individuals who have relatively fewer familial responsibilities are expected by their siblings to look after the elderly parents. Our informant, Jerry, who was gay, was also the eldest son in his family. Because of traditional ideology and the circumstances of his gay life, the responsibility for looking after his aged parents as well as children of the extended family was "naturally" placed upon him. Many personal sacrifices and accommodations such as taking work holidays to chauffeur his parents to the doctors and moving in with parents were made to fulfill the son's full filial responsibility as a carer:

> Jerry: I have looked after almost 20 children—my siblings and then my cousins. My sister was the first to get married and she was only 19 and her husband was only 20, so they were very immature and I had to look after her baby girl for two years because I'm the *Dai Cao*[5] and that girl is now 40 years old and she's got her daughters, ten and 16… I have looked after the youngest one. It just goes on and on! I never have time for myself. It's always looking after my family because I am the eldest brother in my family and I naturally became the carer. Now I've been intensively looking after my parents for the last fifteen years. Ever since I came back from China, I was living with them at Eastwood and I was looking after them. All of my holidays were taking them to hospital backwards and forwards. They were always sick and I'm still doing it now, though not as much as I did before, but it's still regular.
>
> Co-author Ngan: Do you share the workload with your siblings?
>
> Jerry: Now we are, but the last four years they had been living in Brisbane and it was terrible.

Similarly, George, who was also gay, explained that he was the only one among his siblings to be unmarried and to have no children. He too became the primary carer for his mother, as all his siblings were "too busy" with their own family life:

> For some reason I did not have a close relationship with my father but was more bonded with my mother. So when my father died earlier, for some years I cared solely for my mum because I was gay. The rest of the family were married, had children and had set up their own homes. The responsibility to take care of my mum was placed back on me as I was gay, meaning single, no child, so I have had to look after my mum.

Respect for the elderly and family harmony were important to male informants, thus reflecting the persistence of the traditional ideology of sons as the main carers for their parents and family. However, even for those informants who were homosexual, such an embedded gendered notion of *Xiao* or filial piety means that, despite their

---

[5] *Dai Cao* are the Cantonese words for one's mother's eldest brother.

gayness, they still performed the cultural expectation of the male role of a dominant carer to the family.

The notion of *Xiao* as discussed earlier is also linked to the obligation to produce a male offspring to ensure continuity of the family line and family name. Such Chinese familial ideology continued to be a deeply entrenched value of the families of long-settled ABCs—as illuminated by the last wish of George's father:

> When my father laid on his death bed dying of cancer, he said, "Would you promise me you would marry a Chinese?" He never knew I was gay and I would never tell him I was gay. Even though born in Australia; and his father was also born in Australia, my father then, in the fifties, believed that Chinese must marry Chinese. The word flowing around in his times was half-caste, not Eurasian. So the context of mixed-blood was totally awful to him. He said to me "would you promise me to marry a Chinese girl?" And I said, "yes, I will marry a Chinese girl"—cos I wouldn't tell him I couldn't marry a girl at all because I was gay. I promised that I would marry a Chinese. When my sister went off and married this Norwegian boy, Eric, my father was furious. He couldn't accept that. He felt his daughter should have married a Chinese boy, even though my father was very Australian in many ways.

Even at his deathbed, George's father's last wish was that his son would marry a Chinese. Keeping the secret from his father that he was gay and would never marry, George promised him that he would marry a Chinese woman. The social stigma of homosexuality and the unfulfilled obligations of a son led to a profound sense of guilt.

Gay men often have conflicting relationships with their parents in their youth because as gay men they are unable to fulfill the Chinese obligation of marriage to produce a son to continue the ancestral line. Jerry explained that his unmarried life meant he would not be able to pass down the name of the family. As such, as a son, he had failed:

> I don't think my parents and I had a close relationship. I think they had kids for the sake of having kids and what they did was a fulfillment of their obligations. That's how I see it and I feel sorry for them for having a son like me. I will never have kids.

Conflict within the family and their inability to fulfill a son's obligation led to an intense sense of guilt that was emotionally devastating. George's recollection of his adolescent years, prior to his coming out, illuminates the emotional trauma and intensity of guilt about his homosexuality:

> You are living constantly in guilt. I was always praying, God forgive me, God forgive me, change me by the holy power of spirit, let me not think of men and boys, let me think of women, and so it was awful. It was awful to be living in constant guilt, feeling terrible about confessing. I want God to help me, to change, to be straight. I asked god to help me to marry and become a heterosexual, but I just couldn't… But gradually by accepting a gay lifestyle, I have learned to be more accepting of myself because I am no longer in tension, no longer in conflict. I am no longer living a life in guilt.

Jerry was similarly traumatized by a sense of guilt about his gayness and his inability to fulfill his filial roles as a son. The pain in negotiating familial expectations, dealing with cross-cultural pressure, and confronting his own sexuality led to his attempted suicide when he was in his 20s.

Studies have found that intolerant attitudes toward gayness among Chinese men are directly related to internalized filial piety since a gay lifestyle was largely seen as a threat to the continuity of the family (Hsu, Hui, & Waters, 2001; Wang, Bih, & Brennan, 2009). Comparing the experience of coming out between Westerners and Chinese, "the greatest obstacle a Chinese homosexual faces lies not with religion or the workplace, but with the family; parents being some of the most difficult of those to come out to" (Chou, 1997 in Wang et al., p. 286). George explained that he never told his parents about his sexuality as they "never would have understood the concept of gay." He also noted similar experiences of other homosexual couples:

> I met two gay girls at a party six months ago, one was a European girl and her partner was Chinese. Both of them have been living together in a gay relationship for many years and interacting with each other's family, but none of them would dare to talk about or mention that they are gay. Their families just think that they are simply good friends who live together in the same household. The Chinese girl would have never told her family, "I am a lesbian." Their families just treat them as good friends. They would never come out, they *can never* come out. So there is still a degree of secrecy that threatens people to tell who they are sexually.

While internalized values of filial piety prevented gay informants from coming out to their parents, the social context of the wider Chinese community also contributed to the suppression of their homosexuality. Until recently, the Asian homosexual community in Australia was very small and homosexuality has largely been unspoken about in the Chinese Australian community. George described how the social environment of the Chinese gay community in Sydney has changed since his youth in the 1960s:

> I think the Chinese community in Sydney in the early days wouldn't recognize that Chinese were gay. The Chinese community in Sydney then was a straight community, and everybody went "when are you going to get married? When are you going to get a girlfriend?" Now the Chinese gay community is more open because of Mardi Gras. People can see gay Chinese men marching on Oxford Street. There is recognition that Chinese can be gay and being gay is not just a Western phenomenon.

While social attitudes toward homosexuality have changed in Australia, particularly within the recent decades with the establishment of Asian gay and lesbian organizations, homosexuality is still a taboo subject in the Chinese Australian community. Because of the continued conservatism of Chinese families, gay informants both young and old, who lived by the virtue of filial piety, were unable to "come out" to their parents. In this way, the notion of "being Chinese," or being a member of a "Chinese family," had a detrimental impact on self-identification as gay for our homosexual male informants. As such, together with the relative flexibility of their unmarried and childless life, as well as a sense of guilt, gay sons continued to meet the cultural expectation of the male role and take on the dominant responsibility for caring for their aged parents.

Conclusion

Chinese diasporic communities and their life trajectories provide critical spaces to examine the ambiguous and ambivalent notion of Chineseness that has defined and differentiated diasporic lives. In the case of long-settled ABCs, although their families had departed from China over three generations earlier, and have been socialized in the western culture of Australia, they were still intimately influenced by traditional Chinese ideologies in varying ways and at different stages of their life course, which was dependent on fundamental factors such sexuality, gender, and class. The inscription of Chineseness was largely by their families, mainstream Australian society, and the Chinese diasporic spaces they inhabited which established a sense of their social location. At the same time, as they took on different social, gender, and familial roles through age transitions into childhood, adolescence, marriage, parenthood, and old age, multi-generational ABCs were compelled to confront and interrogate their Chineseness. Due to varying social experiences and biographies, their sense of identity changed over time in different localities and social eras.

What we have discussed in this chapter is the complex interplay of processes that intricately influence the formation of one's cultural identity. For our informants, Chineseness and social identities were constantly being negotiated and renegotiated, a process that was contingent on their differential meaningfulness in different age-related social identities. Yet they were at the same time shaped by a sense of Chineseness and its associated set of social practices, which had implications for how they comprehended themselves and the world. On the one hand, one's daily experiences establish one's social location; yet, on the other hand, one's social location also determines the experiences an individual is likely to have. For example, as a mother, Mary's Chinese heritage was of less importance, but as a widower, Chineseness became a matter of acute awareness. As such, her sense of Chineseness changed across the different stages of her life. For Donna, it was her sense of Chineseness that influenced her decision to marry a man with "Chinese blood" and adopt a Chinese child.

While highlighting that the dynamic negotiation of Chineseness was an embedded part of an informant's identity, being Chinese was also a matter of lifestyle in the "habitus" of everyday living which changes across the stages in the life course. Different generations negotiate Chineseness in their own ways where certain customs, practices, and values of the previous generation are maintained while other aspects that appear irrelevant are modified, resisted, or discarded. In this manner, Chineseness becomes, to a certain extent, a consumed affair as subsequent generations make choices central to the ways in which it is constructed. As Mathews (2000: 5) explains, We seem to be able to pick and choose culturally who we are, in the food one eats and the language one chooses to learn." For our informant Debra Chineseness was impacted by the choice of learning the Chinese language, particularly after marriage to an overseas-born Chinese, while for Dean, our other informant, it was avoidance of eating Chinese food at school. Either way, the choice of what to consume and what not to has cultural implications for their negotiation of identity. The ability to "pick and choose" allows subsequent generations to retain aspects of Chineseness that have positive symbolic value while modifying or discarding other aspects that appear irrelevant. In this manner, our informants reconstructed hybridized forms of Chineseness in ways of their own choosing that were relevant and meaningful to their identifications as long-settled ABCs or Chinese Australians—or as whatever labels that represented and expressed their identity in a particular context in their life course. Variations in consumption across the life course are intrinsic cultural processes which are increasingly central to the definition of identity.

Although "being Chinese" can, to a degree, be argued as increasingly becoming a matter of personal taste, the choices that subsequent generations make throughout their lives are not totally free, but are affected by social constructions of race through mythic racial physical features. While the postmodern literature maintains that identity is fluid and dynamic, the truth of one's social and cultural position is visibly manifested through the social construction of the Chinese face and body—as such constituting an objective location. So the coded and aesthetic physical marker(s) that one has shapes one's sense of identity and difference. For those who are of ambiguous identity such as the mixed race and the multi-generational Australian-born Chinese, their physicalities often encounter an unrelenting skepticism and interrogation when there is no visible manifestation of their declared racial identity. Those situated in a hybrid zone often experience anxiety when essentialized racial/physical features—which have been socially constructed as determinants of identity—fail to match an individual's claim to identity.

Having established that the formation of Chineseness is a fluid process contingent on social and cultural contexts, biographical time, physicality, gender, sexuality, and socially constructed, age-based identities, our next chapter turns to a focused discussion on hybridization and hybridity. We shall show what is in between socially constructed cultural identities that is central to the understanding of Chineseness of long-settled ABCs. We shall direct attention to what happens on the borderlines of cultures—"Chinese" and the "West"—to see what happens in the lives of subsequent generations who are living in-between cultures. It is amalgamation, intersection, in-betweenness and an alternation of cultural identities involving the self and the Other that is central to the creation of new meanings.

Chapter 7
Decentered Linkages and Hybridity: The Ambivalence of Chineseness as Identity

Contrary to assimilationist propositions, and in the same way as many recent immigrants, long-settled Australian-born Chinese are caught in a liminal zone where the formation of identities subsumes being both Chinese and Australian, and not an "either/or" situation. Like a stone, race is "just there"—a hard thing to ignore or change. Racial identities are deeply embedded social constructs on "both sides of the equation," which act as a barrier—a wall that separates the ethnic actor from the dominant white society. Within the family, subsequent generations of the Australian-born Chinese undergo a unique, indeed spectacular, process of hybridization during which their negotiations of home and identity are constructed by decentered connections of memories, nostalgias, stories, legends, and even myths, of the Chinese pioneers—all of which have deep implications for the development of hybridized identities. Regardless of the generational longevity of their presence in Australia, like all nonwhites in history all over the world, to "cope" with racism, these Chinese immigrants do the best they can under the circumstances. Sometimes it works, triumphantly, thus bringing delight and pride; and sometimes it does not, and even fails tragically—thus their plight, embarrassment, and even shame. No matter, the ethnic actor keeps trying, to "take the best of both worlds," as our informant put it.

Recently there has been growing awareness of the inadequacy of older theoretical frameworks that see migration as a once-off movement from the homeland to a new home where assimilation is alleged to occur inevitably (e.g., Basch, Glick-Schiller, & Szanton-Blanc, 1994; Foner & Glick-Schiller, 2002; Glick-Schiller, Basch, & Blanc-Szanton, 1991; Levitt & Glick-Schiller, 2004; Smith, 2002). To more fully understand contemporary migrant's experiences—which often involve unsettling identities as a result of the intersections of crossroads and borderlands—emerging frameworks argue that the impact of cross-cultural and cross-national ties must be addressed from a transnational perspective.

L.L.-S. Ngan and K.-b. Chan, *The Chinese Face in Australia: Multi-generational Ethnicity among Australian-born Chinese*, DOI 10.1007/978-1-4614-2131-3_7, © Springer Science+Business Media, LLC 2012

The concept of transnationalism describes a set of activities that involve "the frequent and widespread movement back and forth between communities of origin and destination and the resulting economic and cultural transformations" (Levitt & Waters, 2002: 7). A heavy emphasis is placed on the flows and networks within a social space that is characterized by "contested cultural boundaries, flexible citizenship, and intensive flows of people, capital, subcontracted goods, technology, and information, all tied directly or indirectly in their own ways with the transmigrants and their place-based social networks" (Ma, 2003: 5). The contemporary advancement of technological innovations (e.g., Internet, e-mails, cheap IDD phone cards) and media intervention (e.g., satellite television, movies, music) have strengthened connections between host country and homeland. Through the transnational framework, it has become widely acknowledged that separate places have become a single community through the circulation of social, cultural, legal, political, educational, economic and religious resources and ideologies that are pooled together, sustained, and shaped by migrants and nonmigrants crossing national borders, which have important ramifications on notions of home and identity.

In particular, the transnationalism perspective has been central in studies of home and identity that go beyond simple bounded notions of all kinds. Diasporic images of "home" often intertwine origin, cultural heritage, ancestral homeland, and local residence, which form an intimate community within a wider "spatial" world that has become important in theorizing identity and politics of location (Kuah-Pearce & Davidson, 2008). Thus, contrary to its traditional conception, "home" can no longer be tied to boundaries of a physical territory nor conceived as geographies of dwelling in concrete places. As Appadurai (1997: 7) contends, "diasporas always leave a collective memory about another place and time and create new maps of desire and of attachment." As different people are drawn, even thrown, into each other, waves of social transformation travel virtually all over the world, transforming ideas about home and identity and engendering hybridized, flexible identities in diasporas.

The transnational perspective rejects the long-held notion that the establishment of ethnic identity is solely due to continuous movement across physical territories and argues that it is conditioned by what Ong (1999: 4) calls "cultural interconnectedness and mobility across space." The exploration into the flexible practices and strategies of transnationality among the Chinese has given rise to figures such as the "flexible citizen"; the "multipassport holder"; "the multicultural manager" with "flexible capital"; the "astronaut father" shuttling across borders on business; the "parachute kid" who is dropped off in a foreign country by parents; the "lone mother" or "mother goose" who is left alone with children to settle in the host country while the husband commutes across borders.

Transnational ties with the homeland play a "crucial, ongoing, and often central role in informing not only notions of immigrant ethnicity but also of one's relationship to society" (Winland, 1998: 7). By incorporating a spatial understanding, notions of home are stretched, to become multifocal, as people conceptualize and act on different contexts of home, and thus are connected to home through diverse and changing social relations. It is precisely because of its fluid nature that home can be unfixed, multiple, and contested. The critical relations between notions of home and identity play a central role in informing not only notions of Chineseness, Englishness, Blackness, etc., but also relations to the host society.

Unlike overseas-born Chinese migrants whose transnational linkages with the homeland often become a resource for maintaining Chineseness, long-settled communities tend to have weaker physical and emotional ties to China. How do those who do not actively participate in transnational activities negotiate Chineseness? How is "Chineseness" constructed by those who only see China as a land of their ancestors rather than a "homeland"? Are only those who consider China homeland "Chinese"? To comprehend the connections between home and identity, conceptions of home need to be "opened up" to unconventional explorations of memories, nostalgias, and stories within the family. These decentered connections act as bridges and overlap spaces, places, and generations within the family—all of which have deep implications for the development of hybridized identities.

Living in a plurality of imagined worlds inevitably impacts on feelings of home and belongingness. The concept of hybridity offers a zone of in-betweenness to narrate, describe, and make sense of the many layers of entanglement of cultural, anthropological, economic, and political forces between the homeland and the country of settlement—all of which impinge, impact, sometimes confuse, even disturb, the everyday life of migrants. The dialectic of cultural contact has significant impact on migrants' continuous negotiation and configuration of identities, which can lead to varied possibilities other than assimilation. Ethnic minorities may adopt and adapt strategies of alternating identities when they learn to oscillate between one identity and another in different contexts to pass, or to practice, what Du Bois (1903) in *The Souls of Black Folk* famously called "double consciousness." Du Bois saw black Americans as caught in a "twoness," between being an American and being a person of African descent. Like Nagata (1979) and Gilroy (1987, 1994), Tong and Chan (2001b), in their essay titled "One Face, Many Masks," explored the plurality and singularity of identities of Chinese migrants. The notion of alternating identities suggests that we have only one face, but we put on different masks, strategically as performances, to impress our audiences for self-gains. Such strategic alternation of identity is somewhat like what our informant Doreen expressed in her autobiography in Chap. 3 as "role playing" or "donning a mask." The point is that humans are dramatic, theatrical in the face of adversity, turning a liability (race, skin color, gender, body shape, height, etc.) into an asset in the best way they can. Another possibility of border crossing is that migrants undergo a process of hybridization when identities are fused and transformed. Bhabha's (1991, 1994) "third space" defines an "in-between" place inhabited by migrants, where they are neither one nor the other but are in a unique spatial condition. This new construction of identity is like fusion cuisine—a combination of elements of various cultures (or culinary traditions in cuisine) while not fitting specifically into any.

Underlying the perspectives of "third space" and "double consciousness" is an intellectual decentering built upon notions of difference and otherness—thus its stance against homogenization of diverse cultures into a single group. Asserting difference is an attempt to abolish the reliance on unitary, fixed, and essentialized concepts embedded in the assimilationist framework. While the postmodern thematizing of hybridity has implicitly informed the anti-essentialist and assimilationist character of identity politics, ironically, the very logic of it has led to the reinstatement of sameness and a redrawing of exclusionary lines. As Dunn (1998: 29) rightly observes, "in most postmodern writings, difference has become another essentialism and universal, whether through inclusionary or exclusionary strategies." In this chapter, we argue that attempts to abandon identity categories through notions of hybridity as currently formulated in the field are fundamentally problematic. The significance of identity still depends on the fact that the organization of society is based, to a large extent, on relative positions between essentialist categories. Moreover, hybridization for subsequent generations of immigrants is a complex process, and aspects of both perspectives of hybridity are equally relevant for understanding their experience.

Through in-depth analysis of our informants' narratives, this chapter begins by maintaining that Australian-born Chinese with long-term residence are situated in a hybrid space which is infused with a variety of experiences, voices, languages and identities. First, we highlight the complexity of the identity of long-settled ABCs. To do so, we take up two distinct concepts of hybridity—namely, "double consciousness" and "third space"—to explore the liminal space in which they are situated, while highlighting the underlying essentialist constructs inherent in these postmodernist perspectives. We then explore hybridity through decentered linkages with the homeland and examine the ways in which forces of imagination, memories, and myths through the generational and locational points of reference can engender feelings of home, belongingness, and identification with their Chinese heritage. Finally, we explore how the manipulation and reshaping of identities can also lead to both contentment and ambivalence for the subsequent generations.

Hybrid Identities of Long-settled ABCs

Diasporic narratives fraught with contentions over belonging and difference are inevitably affected and infected by notions of hybridity. The experiences of hybridity and transnationalism of first- and second-generation migrants have received much attention in the scholarly literature. Somewhat lost in the debate over Chinese diasporas and identities are the experiences of those with long-term residence who have established themselves outside mainland China. The ideological hegemony of models of assimilation, acculturation, or conversion, where ethnic and racial groups are assumed to integrate into the mainstream culture and where minority identities are assumed to eventually disappear through time, has resulted in the lack of research on the experiences of those whose settlement is beyond the second generation. In the Australian context, the common perception is that the more Australian one becomes, the less Chinese one will be; thus, by the third, fourth, fifth, and sixth generations, the ethnic subject *will* disappear, inevitably and eventually. For all intents and purposes, they will be Australian, not Chinese, not anymore.

However, the formation of identities of multi-generational communities is increasingly complex and cannot be defined simply in bounded homogenous categories.

Despite long-term residence, the cross-cultural encounters that emerge from dialectics, contradiction, ironies, and paradoxes between different generations within the family and between in-group and out-group members can have a substantial impact on the negotiations of ethnicity. Unlike overseas-born migrants, ABCs with long-term residence are not necessarily the transmigrants that Levitt and Waters (2002: 5) describe as maintaining "widespread movement back and forth between communities of origin and destinations," or what Nonini and Ong (1997) suggest as those who are conscious of sharing similar conditions with other ethnic Chinese in other countries. As highlighted in a number of autobiographies by Chinese overseas in *Cultural Curiosity* edited by Khu (2001), these individuals may not even be familiar with patterns of physical transnational practices (e.g., phone calls, travels, keeping up to date with local media) that most recent migrants maintain. They may not necessarily regard themselves as participants in Tu's (1994b) "Cultural China."[1] They may have never even been to the "homeland"—mainland China—where their family originally came from, or may not speak the Chinese language. For those with long-term settlement, connections with China are often more "faded" than that of first or second generations. When descendants of early Chinese migrants become integrated into the host society, do transnational processes affect their negotiations of identity? Can they still be situated in a liminal zone?

Although multi-generational ABCs have identities grounded in Australia and a strong sense of belonging, the particular histories of their families mixed with personal experiences often situate them between the master narratives of the dominant, or "white," Australian on the one side, and Chinese culture on the other side. The response of Jenny, a sixth-generation ABC, about her partial belonging to both cultures is typical of informants in our study: "I don't feel I fit into the Chinese community, but I don't really feel like I fit into the white community either. I sort of feel I am floating in-between but I am okay with it." The difficulty of full integration into the mainstream white community *and* the Chinese community, as shall be discussed, tells us that long-settled ABCs can still feel caught in between cultures. Their experiences challenge the common assumption that ethnic identification decreases through time.

Often a sense of otherness separates the long-settled Australian Chinese community from the mainstream Anglo-Celtic community, leading to difficulties of full integration into the mainstream. They are off stream, out of stream. Identities are socially bestowed and approved. The powerful locals can withhold their acceptance or approval of performances of hybridity. For Jenny, being the sixth generation of her family to reside in Australia and despite having a close social network of Caucasian friends and being in a de facto relationship with a white Australian man, she still expressed the impossibility of complete integration:

> I feel I am different. It depends on who I am with and how comfortable I am. So with different people, I feel more Chinese or less Chinese depending on what they do. I remember my friend once said to me, "Sometimes I forget that you are Chinese." I thought that was a weird thing to say. It made me think twice. It made me notice.

---

[1] See Chap. 2.

Although she identifies herself as Australian, she has been continually viewed through a prism of otherness by her friends, as her physical appearance does not fit in with the "white" Australian social imaginary. Her Chinese face has always been a constant reminder of her race, her ethnicity. The human face is an inescapable fact—or is it? In this way, hybrids are like jugglers. They juggle their roles/masks. If one of the balls they throw in the air drops, the result is, to Goffman (1959), embarrassment, even shame.

For Jerry, a third-generation ABC, direct experiences of social exclusions and racism in his daily life inevitably led to a weakened sense of belonging and acceptance in Australia:

> I did have one suicide attempt at twenty-four. There was so much pressure living in the white world and living in the yellow world—and being nowhere… There was the RSL.[2] It's only the last five years that I can actually go into an RSL club because, in my time, when you went into an RSL club and after a few drinks some people there would turn around and shout at you, "Ah you*** Jap! What are you*** doing here?" The feeling you get is what are you doing in our world? Ooh, white man's territory. It used to be like that, but not anymore. But see, I overstepped the boundaries and I was actually participating in the white activities, playing golf and drinking. Meanwhile my parents worked very hard seven days a week. They wanted me to get into the family business but I had a bit of the white world in me so there was a clash … it's not negative. It's just a feeling of not belonging; it's not necessarily negative. For example, after I leave you here I'll walk out, I know I don't belong here because it's all white. I'm not being discriminatory, it's just a white country, a white majority …

Overt and subtle racism involves individuals within the white community identifying those considered not locals through a process of othering. At the same time, deeply instilled Chinese cultural beliefs, values, and traditions that are held and practiced by long-settled ABCs can also impact on their own construction of belonging. For Donna, the difference in family values and filial obligation between Chinese and Western families is a major differentiating factor that has created a sense of having only a partial belonging to Australia:

> Co-author Ngan: Do you feel that you belong to Australia?
>
> Donna: No, not really, because there's this Chinese side of me that isn't fully Australian. I feel I'm fortunate to be able to take lovely things out of the Western world as well. I sort of sit in the middle, and I don't see it as no-man's land. I'm just very fortunate to be sitting in the middle. That's how I feel.
>
> Ngan: Even though you grew up in Australia, and basically you've lived your whole life in Australia you still don't feel you fully belong to Australia because of your Chinese cultural values?
>
> Donna: It may change in another twenty or thirty years, with the way that Australians have accepted multiculturalism, and nothing matters any more—physical appearance doesn't matter. But there are still some things that do matter…even though my mother and I don't have a strong bond, because she has this thing about daughters being second-class citizens, and that's what I grew up with. She's now 84 and she may have mellowed in that way, but before,

---

[2] RSL stands for Returned and Services League of Australia. The RSL is the largest ex-service organization in Australia and represents thousands of former and currently serving defence force personnel. RSL clubs usually have dining and bar facilities and gambling areas for their members and guests.

daughters really were of no value because they didn't carry the family name and all that kind of thing. And I sort of think, well, that wasn't the right way to bring up children, they should all be treated the same…but I still feel duty-bound to her. There isn't the unconditional love that one should have for a mother that I see some of my Australian friends have for their mothers. For me, it's more about obligation, more about duty.

Ngan: So it's this sense of filial piety.

Donna: Yes. All of that. And I think that I wouldn't like to hurt my mother…to make that obvious, it's not love, it's more filial piety. She thinks it's sort of my dutifulness to her, or something like that. That's Chinese.

It is important to point out here that while a sense of otherness often differentiates long-settled ABCs from the dominant "white" Australians, neither do the ABCs fully associate with Chinese communities in Australia. Common among the majority of our informants is a sense of difference that separates them from other "Chinese" groups in Australia. Dianne, a fourth-generation ABC, explained that her marriage with a Hong Kong-born migrant made her realize that she was situated in a liminal zone:

…because I was getting married to a really Chinese family, so that made me feel really uncomfortable, because I was Australian-born. I felt they were different. And I still do, actually. I don't discriminate against them or anything, but I feel there is a difference…I seem to be more comfortable with the Australians than with the Chinese. I don't know why. Maybe because we have common interests because we study together. I don't know. It could be that. But my family practices many Chinese traditions…so I'm sort of in-between, yes. I feel as though, because Chinese are a minority group in Australia, I'm part of that minority group, but at the same time I'm not that minority group, I'm not that traditional Chinese minority, yes…I actually feel that the ABCs are separate from the recent migrants, yes…I don't know why, I just feel a difference. I guess because ABCs are brought up with Australian traditions, maybe retaining some Chinese traditions; but basically Australian traditions, whereas you get your migrants, they're not educated in the Australian way, they're more their own people and they tend to mix with their own people as well.

The sense of difference from other Chinese migrants is also expressed by Rob, a fifth-generation ABC. He recalled a conversation with his wife, a Hong Kong-born migrant:

My wife still considers me to be Australian. She thinks I wear my Chineseness like a—something I can put on and say 'Oh I am Chinese I have a *min larp*[3] on, and take off. She doesn't think I am Chinese at all … My wife says "You are pretending to be Chinese and you are talking about things you don't know anything about. You are trying to take the best of both worlds. You are trying to be Australian but you are trying to be Chinese at the same time."

Although racialized collectivities are stratified within a broader social spectrum where stereotypical identities are often imposed by the dominant groups, as we have pointed out in Chap. 5, in-group members also play an important role in establishing their own hierarchy of identities. The way in which racialized groups shape their own identities can be illustrated by the delegitimization of Rob's Chineseness by his Hong Kong-born wife. Such a sense of cultural chauvinism of the Chinese—in particular, the overseas-born Chinese—is often percolated from the ideology that

---

[3] Traditional Chinese jacket made of silk floss, worn in winter for warmth.

China is the land of the ancestors of the people of Chinese descent and the original source of Chinese civilization. The challenge of authenticity on fellow Chinese who don't read and/or write Chinese (Cantonese, Mandarin, etc.) properly coincides with Gans' (1979) notion of symbolic ethnicity where occasional ethnic behavior is seen as an absence of "real" ethnicity. Although Rob identifies himself as a Chinese in certain situations, because of the hegemonic discourse of authenticity that differentiates him from his wife, he was teased as being "not a real Chinese," thus situating him in a state of limbo. In this respect ABCs' claim to Chineseness is often referred to as lacking substantial cultural content. It has become an empty vessel—all form but no substance.

As such, not only are subsequent generations situated between the East and the West because of internal stratifications among the Chinese in Australia, but they also feel they are caught in between different Chinese groups. Our informant, Dean, explained his belonging to different Chinese groups in Australia this way:

> I probably say there is the old group that has been around for more than one generation and there is that second group that is probably more of a Hong Kong background who are more able to get out and have come here for a better lifestyle. And maybe a third group that consist of more recent migrants from the mainland. These groups I see are more based on migration patterns and history over time...if I had to position myself, I'm probably straddling between the first and the second, because my dad's line is definitely the first group; mum's line is so definitely the second...being able to straddle between these groups is an advantage...it means I can't be placed in any one single group.

Dean's experience highlights the complex segregations within the Chinese community in Australia. Stratification among the Chinese, according to our informants, is differentiated on the basis of length of residency in Australia and language ability, in both Chinese (and its many diverse dialects) *and* English.

The hybrid experiences of long-settled ABCs challenge the assimilationist assumptions which consider integration of second- and higher-order generations as part of a unified, linear, and unidirectional process. Although our informants are grounded in Australia, their experiences reveal that it is not a simple case of weakening ethnicity and a progressive assimilationist path to "complete" integration, but rather of complicated entanglements and negotiations between cultural borders. Inhabiting a state of hybridity, the migrants' sense of identity is often situated in a liminal space as they negotiate and display who they are or what they want to be seen in different contexts.

Double Consciousness

The diasporic literature has highlighted that migrants often maintain a social and cultural foothold in two or more distinct ethnic environments where they find themselves developing multiple identities in transnational spaces. They live a two-legged existence. The concept of "double consciousness" reveals the hybrid character of modern ethnicity and its profound effect on diasporic communities. This notion derives from the circumstances and contexts in which ethnic and racial groups find themselves. The analogy of an international buffet provides a descriptive means of understanding this hybrid oscillation of identity—you can pick and choose a bit of this and a bit of that, as you wish, like "dim sim," a Chinese delicacy, where you literally point your finger at what your heart desires.

However, the switching of identities is not simply a straightforward process of alternation. A person's identity can intentionally or unconsciously vary depending on the context in which they are located. Our informant Sunny, a fourth-generation ABC, expressed, "if I was in Hong Kong right now, I might feel a little Chinese. If I was, say, in an all Anglo environment I would feel very Chinese. So a lot of it depends on my surroundings." Identity is a contextual, circumstantial, and relational positioning rather than a fixed essence. More like a process, less like a "thing."

Ethnic and cultural boundaries are maintained through interpretation of cultural phenomena in accordance with the requirements of particular contexts as individuals strategically express how they choose to be or to be seen. Our informant, Pete, a fourth-generation ABC, explained the role of social context in the way he adapts his behavior:

> You identify yourself situationally. But basically I am Australian. Sometimes, Australian-Chinese. It depends on what you want to present yourself as and what the context is. If people are interested in your Chineseness then you respond in that kind of way.

Similarly, the fluidity of identity can be highlighted by Nelson's appropriation of cultural values according to contextual considerations:

> I think of myself as a mixture of both. Western culture in general is driven by Christianity, so I am religious. Well I also believe in a higher being, whether it be Buddha or God, Allah, Jesus Christ or whatever. I also live by the Chinese way of thinking. Sometimes it clashes, so what do I follow? I apply whatever value I think is appropriate at the time.

Contrary to the impact of multi-identities being largely assumed to be detrimental, hybridity can also positively facilitate social integration. Similar to Nagata's (1979) case on the situational selection of ethnic identity in Malaysia, subsequent generations are able to manipulate or actively assert their identity to enhance their position in social situations. They reorient themselves always temporarily and select a particular group of reference in accordance with the degree of affinity they wish to express in a given situation. The ease in switching between ethnic identities is encapsulated in Rob's simple comment, "I can wear my Chinese so easily. Whenever I feel comfortable."

Through strategic assertions of identity, long-settled ABCs can express either social distance or solidarity, as our informant, Sean, explained:

> I can probably adopt my identity to suit my friends, to make them comfortable. So with my Australian friends I probably adopt "Australianism" to make them more comfortable. For my Chinese friends I adopt Chinese habits to make them feel more comfortable.

Similarly, Martin spoke about the way he is able to adopt different behaviors when he is with Australians or Asians:

> When I am hanging out with ABCs I don't talk about this cultural identity thing. They don't like talking about it. They don't find it a problem. They probably just see themselves as Australians with Chinese background but they are in a new country so they have to become part of society. When I am hanging out with Western people, I tend to be more quiet because I don't feel as comfortable. When I am hanging out with my Asian friends I can be *more relaxed.*

> They understand the jokes that I tell. But with my Asians friends I can't talk about political issues. With some of my Western friends at least I can talk about political issues.

Strategic oscillation of identity is a positive trait enabling subsequent generations to avoid conflict caused by inconsistencies of role expectations of both white and Chinese communities.

While this notion of circumstantial identity represents a new kind of cultural space that challenges the homogenous conception of identity as a single entity, the orientation toward a discourse of "double consciousness" is in itself ironic. The privileging of multiple "groups" of identity is nevertheless constructed within the boundaries of a unified and collectivist paradigm. Such discourse is motivated by another kind of centrism, this time along the conglomeration of multiple groups of identities.

Furthermore, the limitation of such a perspective of hybridity is in its assumption of an individual's anchorage to multiple homogenous identities. It must be acknowledged that the switching of identities is not a straightforward oscillating process between one "full" identity (i.e., Australian or Chinese) to the other (and different) end of the spectrum, because cultural boundaries are often unclear and ambiguous. The ethnic actor is often only able to perform certain aspects of a particular culture but without having a complete sense of belonging to that particular cultural group, thus situating them in a zone of in-betweenness. Consider Sunny's statement, "To say oscillating between both implies you can totally fit into one camp or totally fit into another camp, which I don't think I do." While subsequent generations strive to achieve a strategic adoption of particular expressions of their identity, they are also situated in a peculiar space of in-betweenness, belonging neither to a Chinese nor to an Australian entity.

Third Space and In-betweeness

An alternative approach to hybridity found in the writings of Bhabha (1991), Hall (1996), and Ang (2001) problematizes the rigid nature of boundaries. They argue that hybridity is an opening within which different elements encounter and transform each other. In this way identity is seen as a dialectical construction with "the original" as well as its counteridentity, yielding a new form known as the "third space" or "in-betweenness." They are symbolic spaces where identities are hybridized, the self and the other are unsettled, and truths are ruptured (Ang, 2001: 164). Bhabha (1991) asserts that, to adequately understand this liminal space, one should not conduct an analysis as if there really were pure cultures to compare discretely in the first place, as this in-betweenness is *not* a consequence of other allegedly "pure" identities intertwined together.

For the long-settled ABCs, the suspension in a third space is evident where complicated entanglements of cultural boundaries embody their daily lives. This notion of crossroads was highlighted when Tanya spoke about her sense of identity: "What am I? I am a person. I never ask "Am I Chinese or Australian?" Because I am a mix I can't think of any other way except as a mix. A crazy mixed up kid, you see!" Her location of identity was in a third space where difference was neither one nor the other but something else besides. Then there was Martin's acknowledgment of an "in-between culture":

> I think there is a culture of in-between but it is hard to know who belongs to that culture. A lot of people are marrying Western people. Do you include them or not? Realistically I am a hybrid of both, but I would like to be more on the Chinese side.

The suspension in a space of in-betweenness implies a crossroads of cultural boundaries. The point becomes even clearer through Marco's response about his sense of identity, which was complicated by his migratory movements between Australia and Hong Kong. Marco left Australia for Hong Kong during primary school and then returned to Australia for higher education:

> When I came to Australia there was just a growing realization that to be an Australian is to be more than just where you were born—although it is a birthright, it's also where you were brought up, where you can sort of identify strongly with particular values... I guess it's where you can identify more, and I don't identify with Australia as strongly compared with someone who was brought up here and who can name their favorite football club or the entire cricket team! I mean, I can only name three or four players! So it's really hard to identify myself as Australian but I'm certainly not someone who can really identify strongly with Hong Kong either... as in the mainstream local Hong Kong person who can speak the language very fluently and who uses primarily a Cantonese language. If I were to make a self-statement it would be an overseas Chinese who was brought up in a British or Western system of education in Hong Kong. That would be the group I would identify myself with. It's probably a very small group, but that's a group for me to associate with when I go back to Hong Kong, that's the people I know well and they probably have the same sort of identity.

Marco's experiences suggest that he was located in a liminal zone where he did not fit into either mainstream Australian or Hong Kong society. This state of being would be accounted for by postmodernism as the "third space." However, this notion, based on fluidity and transforming identities, does not fully explain Marco's experience. While his sense of identity was situated liminally, the significance of it was still based on predefined social categories. This is evident in the way he located himself relative to cultural boundaries of language and social values that define being Hong Kong Chinese and being Australian. Similarly for Martin, his sense of in-betweenness was articulated precisely in reference to the bilateral ends of Western and Chinese cultures.

Ironically, although the notion of third space attempts to abandon identity categories altogether by emphasizing the nonexistence of discrete cultures, the process of identity formation is nevertheless articulated on the basis of positioning between particular constructed collectivities. The fact is that identity categories are crucial in providing modes of articulation of significant correlations between the lived experience and social location. This perspective of hybridity is a reinstatement of unifying concepts of sameness, albeit a new dimension but in an inclusive space of in-betweenness.

Furthermore, while hybridity as a floating identity means combination, amalgamation, fusion, and a condition that cannot be definitely defined (Bhabha, 1991), we argue it is possible to develop a stock of reliable knowledge about how and where one fits. For example, Janice's sense of identity was largely based on the shared similarities and differences of particular cultures:

> I think our upbringing was very Asian-based. When I was at school there were hardly any Asians in my class—there were probably none! So all my friends were Australians. But I have always realized that not only did I eat different food but I had a different lifestyle! I have always moved towards an Asian lifestyle. Maybe they always liked the beach, sports, swimming and stuff like that, but we weren't that kind of people. Maybe we always had that problem because we looked Asian. There was a lot of name calling when we were growing up as there weren't many Asians around. Basically we just stuck to ourselves, we just didn't mix very well. I found that, even with my school friends, their way of thinking was different from mine, so when I got older I gravitated *back* to the Asian people or even just with the Australian-born Chinese who thought alike.

Individuals are often bound to one another by their participation in a common culture—that is, a set of more or less shared understandings and interpretations including ideas that guide actions. These ideas may be communicated implicitly in processes of socialization or learned through shared experiences. Not only do they provide conceptual interpretation of a world at large and guide action, but they also specify and exalt the identity of a particular group. "What links group members to one another…is the perception that to a large degree they think alike, or at least view aspects of their own lives and certain critical features of the world similarly" (Cornell & Hartmann, 1998: 87).

Indeed the way in which identity is established largely depends on how the self and the other are interpreted. Thus, the subjective experiences of any social group membership depend fundamentally on relations to memberships in other social groups. A contributing factor leading to one's sense of difference/sameness is located in complex notions of recognition and belonging where the central question concerns how individuals interpret, construct, and reconstruct themselves and the culture of which they are a part (Anderson, 1999). As such, for the long-settled ABCs, the experience of group membership is located in the very definition of racial categories of Chineseness and Australianess since the significance of any identity depends on one's association with others. Nelson explained the process of adopting particular cultural behaviors this way:

> I am sure a lot of ABCs can understand when you are around Australians you may do things that may be regarded as more Asian such as Karaoke. But then when you hang around with your Asian friends and you play rugby they say you are quite *Gweilo*.[4] So I try to maintain a balance. I take the values which I regard as important in both cultures. When people ask me, I say I am Australian. I was born and raised in Australia but in terms of ethnicity I am Chinese.

In Nelson's situation, the way in which he positioned himself in relation to cultural boundaries points to the fact that he was clear about where he fit according to essentialist categories of Chineseness and Australianess, although the meaning of

---

[4] *Gweilo* (Foreign Devil) is a Cantonese/Southern expression which essentially means White Westerners. The identification of Australians as *Gweilo* is suggestive of an inherent social barrier that segregates long-established Chinese migrants from mainstream white Australian society.

these constructs was dynamic. Nevertheless, these imagined social constructs still serve as the organizing principle of life and living. Certainly, there may be variations of experiences such that one may identify with multiple cultural groups or may feel suspended in-between or, in more extreme cases, may not feel any sense of affiliation with any cultural group at all. However, the manner in which members of diasporic communities position themselves according to specific collectivities suggests that essentialist structures still shape our perceptions of the real world.

Despite postmodernist attempts to delegitimize identities through a discourse of in-between identity, collectivized homogenous notions still perpetuate in the carving of identities in daily life. Since cultures are effects of social stabilization and historical process, it is pertinent to understand the formation of social structures (Huddart, 2006: 126). We emphasize that in understanding identities we cannot totally dismiss the historical and social significance of collective cultural constructs, as they are tools that enable us to account for the role of multiplicity in an enabling way. Moreover, while various perspectives of hybridity have been developed as alternatives to understand multiplicity, on the basis of the experiences of our informants, we maintain these perspectives complement each other in our understanding of the identity formation of subsequent generations.

Doing Transnationalism Multi-generationally

Studies on transnationalism indicate that migrants' cross-border ties contribute to the development of unsettling identities; in particular, the intersections of crossroads and borderlands can lead to coexisting homes that link the homeland with the host country (Phizacklea, 2000; Ryan, 2003; Waters, 2002). In the case of diasporic Chinese, the negotiation of their identities is assumed to be associated with the intensity of transnational links they maintain with China, and cultural identification with homeland as "China" per se becomes a defining factor of their Chineseness. However, those with a long settlement history take on new elements in the construction of Chineseness through decentered connections with the homeland.

To precisely illustrate this point, the majority of our participants in this study do not share the common transnational practices of recent migrants and they do not hold strong emotional attachment to China as homeland. Jane explained, "China is just a foreign place, it means nothing much to me." For Jenny, although her father's family was based in Hong Kong and visits were primarily family-based, the idea of Hong Kong as homeland was not cultivated:

> When I was little we used to go back to Hong Kong quite often and stayed with my grandparents for a few weeks. Being in those environments made me more Chinese but I don't really feel that Hong Kong is home. It is hard for me to explain!

Contrary to the transnational paradigm, frequency of return does not necessarily engender a sense of home or intimate attachment to land. Despite her lack of attachment to China as homeland, Jenny felt that there was a unique connection with Chinese people in Australia, as she expressed: "I feel that there is more of a connection with Chinese people even if I don't like them or they don't like me or we don't know each other. I sort of feel like there is." The centering device of physical returns and attachment to land as a means of evaluating identity is clearly problematic.

Rodney justified his distant attachment to China by arguing that, first, his family has resided in Australia for three generations; second, he has never been to China; and third, he has no intention of going. Co-author Ngan's usage of the words like "going back" and "returning" to China during interview sessions with her informants was at times questioned as inadequate and inappropriate to their experiences. Rodney contended, "We still have a traditional family house, which I have no interest in. Realistically what's the point! I will never go there, I have no association. It's a bit bizarre! I often say just give it away, we don't need it." While he had a definite position of no return to a real or symbolic homeland, connection with a Chinese identity was still evident:

> I am Chinese because by definition I am. My cultural roots are Chinese. If you ask me what country I come from, it's Australia, but my cultural background is Chinese. That is by definition, but I consider myself an ABC. If you are asking me what makes me think I am Chinese, I don't know!

The fact that he did not maintain physical and emotional links with China, yet still defined himself as Chinese and more specifically as ABC suggests the presence of an exclusive Australian-born Chinese social space in which members are able to share past experiences of adaptation and connections in Australia but are, at the same time, innately connected to a larger imagined origin that is shared by all diasporic Chinese.

Some informants had distant relatives in China but they did not maintain close familial connections with them. Sunny explained his loose connections with China:

> I don't consider China as my homeland because Australia is my home. But I have connections with it—that is how I view it. I guess I do have some contact with my cousins … My mother always wants me to go back. The relatives want to see you and this and that. I say ok I'll go back and say hello. For me it's a place where my family grew up and there was connection before me, but it is not a total connection.

For Sunny, while he did not totally encapsulate the notion of homeland as China, persistence of physical and emotional linkages maintained within the family created a sense of ethnicity for him. Underlying such kind of connection common among informants was an allegiance to an imagined past which instilled in them a sense of cultural heritage.

Indeed, the experiences of long-settled ABCs do not meet in any neat way the transnational criteria of a strong attachment to, and a desire for literal return to, a physical homeland. There is little room in the transnational paradigm for an ambivalence about physical return and attachment to land. The particularity of feelings of home, belongingness and identification of long-settled ABCs is constructed, not by distinctive relations with a particular locality, but through decentered connections of intergenerational connections, memories and myths within the family.

These porous connections established within the family become a part of daily life, which continuously shapes their hybridized identities. The proceeding section brings to light such dimensions in relation to the significance of intergenerational ties that bring in the force of imagination as both memory and desire that are shared by our informants.

Intergenerational Influence

The establishment of Chineseness is often articulated through circuits of memories, travels, and histories with the homeland, China. Unquestionably, memories provide an intimate means of connecting life worlds of the past and the present, and home has been celebrated as a site of authentic meaning, value, and experience, imbued with nostalgic memories and love of a particular place. In Kuah-Peace and Davidson's (2008) edited volume, *At Home in the Chinese Diasporas*, the essays point to how memories are reproduced and how they impact on constructing identities and belongings of diasporic Chinese. In her essay "Identities and Decentered Transnational Linkages: Returned Migrants in Hong Kong" (2012), co-author Ngan writes about how memories as decentered transnational linkages with Australia impact on the construction of her identity as an overseas Chinese returnee in Hong Kong. Increasing numbers of studies of personal testimony and cultural memory also testify to the impact of momentous events in previous homes on diasporic lives. Memories can be a source for relaxation for those in diasporas, but endured nostalgias, or what psychiatrists call nostalgic fixation, can lead to psychosomatic symptoms affecting an individuals' mental and physical health.

Memory fragments have been questioned as a source of authenticity. Cook (2005: 3) explains, "the fact that the eyewitness was actually present at the time invests their recollections with an aura that transcends the knowledge that their experience is reconstructed for the purposes of current agendas, and endows with it authority and emotional power." Memories, therefore, are not simply dissociated pieces of past events but are continually reconstructed to provide a new take on the old and are reshaped to provide different perspectives (Davidson, 2004). Nostalgic memories, in particular, intensify the intergenerational influence on the construal of home and identity. Nostalgia can be defined as a state of longing for something that is known to be irretrievable, but is sought anyway (Cook, 2005); in so far as it is rooted in disavowal or suspension of disbelief, nostalgia is generally associated with fantasy and regarded as even more unauthentic than memory. The intensity of longing inevitably impacts not only the overseas-born migrant's sense of identity but also, because of emotional power, that of their descendants. The distinction between memory, nostalgia, and history as sources of imagination are often blurred and dynamic—as such, notions of home which shape identity are always changing. Kuah-Pearce (2006: 230) explains, "the self marshals its understanding of the social history of its kinship and social groups, selecting and negotiating its memories to suit its individual needs." Thus, at any moment in the diasporic trajectory, tensions are released in different sites of home as well as in different feeling states of belonging. In this way, intergenerational influence on the construction of homeland often produces varied notions of homes, contributing to the development of hybridized lives.

When subsequent generations reproduce collective memories of the homeland, the details tend to differ from one generation to another. The imagination of a notional homeland is often situated between different generational and locational points of reference that percolate from the nostalgic memories of their own parents, grandparents, and other relatives. Our informant, Vera, was born in 1966 and grew up in Sydney. Her paternal grandfather moved from China to Australia in 1917 to make a living; although he settled in Australia there was, nevertheless, the maintenance of intense transnational activities with China through constant physical movement, remittances, letters, etc., between the two places. Her father was born in China and that was where he married her mother. After the first few years of marriage Vera's father moved to Australia to assist her grandfather's market garden business, and while waiting for approval to migrate to Australia, her mother endured the Chinese Cultural Revolution. Because she was identified as a landowner, a capitalist, she was persecuted by the Chinese government. Her father tried hard to speed up the immigrant application process but because of the restrictions under the White Australia Policy, it took many years before her parents could reunite. Vera recounted her connections with China this way:

> I have only been to China a few times over the many years. I don't have contact with any relatives over there. I don't know anybody there, but I don't mind going on visits. My mother doesn't want to go to China because she was tortured and suffered quite a lot—she never wants to go back again. Only my father went back to the village a few times after they came to Australia. My mother used to talk about what life was like in China and she still talks about it now. She suffers depression and it actually gets worse when she recalls about how she was persecuted. But for my father, when he talks about it, he only talks about the good times. So they have totally different perspectives in their memories.

This is a classic narrative that can undoubtedly be told in countless variations by many long-settled diasporic Chinese throughout the world, articulating the shared experience of the weakening linkages with homeland as a locality—that is, geographical China per se. Yet, there are intimate connections established through intergenerational influence of stories, memories, and myths which have significant effects on the diasporic imagination of "being Chinese." Vera revealed that she had only been to China a few times and she did not have any emotional ties with relatives. Nevertheless, there was fascination about the place that her grandparents and parents had left behind. She reckoned, "I hear different stories about life in China and I sometimes imagine what my life would be like if I was brought up there." At the same time, Vera has never lost a sense of certainty about the self-declared fact of her Chineseness. Although she was well integrated into the Australian society, she was still proud of her Chinese heritage. She said, "I feel I'm very lucky as I have a unique quality to my situation. I was born in Australia but of Chinese heritage." The connection which she had with the "Chinese race" was emphasized by the intensity of her statement that "a political attack on the Chinese community is like a personal strike" on herself. Although well integrated, the stance on such issues highlights an identity which is established through connections with an imagined "Chinese" collectivity.

This glimpse into one ordinary individual with a long history in Australia indicates the fact that individuals who hold weak physical and familial linkages with "homeland" as China per se do not necessarily have direct impact on the establishment of Chineseness. Through intergenerational connections, memories of stories, myths, events, and old photos of the family become a part of daily life, continuously shaping identities and establishing a sense of attachment to the "homeland."

The power of intergenerational influence on the establishment of identity for diasporic Chinese can further be highlighted through Sean's experience. In a similar situation to Vera, he maintains no physical linkages or familial networks with China. His connections with China have largely been influenced by his grandparents as well as through the media during his childhood years. Sean explained that the *Kung Fu*[5] movies that his grandparents encouraged him to watch when he was young played a major role in the establishment of his Chineseness. Because *Kung Fu* movies were symbolic of the Chinese culture, through watching these movies he developed an interest in Chinese traditions and history and cultivated a sense of patriotism:

> I think my grandparents were worried about our Chinese so they got us *Kung Fu* movies to watch. The videos! I think they wanted us to watch the soaps but I didn't like them so they had to settle with the *Kung Fu* movies. I still watch them on occasions. If someone has got all the tapes then I will borrow them and watch them. But I guess I don't watch them as much now because my wife can't speak Chinese. But definitely during university days and the first couple of years after university, I listened to tapes, CDs, Chinese songs. Even though I didn't understand them, I still listened to them … I think my love of Chinese history comes from those *Kung Fu* movies. All the military fights, the emperors, I wanted to understand the culture behind the empires of China, one country, three kingdoms, the classic stories!

An important aspect of the electronic media is that there has been a reinforcement of the stereotypes by which Chinese are represented. As Said (1978: 26) expresses it, "All the media's resources have forced information into more and more standardized modes." Although Sean had never been to China until recently, the ideology of an imagined China as homeland was largely developed through the reinforcement of stereotypes in movies, TV, music, and also through intergenerational influence throughout his life course. The interest in Chinese *Kung Fu* movies was due to his grandparents' conscious effort in maintaining his attachment to his Chinese roots. Consequently, he developed a cultural attachment to a long glorious history of the Chinese race, which contributed to his sense of the Chinese heritage. His diasporic imagination of "being Chinese" has direct consequences for the way in which he is determined to raise his own children:

> I want to raise my kids definitely with a Chinese identity. It is a conscious thing. I am proud to be Chinese and I want them to think that way. I am not going to teach them that the Chinese are better but definitely that the Chinese have contributed to world development. And I will teach them the key historical facts about Chinese history, that the Chinese empire was better than the Roman Empire!"

---

[5] *Kung Fu* is the Chinese name for Chinese martial arts.

The diasporic experience is a dynamic process of interactions between places and ideologies, as identities are not established in a vacuum but are intergenerationally influenced. Although the differences between memory, nostalgia, and history as sources of imagination are often blurred but dynamic in the passing of generations, they are of much import in the construal of ethnicity for people in diasporas. Contemporary images of "home" often intertwine between origin, roots, cultural heritage, ancestral homeland, and local residence to form a significant part of the diasporic imagination of Chineseness.

Of importance here is that transnational links maintained by the older generation and their influence on the younger generation often produce varied notions of home, leading to the development of hybridized lives (Wolf, 2002). These notions often lead to situations in which the negotiation of identity for migrants and their descendents often occurs in a space of liminality. Martin discussed the way in which intergenerational influence had consequential impact on the way in which he (re) negotiated and (re)articulated his identity. He explained that his interest in Chinese culture and heritage all stemmed from his relationship with his grandfather who played a central role in his childhood, often telling him Chinese myths and legends and about the people's way of life in China. Although his grandfather insisted on the maintenance of a Chinese identity, his parents, however, never really wanted to associate with their Chinese past because of the difficulties they had had in establishing their lives in Australia. While both his father and he experienced racial assaults, for Martin these racial incidents have led to stronger affiliations with "things Chinese," whereas for his father, to be accepted by the white society, he often intentionally conceals his Chinese past. Martin constantly struggled between his desire to maintain his Chinese heritage and his father's wish for assimilation. Negotiations of identities, home, and belonging for subsequent generations are inevitably influenced by the family's imagination of "home" and experience of displacement.

The negotiation of Chineseness as deployed in migration narratives often involves the interplay of feelings of home and a cultural identification with homeland, which is inevitably associated with China. These stories illuminate the precarious establishment of Chineseness through diasporic imagination, which is largely neglected in the current transnational paradigm. In the case of our informants who have long lived away from China, their imaginary and subjective relationships to their imputed homeland are an important part of the construction of Chineseness. In other words, identification with China as homeland is constructed in a context of coexistence with a diasporic imagination that is influenced by the previous generations.

While the transnational framework is certainly important in understanding the physical and emotional linkages that migrants maintain, it is often bounded to particular localities as it concentrates largely on the experience of recent migrants. As such, the prevailing theoretical framework of using transnational linkages as a centering device for the construction of ethnicity and attachment is problematic. Notions of home which shape identity should not be solely assessed in terms of the intensity of transnational linkages—intergenerational influence in the form of stories, myths, secrets, photographs, etc., actively shapes the construal of an "imagined" homeland.

The negotiation of identity for those with long-term settlement is not merely a passive process of participation in transnationalism, but is also actively influenced by the force of memory, nostalgia, and the imagination of the family, as they become a part of daily life. So one could ask, if memories are constructed, identity is fluid and home is an imagination, why are they still significant in diasporic lives? Although there is no unchallengeable authentic grounding of identity, notions of home and identities are often designated as an authentic site for the migrants' reaffirmation of identity.

The Upside and Downside of Hybridity

The postmodernist literature maintains that we are living in an era where the preset destination of security and a sense of belonging through unity have become unattainable and there is a bleak vision of progress and control (Bauman, 2000). In particular, hybrid identities are problematic for diasporic communities as their experiences are often seen as a struggle against marginalization and its detrimental impact on social mobility. Such dissolution is similarly expressed by Ang (2001: 17): "The very condition of in-betweenness can never be a question of simple shaking hands, of happy, harmonious merger and fusion." While complicated entanglements exist, missing from the debates is an interest in those who have accepted and embraced hybridity and view it as a positive force in their lives. Both upside and downside need to be taken into account to fully portray the experience of hybridization of subsequent generations of migrant families.

Ambivalence of Hybrid Identities

Contrary to the assimilationist position, the formation of identity of subsequent generations, as we have argued throughout this chapter, involves entering a state of hybridity where cultural borders are blurred and transgressed. Ang (1998) argues encounters at the border—where the self and the other, Asia and the West, meet—often result in potential intercultural conflict and miscommunication. Rob shared his experience of disillusionment this way:

> I have worked so hard to reconcile my Chineseness; in a sense it has been very painful. You may not admit it but it was painful being Chinese in Australia. You try to repress it all the time. You spend so much time repressing it that you can't be normal. You think to yourself, "Do they dislike me because I am Chinese or is it just me?" That is why I would love my Children marrying Chinese. You are ticking off the boxes that make life easier.

Encapsulated here is the very condition of in-betweenness. Borders are not easily crossed; as such, those who are straddling cultures experience complicated entanglements. The paradox of hybridity in the postmodern context is that while the meaning of "Chinese" can no longer be described in clear-cut terms, there is an increased salience of the very term as a self-conscious marker of identities for diasporic Chinese. Certainly differences and hierarchies exist, but they are becoming much more difficult to separate out. For Rob, the only way to find some sense of security was to identify with a collective whole—a whole that allows one to cleanly fit into a single box. Thus, it is the very difficulty of positioning their identities in relation to others that leads to the ambivalence in their daily lives. As we have stressed in this chapter, identities emerge in the midst of social relations involving the assertion of difference within a stratification system of the wider society. The difficulty of such conditioning is expressed by Marco when he recalled his high school encounter with a Caucasian student who questioned his identity as Australian:

> In early high school, I encountered a girl who questioned why I would call myself an Australian if I wasn't Caucasian. I don't think she meant any spite by it, but it was just something she was probably brought up to think, and I explained it to her that I was born in Australia and my family has been here for generations, which didn't really make sense to her. But that was the first time that I encountered someone who believed strongly that an Australian should have some sort of Caucasian background...so I don't see myself as an "Australian." I had a concept of being an "Australian" when I was growing up in Hong Kong because essentially my peers in school would identify with where they were born. A lot of them were born in the UK, the US, Canada, other regions around the world, so that was the identity in terms of them saying, "I'm an Australian," "I'm an American," "I'm a Canadian."

The way in which Marco and his peers articulated their identities illustrates that the social context in which people are situated invariably influences the priorities and responses that shape their identity (Papastergiadis, 2000: 31). The construction of identity becomes constrained or motivated in relation to the ascriptions and expectations of the wider society. Since a collectively assured sense of solidarity is built upon the ideal of homogenous, clear-cut identities, people are often uncomfortable with fragmentation and multiplicity. It is this process of rethinking the relationships between the politics of hybrid and embedded essentialist dispositions which is disturbing for many people—partly because of the impossibility of reconciliation. As such, much contempt is often placed upon those who do not "fit" the "familiar" social norm as defined by the wider society; the tendency is to attack everything that separates the individual from the wider group. Thus, questions are raised about the construction of categories for self-definition and the way they constrain choices and possibilities.

Furthermore, for subsequent generations, the condition of in-betweenness created by elements from a diversity of contexts as they encounter a variety of memories, experiences, voices, languages, and identities can lead to disillusionment. Martin commented:

> My home village in China is a place that I definitely have to go to. I can picture myself. It will be so emotional...I guess it is a sense that you are stuck in between two cultures so you don't really belong to either. I can't really say that I feel like Australian. I definitely want to identify as Chinese but I can't say that because I can't even speak the language and I haven't been taught much about the culture. I can imagine if my grandparents didn't decide to migrate out of China, what life would have been. I just feel that I have a sense of belonging that I don't feel when I am in Australia.

Subsequent generations are often suspended between different generational and locational points of reference—the previous generations, the wider society, and their own generation—resulting in experiences of ambivalence as they try to locate a sense of belonging.

I Love Being a Hybrid

The postmodernist concept of hybridity indeed has made possible new and different ways of understanding the "ambivalent" experience of diasporic communities. While recognizing the diasporic feelings of alienation and insulation of subsequent generations, it is also important to acknowledge that not all are marginalized. Pluralization or fragmentation of identities is not necessarily a "wounded attachment" but can provide positive and enriching structures of belonging and identification. Much of the postmodernist writing on hybridity overlooks this, consequently failing to explain important modes of behavior by which individuals experience and understand their social world. The following are examples of informants' positive sentiments toward their hybrid identities:

> I feel I'm fortunate to be able to take lovely things out of the Western world as well. I sort of sit in the middle, and I don't see it as a no-man's land. I'm just very fortunate to be sitting in the middle. That's how I feel. (Donna)

> I feel I'm Chinese Australian—there are no two separate things. It's actually unique because as I said before I'm bi-cultural so I fit in Western society very easily because I love going to Europe and I can speak French. I've lived there for a few years, things like that, and I can really appreciate European culture. But when I go to China I can also really appreciate Chinese culture, I mean really enjoy and fit in! Whereas someone who is mono-cultural—say if you're an Anglo and you go to China—you would feel uncomfortable. Just like if my mother went to Europe, she won't feel comfortable too. So I feel I'm very lucky in that way. And that's unique to my situation because I was born in Australia of early Chinese migrants. (Vera)

> I have the best of both worlds. I have multiple influences from Hong Kong, China, and obviously from Australia, although I feel slightly torn between the two sides. (Don)

> … being able to straddle between these groups is an advantage…it means I can't be placed in one group only. (Dean)

> It's very difficult to separate both sides of my identity coz[sic] it's kind of fused. Clearly being Chinese is not an absolute barrier. Depending on what field you are in, it may even be an advantage." (Phillip)

Common to our participants' responses is that while the hybrid zone in which they are suspended is often the source of racial contestations and delegitimization, such a condition has intrinsic value and is a precondition of their social advancement. Our respondents were able to effectively manipulate their cross-cultural experiences and skills to respond to the everyday racial tensions in their lives. This can be illustrated by Andrew as he shared with co-author Ngan his strategy in responding to racial discrimination:

> Dad always told us, even if you don't want to speak Chinese you can't change your face. You are always forever Chinese so you might just as well get the best of it. So this became my philosophy. When I was growing up in Sydney, when people called me "Ching Chong

Chinaman" or gave me names or graded my group, I just said, "I am better than you, I got two languages and I can pick the best out of the two worlds!" That was how I got over discrimination which I didn't suffer too much…. I was sort of the minority. When I first went to school there was only a Chinese boy in the class, so in a class of about twenty or thirty there were only two of us. But nowadays, half of them are Chinese… It's all changing, the West is meeting the East … the beauty of my situation is that I can pick the best of both worlds."

Despite the struggle in transcending boundaries, subsequent generations have learned to rearticulate and recontextualize their complex identities in unprecedented ways. Over the years they have become used to the awkward position of being a minority in an otherwise "white" environment. With increasing arrivals of Asian migrants, they are no longer an anomaly but a regular presence in the western-dominated society of Australia. This has a tremendous impact on the experience of "being Chinese." While cross-cultural anxiety certainly exists, the malleable quality of their identities, however, allows them to absorb cultural differences. Overall, our informants projected a positive tone highlighting their acceptance of a hybridity and, in particular, the unique advantage of an ability to enjoy varying aspects of Australian and Chinese cultures—as they like it. Thus, contrary to the diasporic literature that sees hybridity as largely a negative experience, or in Ang's (2001: 1998) words, "uncomfortable and threatening," the experience of hybrid multiplicity can be potentially positive and empowering (Chan 2011).

Conclusion

While Australia is known for its culturally diverse society and for its official embracing of the policy of multiculturalism, a major challenge that Chinese Australians still face daily (*including those whose families have resided in the country for three, four, five, and even six generations*) is that of identity. The portrayals of images regarding integration and assimilation, which result in the lack of research on subsequent generations, have indeed led to misconceptions being formed about the nature of the Australian-Chinese community. While the assimilationist models are not completely unknown in the realities of early migrants and some overseas-born migrants, the experiences of long-settled ABCs suggest that a much more complex process of identity negotiation is present which has subsequent impact on their incorporation into Australian society. Indeed, a contributing factor leading to the production of assumptions noted above is located precisely in the definition of Chineseness (and Australianess). Pertinent to the discussion in this chapter, however, is the problematic nature of assimilationist models, which consider cultural identities as bounded and mutually exclusive. As previously argued, what is reflected is the static nature of essentialist conceptions of "Chineseness" and "Australianess" held by Chinese and non-Chinese alike, which intertwine with notions of "race," culture, and identity. The problem lies in the inability of assimilationist models to reflect the identity processes involved in the construction of multiple, hybrid, and fusion identities.

Skinner's hypotheses on the assimilation of the Chinese in Thailand have been challenged by Tong and Chan (2005a), who argue that descendants of Chinese immigrants do not naturally merge with the local society and become indistinguishable from the native population. If Skinner is right and assimilation takes place with regularity then the Chinese cannot survive as Chinese in Thailand; as a minority group they will be absorbed by the third and fourth generations, meaning that there should now be no ethnic Chinese community in Thailand. Yet, in present-day Thailand, there are still a substantial number of ethnic Chinese. In the same way, in Australia, even in the fifth to sixth generation, long-settled ABCs still identity themselves as ethnic Chinese. Theories of assimilation often exaggerate the absorptive power of the mainstream society and fail to account for the complexity of cross-cultural relationships between the mainstream and ethnic communities, while overlooking the tenacity of ethnicity as well as the hybrid process of identity formation.

Certainly the concept of hybridity has been useful as a conceptual tool to understand the unsettled and unsettling identities which are characteristic of the diasporic experience. Different approaches to hybridity have emerged as means to unwrap the complicated entanglements of identity and self. The "third space" and "double consciousness" are two theoretical dimensions of "hybridity" that have increasingly received much resonance in our understanding of the syncretic complexities of identity formation which shape social incorporation in fundamentally different ways. Both perspectives are intellectual decenterings built upon notions of difference and otherness and are largely a means of delegitimizing the homogenization of diverse cultures into a single, solitary group.

However, the very logic of both perspectives, which attempt to abolish the reliance on unitary notions embedded in the previous assimilationist framework, is, paradoxically, a reinstatement of homogeneity based on exclusionary lines. The celebration of difference has unintentionally created a kind of universalizing sameness such that we are all marginal. Attempts in the abandonment of identity categories through notions of hybridity as currently formulated are thus fundamentally problematic as the significance of identity still largely depends on the relative positioning of collective essentialist categories. The switching of identities is not a straightforward alternation process from an identity at one end of the spectrum to another at the other end. While long-settled ABCs are able to don different masks and perform Chineseness, or Australianess, in varied contexts, they do not feel they fully belong to either cultural group. The formation of identity of subsequent generations is a fluid process and a number of different identities can be held and merged simultaneously without one identity necessarily predominating over, or resulting in the erasure of, the other. Moreover, the alternation of identities is at times purposeful but, at other times, unintentional or wholly circumstantial, even forced. The complexity of their identities situates them in a peculiar zone of in-betweenness, belonging neither fully to a Chinese nor to an Australian entity. The purpose of this chapter is not to applaud or delegitimize a particular perspective of hybridity, but rather to bring to light that subsequent generations of the Australian-Chinese may engage in multiple processes of hybridization.

We have discussed the critical relation between notions of home and identity—one that is central in the hybrid construction of Chineseness. We have highlighted the inadequacy of transnationalist models in their incorporation of the experience of long-settled migrant communities and the problem of utilizing transnational linkages as a centering tool for the construction of Chineseness and attachment to Chinese heritage. Those with long settlement cannot be adequately incorporated in the transnational paradigm as their negotiation of ethnicity is invariably different from that of the recent migrants. Through the experience of subsequent generations we brought to light a decentered dimension of linkage with homeland through intergenerational ties that invoke the force of imagination as both memory and desire. Linkages connecting diasporic communities do not necessarily need to be articulated predominately through a real or symbolic homeland—decentered connections are as significant as those formed around notions of origin or return. The politics of multiple hybrid identities, as Papastergiadis (2000: 31) points out, are "often perceived as the collapse of the political because it is considered impossible to reconcile solidity with difference." Since all identities are subjected to change, how do members of diasporic communities make sense of themselves when identity seems to be changing and there is no sense of stability and truth? The answer lies in the relational positioning of the self to the other, which is always determined upon references to a number of essentialized collectivities. In Dunn's (1998: 21) words, "identity politics involves a preoccupation with group membership, the determination of group boundaries being a necessary condition for definition of the self." It is important to emphasize here that no matter whether one positions oneself within or outside a cultural group, collective identities are definitely utilized as a point of reference for making sense of one's experiences. Collective identity may emerge as part of how groups meet their perceived needs, or it can be part of a gradually assembled view of a group, conditioned by the social context in which the group is embedded. What follows is a narrative that indicates what separates one from the other and that gives significance to the meaning of separation resulting in the establishment of identity categories. Whether we may perceive identity as artificial or real, fluid or static, the fact is that cultural identities are potent social and symbolic forces in histories and politics—they give meaning to people's lives.

Despite postmodern theoretical discourses that maintain identities are constructed, and thus somehow not real, identities are generally expressed precisely because they feel "natural" and "essential" and are inherently political. While the general emphasis of "hybridity" discourses has been on the negative, ambivalent experience, it is necessary to acknowledge those who have accepted, even embraced, multiplicity and plurality as a natural part of their lives. In the case of long-settled ABCs, the manipulation and reshaping of identities can lead to both contradictory feelings of ambivalence and contentment, plight and delight (Chan 2005a, 2005b, 2011). To adequately comprehend the complex process of hybridization, it is vital to portray both the upside and downside of hybrid experiences in the lives of diasporic communities—and their people.

Chapter 8
Conclusion

The concept of diaspora usually presupposes cultural connections between multiple communities of a dispersed population who feel, maintain, revive, or reinvent a connection with an imagined homeland in various ways. The concept of identity provides an important framework for conceptualizing individuality, community, and solidarity, and a tool to understand the complex social experiences of diasporic lives. However, the traditional essentialist concept of identity—which conceives a single aspect of identity such as race (e.g., Chinese) as the fundamental essence of an individual's experience—has been delegitimized by postmodernists because of its inability to capture the multiplicity, fluidity, and dynamics of identity as process and in process. The postmodernist discourse insists no single frame can represent the truth about individual's experiences and histories since they are socially constructed and dynamic. In this book we contest the postmodernist view on identity and argue that socially embedded essentialism has been and is still the fundamental organizing principle of human interactions. One of the most important functions of identity, we insist, is providing a means of understanding one's social location in diasporic life.

Certainly, as we have demonstrated through the experiences of long-settled ABCs, the construction of identity is a complex process; identity is constituted variously in different historical, cultural, and social contexts across the life course, intersecting gender, class, sexuality, age, ethnicity, and race. Among the long-settled ABCs, it is evident that common birth cohorts and life stages do not necessarily equate with similar life experiences. Interactions with the dominant white Australian community, intracommunity dynamics among the conglomerate of "other Chinese communities," and the interplay of age-based transitions and personal biography across the course of life have profound impact on the varied ways Chineseness is negotiated, leading to different life trajectories. Furthermore, gender and sexuality are also crucial factors in the formation of social and cultural identities; at certain points in life they are distinctively meaningful and impactful on the construction of social roles. Surviving within the collective social spaces of the Australian society and Chinese diaspora, long-settled ABCs are often caught in a liminal zone, suspended in a space of in-betweenness, not belonging to any one collectivity.

L.L.-S. Ngan and K.-b. Chan, *The Chinese Face in Australia: Multi-generational Ethnicity among Australian-born Chinese*, DOI 10.1007/978-1-4614-2131-3_8,
© Springer Science+Business Media, LLC 2012

Nevertheless, we maintain a sense of "being Chinese"—however one may define it—is still crucial to making sense of the identity of long-settled ABCs across the life course. This argument is particularly pertinent considering that the most recent literature on Chinese in Australia or Chinese overseas has veered toward a more flexible and fluid set of multiple or hybrid identities, as the latter are impacted by rapidly emerging transnational forces.

In addition, for those with long-term residence, issues concerning racial relations and ethnicity have generally been dismissed because of one-way, unidirectional assimilationist assumptions and melting-pot concepts—such as the perception that ethnic identification decreases over successive generations and attempts at unifying sameness that lumps all "Chinese-looking" persons into one group. Thus, it is often assumed that long-settled ABCs have by now completely assimilated into the Australian way of life and have consequently lost their Chineseness. This assimilationist assumption reflects the persistence of essentialist perceptions of Australian and Chinese identity such that each is homogenous, separate, and mutually exclusive. These perceptions have contributed to a lack of in-depth research on the negotiation of identity of subsequent generations of early Chinese migrants in Australia.

Through the experience of multi-generational ABCs whose families have resided in Australia for three, four, five and six generations, we demonstrate that Chineseness is in fact a historical constant that still continues to shape their identities. Regardless of their families' generational longevity in Australia, their cultural integration into mainstream Australian society and their varied transitions into different life courses, Chineseness remains a salient part of their lives. We challenge the current simplistic notion that identities among subsequent generations are unproblematic and uniformly "Australian." In this way, mental constructions of Chineseness do, in fact, continue to help them to make sense of their social experiences and enable them to read the world in specific ways. By exploring how Chineseness has been nurtured, maintained, negotiated, forced upon, or reinvented in the lives of subsequent generations—within the family, Chinese communities, and mainstream white society—we stress the tenacity and persistence of race and ethnicity, thus highlighting the invalidity of assimilationist assumptions and postmodernists perspectives on identity.

The Racial Discourse

While Chineseness is frequently criticized as a construct of essentialism, we demonstrate that, in reality, it remains important for long-settled ABCs in defining and asserting their identities. The persistence of Chineseness is largely associated with the fact that the ethnic actors are compelled to confront Chineseness as an *inescapable* "reality" throughout their lives because of the visual physicality of the Chinese face in a "white" society—whether or not they willingly choose to identify as "Chinese." This "reality" of physicality inscribes them as *others* throughout their life course; it is a constant reminder of their marginalized status, despite their generational longevity and their strong national and cultural identities grounded in Australia.

The experience of being continually seen through a prism of otherness by the mainstream white community, as what Simmel (1950) calls the "stranger," has become an important source of reinforcement of Chineseness. As such, in a "white" society, long-settled ABCs with a Chinese "look" have found it impossible to achieve complete integration because of the power relations of "difference" and "sameness" underlying the social construction of race within dominant "white" Australian society as well as the wider Chinese diaspora. The intense desire for group recognition has consequently led to differing responses and attitudes of belonging; for some it is a negative association with being Chinese, while for others it is a gravitation toward the Chinese community as individuals entered into different age-based identities across the life course.

As an instrument of cultural authentication, language retention has often been used to pass the judgment as to whether someone is a "real" Chinese. While Chinese often prescribe stereotypical labels of "real" or "unreal" Chinese based on an individual's ability to speak the language, Chinese in-groups also play an important role in establishing their own hierarchy of identities. To a Westerner, those who can speak any form of Chinese are "true" Chinese; to a Cantonese-speaking Chinese, those who can speak Mandarin are more "authentic"; to a Mandarin-speaking Chinese, only those who speak Beijing Mandarin are "pure" Chinese. For multi-generational ABCs, variations in Chinese fluency led to hierarchies of Chineseness being formed as they positioned themselves against the different groups of Chinese immigrants in Australia. A sense of "superiority" or "inferiority" to others varied, depending on the perceived "authenticity" of their Chineseness.

Our findings have revealed important cross-cultural issues of identity facing long-settled ABCs as a radicalized minority. In particular, they highlight issues of "race" that preclude ABCs from gaining acceptance in Australia as "real" Australians on account of their visible manifestations of physicality, suggesting a continued sense of their being outsiders within Australian society. Yet, at the same time, they are also precluded from gaining group identity in local Chinese communities on account of their lack in cultural attributes. Though they have acquired a broad range of symbolic cultural capital esteemed in Australian society and have maintained values and morals of the Chinese culture, they are still unable to totally fit into either community because of the hierarchical stratifications by Western and in-group Chinese diasporic ascriptions. This shows that essentialist ascriptions are not a consequence of the only Western hegemonic discourse; within the Chinese community that is divided largely by the differing cultural capitals of recent and old migrants, stratification based on essentialized qualities also exists.

Evidently, the prevailing discourse of authenticity based on essentialized attributes continues to be a "real" factor in determining group belonging despite the delegitimization of identity in postmodern discourses. The construction of Chinese identity thus depends heavily on physicality and language fluency. By analyzing the significance and impact of these racial markers we highlight that essentialized racial boundaries are an authoritative stamp of authenticity that consolidates the social positions of subsequent generations. As such, rather than dismissing the significance of socially constructed constructs, preset boundaries need to be fully acknowledged

and explored in their own ramifications. The theorization of Chineseness would be incomplete without a concurrent problematization of the configuration of power that stratifies social positions within the Chinese diaspora.

Life Course

Recently, the life cycle theory has come under scrutiny because of its inability to account for the variation and diversity of one's biographical movement through time. In recognition that cultural identities are influenced by ever-changing histori-cal, social, and biographical contexts, the life course orientation has emerged to challenge the supposedly fixed and repetitive sequence of ages and stages of the life cycle. While the life course approach celebrates variability and dynamics of human maturation and growth, visible manifestation of stages within the life cycle is an unavoidable feature of the present-day operations of social identities.

Life stages are signifiers which do play on people's lives. In other words, although the timing of transition into different socially constructed life stages may vary for each individual, we can still speak of continuity, and there is something that we call adolescence or parenthood on which we "hang" our social identities. As such, if these stages within the path of life are totally dismissed, it would be difficult to construct any conclusive account of the meaning of the variability of individual lives. In this respect, we argue that since age-based transitions are a significant resource individuals use to construct their biographical narratives as well as their interactions with others, they should not be casually dismissed. In the same manner, although the notion of Chinese identity is socially constructed and fluid in nature, there is nevertheless something we call "Chinese." Contrary to postmodernist per-spectives, essentialized social collectivities should be utilized as important guiding markers for our analysis of the changing nature of identity formation across the life course. The innovative aspect of the conceptual framework of our study lies in its use of both the life course and life cycle orientations in examining how Chineseness is socially organized and evolves over time.

During the years of growing up, visible manifestations of the face are fundamen-tal for the ethnic and racial awareness of long-settled ABCs in the social context of Australia where Chinese are a minority. This was conditioned through ongoing interactions of the "self" with the "other." In the transition to marital life, familial manifestations of Chinese cultural ideologies take over, defining for subsequent generations the expectations and requirements that they must meet in their mar-riage. While marriage is a personal matter between two individuals, the pressure to marry within one's ethnic group highlights that cultural–familial ideologies medi-ating intergenerational relations have genuine implications for life decisions. The choice of a partner is thus often perceived as a cultural statement that embodies one's sense of Chineseness. Consequently, those in interracial marriages, particu-larly women, become the subject of objectification. While the experiences of Chinese women as the objectified—the hyperfeminine women—are crucial to adequately encapsulate the entirety of the self/other relations, the hegemony of western ascriptions on Chinese males—typically portrayed as the asexual men—must not be lost sight of. The articulation of Chineseness thus goes hand in hand with the articulation of sexuality. The transition to parenthood has brought Chineseness into the consciousness as parents decide on what values are to be or not to be taught to their children. In the later years of life, Chineseness becomes a matter of lifestyle in the "habitus" of everyday living as old age brings with it much time and space for a kind of self-reflection that is not possible in the busy middle years of life.

Furthermore, familial–cultural values of duty and gender role obligations toward aging parents have continued relevance for the way in which generational relations are acted out in the lives of long-established ABCs. Sons have traditionally assumed the duty of caring for the parents. However, our findings show those who are gay are bestowed even more family responsibilities. Gay men are compelled to take on the role of a carer for their elderly parents as a result of their homosexuality, meaning an unmarried life and no children, thus more free time. Our findings on the interplay of sexuality, gender, and duty for the aged have uncovered rather valuable insights to guide future research.

This study is built upon a dialectics that argues that daily experiences establish social location (Clausen, 1986) and one's social location also determines the experiences one is likely to have (Moya, 2000b). We hold the view that aging is a significant resource used by individuals to construct their biographical narratives as well as their reportage on social interactions and is intricately linked to the establishment of cultural identities and belongingness. Since generational relations in later life are interconnected with experiences and transitions from earlier life, different life stages are therefore part of an overall process of generational interaction rather than as isolated stages. The interplay of age and societal dynamics is fundamental to the ways in which subsequent generations negotiate Chineseness. A recognition of such important linkages between ethnic identity, social pathways, developmental trajectories, and changes in society thus lay the groundwork for further studies in the life course trajectories of ethnic minorities.

Hybridity

Notions of hybridity have been employed to confront and problematize the unsettling boundaries of identities of recent migrants. However, as evidenced in the experiences of long-settled ABCs, those with long-term residence can also be caught in a plurality of imagined worlds. Similar to recent migrants, they too can engage in multiple processes of hybridization. The complexity of their identities lies in the dynamic process of hybridization where different identities can be held, manipulated, and merged simultaneously or in turn without one identity predominating over, or resulting in the erasure of, the other. While the ethnic actors consciously manipulate their identities according to their audience, at times alternation of identities can be unconscious and unintentional. The multiplicity of identities situates them in a peculiar zone of in-betweenness, not fully belonging to a Chinese or an Australian entity.

While concepts of hybridity such as "third space" and "double consciousness" have been useful in delegitimizing the notion of Chineseness as a collective racial category, paradoxically, they are themselves reinstatements of homogeneity based on exclusionary lines. The essentialist notion of a "Chinese identity" is nevertheless fundamental in constructing notions of sameness and difference between in- and out-group members. Identity gains its significance by relational positioning between the "self" and the "other." Such conditioning, based on an authentication process of labeling and representation of the "other" through essentializing cultural attributes, is critical for locating one's identity—thus the continued significance of race and ethnicity. So it is what exists between collective essentialized constructs that gives meaning to those in hybridity.

Moreover, although Chineseness may be unavoidably inscribed onto the lives of long-established ABCs, we do not necessarily support Ang's (2001: 44, 50) contention that Chineseness forms a kind of "prison house" that bounds the identities of diasporic Chinese, making it virtually impossible for one to escape from such inscriptions. The diasporic literature in general has tended to portray hybridity as a negative experience; missing from the debate are those who have accepted, even embraced, complex identities in their lives. The experiences of our informants show that the hybrid nature of their identity is not always "wounded attachments"; rather it is at times an enriching source of identification. Their experiences highlight a positive acceptance of hybridity as they take advantage of their unique ability to "pick and choose" among their Australian and Chinese identities as they like, enhancing group belonging and, at the same time, bringing about feelings of enrichment and social advancement. To fully comprehend the complex process of hybridization, it is vital to take into account the ambivalence and contentment of hybridity—the downside and the upside.

Decentered Linkages

Hybrid experiences of subsequent generations are often associated with the nature of linkages with homeland in a peculiar way. Notions of "home" are infected with meanings, emotions, experiences, and relationships that create a sense of belongingness—an important element in theorizing identity. It is clear that due to their long-term residence in Australia, they do not engage in transnational practices or have the deep cultural memories of recent Chinese newcomers to Australia. There is little room in the diasporic paradigm for the principled ambivalence about physical return and attachment to land. Their experiences of Chineseness are established through decentered linkages with an imaginary homeland.

Such decentered connections are intergenerationally influenced through a variety of memories, experiences, and voices within the family that usher in the forces of imagination and desire. We argue that transnational linkages connecting diasporic communities do not necessarily need to be articulated predominately through a real or symbolic homeland—decentered connections are as significant as those formed around notions of origin or return. By exploring "new" and "unique" forms of linkages, we have contributed to the understanding of Chineseness among heterogeneous groups across the Chinese diaspora.

Theory and Mixed Methodology

This book has utilized diasporic and cultural theories on identity to explore the construction of Chineseness through the multifarious ways long-established ABCs negotiate Chineseness within the contexts of the family, mainstream Australian society, and Chinese diasporic spaces. Our informants' biographical narratives of encounters with ethnicity as well as their reportage on their interactions with others in their daily lives contain deep sources of information on their Chineseness. Our informants are able to be active agents in reestablishing and reconstructing the notion of Chineseness through a long-term perspective. While personal accounts are dynamic in nature as they involve an interplay of memory, recollection, attitudinal response, and changing contexts, systematic illustration through excerpts from in-depth interviews, autobiographies, and visual materials provides a way of understanding the contemporary process of identity negotiation which goes beyond analysis merely based on quantitative "facts" and historical events.

Our findings show that different generations share more commonalities than differences as they are similarly influenced by sociocultural contexts, social networks, and intergenerational forces. The common cross-cultural experiences during childhood and youth through the process of socialization within the mainstream and Chinese communities in Australia create a frame of reference and a shared worldview which subsequently influences their sense of identity.

In contradiction to the assumptions that ethnic identification is lost over subsequent generations—and thus is of little research value—this study points out that long-established ABCs are of immense value in analyses of identity politics and political economy.

We do not imagine that the accounts we have given of identity are exhaustive or completely universal, as differences arguably exist due to the dynamics of social contexts and histories of each and every community. However, we believe fundamental processes of identity negotiation are applicable to the social identities of race and ethnicity within the Chinese diaspora and are also shared by members of other societies. Chineseness, like all cultural identifications, can be reconstructed, passed on, and renegotiated with whatever is current in political and social developments. The Australian-born Chinese is not an exceptional case. Far from it.

This book contributes to the difficult project of figuring out the methodological and analytical strategies necessary for the development of new understanding of identity politics. As it happens, we challenge the skeptic postmodernist on the one hand and dismantle the certain essentialist on the other. Undertaking the task of examining the formations of Chineseness is difficult, because to adequately analyze identity, as Mohanty (2000: 64) reminds us, there is "no easy way out." If we deny the validity of all identities because they are socially constructed and tied to subjective judgments, we lose the capacity to make useful and important distinctions between different kinds of identities, values, and judgments. For significant theoretical advances to be made in this field, future studies must not take for granted contemporary theoretical orientation. Rather, they need to continue the challenging task of problematicizing existing theories and draw from across a range of disciplines to develop innovative, interpretative, and analytical tools of theory and methodology that will uncover and discover.

Epilogue

When we assume the vantage point of dialectics, the shortcomings of the "postmodern" critique become evident. The Chinese in (not of, not yet) Australia are embedded in complex relationships constructed along divisions of birthplace, language, gender, generation, occupation, politics, and religion. The word "Chinese" does not necessarily signify any unified position regarding ethnic identity. As such, there is really no single or any one Chinese identity at all. There is not and never was a single community we can call the Chinese community in Australia. Instead, great diversity is found within the broad category of Australian Chinese through their different life experiences and ethnicities, and this diversity may partly explain why some individuals may see themselves as Chinese, yet others may feel the term is imposed on them. As such, Chinese identity is a negotiated and unstable assemblage of perceptions. Nevertheless, as an essentialist construct, it has been critically significant in organizing notions of sameness and difference between out-group and in-group members.

We quarrel with the postmodern theorists for their exultations in the limitless metamorphoses that "liquid modernity" (Bauman, 2000) has made possible for affluent and mobile white men and women. Invoking the Marxist concept of the "real abstraction," we urge the theorists to work toward a nuanced reconsideration of identity. We must take this statement literally (to the *letter*):

The fact is that "Chinese" is real in giving meaning to everyday life, as there are millions of people in the world who would identify themselves as Chinese in one way or another—either voluntarily or imposed upon by others.

In Lacanian terms, "Chinese" is a symbolic quilting point that weaves together a set of symbolic predicates, giving consistency and significance to "everyday life." We must remember that the quilting point, as that which gives some provisional oneness to a symbolic field, is that which guarantees the presence of meaning *without* actually meaning anything in itself. It is, thus, an *empty* signifier that is ultimately tautological—a stopping point that puts a halt to the incessant sliding of meaning. This, as we know, often leads to the illusion of there being some "hidden meaning," some authentic richness that is behind it: when asked about what

L.L.-S. Ngan and K.-b. Chan, *The Chinese Face in Australia: Multi-generational Ethnicity among Australian-born Chinese*, DOI 10.1007/978-1-4614-2131-3,
© Springer Science+Business Media, LLC 2012

"Chineseness" involves, an urbane Shanghainese man would perhaps respond with a clever evasion such as "Oh, I don't know, I can't explain it, you have to be *in* the culture to understand it; you can't *explain* these things in plain speech, you have to *feel it!*" The following response of our informant reflects the hidden meaning of "being Chinese" to the same effect:

> I am Chinese because by definition I am. My cultural roots are Chinese. If you ask me what country I come from, it's Australia, but my cultural background is Chinese. That is by definition, but I consider myself as an ABC. If you are asking me what makes me think I am Chinese, I don't know!

In other words, Chineseness is Chineseness, and the very failure to speak about it is taken as a guarantee of its sacred ineffability. Slavoj Zizek's "ingenious" analyses of ideology (see his *The Sublime Object of Ideology* (2009) and *The Plague of Fantasies* (2009)) utilize this Lacanian insight to decrypt the obscurantist claims of modern advertising, which mobilizes this very emptiness to generate some sort of supplement to the advertised product, thereby baptizing it with a spectral halo. Think, for example, of an advertising slogan such as "This is it. This is the Real Thing," which Zizek takes to indicate the workings of the quilting point as such. Also, when we evaluate symbolic subjectivations (in this case, the assumption of the predicate "Chinese") from the point of view of *the political*, it makes all the difference whether this assumption is done "voluntarily or impinged upon by others." This, we must add, is something that we have long been conscious of. Also of particular interest to us is that the problem with essentialist conceptions of identity is the tendency to posit *one identity* as the single cause that determines the total meaning of an individual's experience. We would like to read this particular sentence against the grain, supplementing it with an in-depth discussion of "hegemony" as we understand it.

So, what is hegemony? It would need to be coupled with a biting discussion of racism in Australia, which we can translate into our Lacanian-Marxist vocabulary. Here are four first-person accounts of discrimination provided by our informants:

> I was always aware that I was different because in primary school I was picked out all the time. You got all these Italians. They were migrants themselves ....You know little kids, they are very cruel, they call you "Ching Chong," slant eyes and so on. You look very different. But Italians don't look all that different from Aussies. The Chinese were very different straight away and you got segregated. So I knew I was different from primary school onward.

> Being Chinese was only a negative identification coz when we grew up in Ryde there were no Asians. All the migrants were Italian or Greeks. Most of them have now moved out. We were one of the few Chinese families. It was quite conspicuous. So you develop a negative identification. So you are Chinese because they call you Ching Chong Chinaman or something like this.

> ... when I was six years old or something ... for a few months I would stand up in front of the mirror and I would try to give myself a crease above my eye and to try to be like everyone else at school and of course later found out it wasn't going to work. It's a very sad thing that I had to do that if you think about it!

> I knew that I was different from other people because people would ask me, "Where are you from? What nationality are you?" and all that sort of thing. And I just used to take it for granted that I was Chinese, but when they used to ask me—they couldn't tell what I was

sometimes! I thought that was a bit queer, because I just automatically thought I was Chinese, but even last week somebody said, "You don't look Chinese!" and I said "Oh, don't I?" She was a lady from Beijing ... When I went to Hong Kong in 1958 a Chinese man on the plane walked by and he said, "Are you Filipino?" He went through a lot of other nationalities because he didn't know what I was and in the end I just said, "Sydney" ... So, I think the best answer is to say you're Australian with Chinese roots.

Here we are given insight into the deformations that the symbolic exerts upon those who enter its dominion—the pound of flesh that it exacts from its faithful. We mentioned above that the subject does not have a free hand in giving form to the imaginary avatar that constitutes its ego. An ego can be forced upon you—a prefabricated image fully equipped with all manner of symbolic transplants (predicates). The third quote demonstrates, in a rather tragic way, the Freudian maxim that "anatomy is destiny"—here, "ethnicity" (as a hegemonized symbolic quality) is a cruel fate that one cannot seem to escape. The last quote is highly revealing of the procedures of identitarian interpellation today, identificatory procedures that Deleuze and Guattari (2004: 195–196) have called operators of "faciality": "We are certainly not saying that the face, the power of the face, engenders and explains social power. *Certain assemblages of power require the production of a face, others do not ...* Primitives have the most human of heads, the most beautiful and the most spiritual, but they have no face and need none. The face is not a universal. It is not even that of the white man; it is White Man himself, with his broad white cheeks and the black hole of his eyes ... Not a universal, but *facies totius universi ...*" (emphases ours).

When Foucault (1977) discusses the gradual shift from disciplinary procedures (confinement, corporeal punishment, and other obtrusive forms of correction) to strategies of control, he supplies an outline for the analysis of contemporary racism. Baudrillard's (2008) pithy observation that "the medium is the model" in postmodernity captures the crux of Foucault's argument perfectly: with the proliferation of all manners of tests, trials, and evaluations, power establishes a means by which it can measure and hierarchize deviations from a dominant model of normativity. Deleuze and Guattari's (2004) notion of the "face" can be seen as being directly correlative of this turn in Foucault's thinking, and the "soft racism" that it enforces is plainly demonstrated in our "multicultural" metropolises: is it not true that "multiculturalism" affirms the difference of the Other as long as he or she accepts the ground rules of Western civility? Multiculturalism, in the last reckoning, amounts to nothing more than the reduction of cultural difference to a series of weak variations on liberal-democratic consensus, which polices the limits of political correctness and moral acceptability. This is precisely why the placid benignity of liberal-democratic "tolerance" can scarcely obscure the paternalistic condescension that it assumes toward all of its errant stepchildren—the Other is tolerable insofar as he submits to the proprieties of our civilized life. This derision toward every form of dissent and heterogeneity finds its consummate expression in the "American way of life" that has become the operative logic of late capitalism. Hence, there is an element of truth in the former American government's denunciations of "undemocratic" people, likening them to delinquents that must be liberated from their self-destructive habits and initiated into the ways of the free market. Thus, the operative maxim of our liberal-democratic market societies is: the Other is alright insofar as he or she is more or less the same as myself. If Marxism continues to exert its claim as "the only living philosophy of our time" (Sartre), it is because it allows us to think this problematic of the Same and the Other, Identity and Difference in a world that would have us believe that it has resolved this tension for good.

We would do well to return to our earlier discussion on the logic of the "quilting point." Let's pay close attention again to the ways in which the discourse of Chineseness is reproduced through internalization, as we tease out the symbolic relations that are constitutive of cultural identity. We juxtapose accounts of discrimination from without with familial impositions of identitarian predicates, showing that there is a certain homology between the two forms. Allow us to share with you one more time these quotes from our informants:

> ... even though I wouldn't mind my children marrying whoever, it would be nice if they could maintain their Chinese looks. Their cousins already look Australian; they are *looking that look* so people won't treat them as Chinese. If no one is going to *treat you as Chinese*, then you won't feel you are Chinese!

> (Being Chinese is about) ... having a family dinner where we all have rice together. With an Asian meal it has to be steamed up and everything put on there on the table and everyone sits down and eats together. To be able to go to a Chinese grocery store and know your sauces and to know how to stir fry and cook.

> My parents are really into that Chinese festivals and rituals like *Ching Ming* but I do that out of respect. The actual rituals mean nothing to me, I didn't understand it, I still don't understand it but I can do the motions. It means something to someone in the family.

A few comments are in order apropos the last two quotes, which evoke Bourdieu's (1972) notion of the *habitus*, with its rhythms, rituals, and practices. The second quote, in particular, is reminiscent of the thought of Pascal (1996: 98)—one of Bourdieu's foremost influences:

> Belief is natural to the mind, and it is natural for the will to love: so much so that if valid objects be lacking they will necessarily attach themselves to false ones ... For we must not misunderstand ourselves: we are as much machine as mind ... The strongest and most widely accepted proofs are provided by habit. Habit inclines the machine, and the machine carries the mind with it *even before the mind can consent* ... It is habit [in the more general sense of custom] that makes men Turks and pagans, traders and soldiers, etc ... We need to develop a simple faith which becomes a habit and which leads us to believe things, and inclines all our faculties in favor of belief, *so that without violence, without tricks, without argument, our soul absorbs it naturally* ... Both parts of our nature must be made to act according to belief: the mind must be persuaded by reasons, which it is sufficient to have seen once in a lifetime, and the machine must be run in by forming it to habit, and by not allowing it to go into reverse." (emphases ours) This is precisely why Pascal (1996: 93) offers the following advice to an unbeliever who, while skeptical of the spiritual truth of Catholic ceremonies, seeks repose in the Church: "You want to cure yourself of unbelief, and you ask for the remedy? Learn of those who have been fettered like yourself, but who have now staked all that they possess ... Follow the method by which they began, which was, to *behave as though they believed*, by taking holy water, having Masses said, etc. This will lead you naturally toward belief and will calm you ... drive the beast out of you.

So, while Pascal seems to suggest that Man is a rational creature just as much as he is an unreflective, habitual one, this is really a ruse: Pascal is implicitly aware that the force of scientific reason unleashed by modernity and the Cartesian revolution, having emerged from the cloisters of faith, threatens to burst its theological chains asunder.

Because Pascal is so fearful of the eviscerating power of the Real and the world-shattering anxiety that it produces in a subject that has lost its moorings in symbolic reality, he desperately attempts to mend the link between Man and his erstwhile order (Catholicism) by tethering rationality to the taskmaster of habit. Pray, receive communion, perform the Eucharistic rituals and *belief will come*, because when you submit yourself to these ceremonies, you already *believe despite yourself*. Why? Because, as Lacan tells us, you don't need to believe "directly"—you can defer your belief to an Other, a "subject supposed to believe." It is *this* intersubjective dimension of belief that is totally missed by nonpsychoanalytic theories that continue to move within the ambit of intentionality. In our disenchanted postmodern metropolises, we are all skeptics, yet many of us continue to "keep our traditions alive," going through the motions of reproducing the supposed "authenticity" of our cultures while maintaining an ironic distantiation toward our own actions. What sustains this authenticity, when we clearly are barred access to it ourselves? The answer is that it exists somewhere "out there"—somewhere somebody *truly* believes in the essence of these perfunctory gestures, and we have to keep the charade going, foregoing our own lack of conviction so that we may act *as though* we believe. Pascal's incisive point is that this second-order, reflexive belief (believing in the authenticity of the belief, even if we cannot participate in it directly), sustained by a mythical "somebody" that *truly believes*, is already an unequivocal triumph for *belief itself*. In reality, we *are* the somebodies that we hypothesize, since it is through this very mythical presumption that the belief is incarnated and transmitted. Slavoj Zizek (2009) has constructed a remarkable, neo-Althusserian theory of ideology on precisely this point—in the words of Marx, ideology can be simply expressed thus: they do not know it, but they are doing it. In a remarkable "correction" of Althusser's concept of ideological interpellation, Zizek asserts that the ironic distantiation that characterizes postmodern subjectivity is no proof of Althusser's irrelevance—on the contrary, it is precisely when we dissociate what we do with what we believe that we are fully within the grip of ideology. As an example of this, Zizek gives the example of the self-avowed atheist who reads the daily horoscope with a cynical smirk, insisting that he does not take its prophecies seriously.

We can now pose the following scandalous hypothesis: what if *nobody* really believes in the formal rituals that give some cultural "richness" of experience, some ineffable *je ne sais quoi* to the notion of "Chineseness?" What if the deferral of belief from one unbeliever to the next is grounded upon nothing beyond a presumption that cannot be validated? The quote that we reproduce below is so apposite to our purposes that it almost reads like a textbook example of belief today. Let us read it *once more*:

> My parents are really into those Chinese festivals and rituals like *Ching Ming* but I do that out of respect. The actual rituals mean nothing to me, I didn't understand it, I still don't understand it but I can do the motions. It means something to someone in the family.

Our point here is that custom is, as Pascal has shown us, precisely that which does not need to be understood, nor *believed* on an intellectual level.

So, having said all this, it would perhaps be fair to suppose that we are advocating the nullification of any cultural predicate whatsoever, in lieu of a real cosmopolitanism in which all imaginary differences are abolished. This is not at all what we have in mind. The extraordinary explosion of subjectivities and the demands that postmodernity have made possible are developments that we welcome. Additionally, you need to only remember that we stated, some pages ago, that sometimes it makes all the difference whether an identity is treated as a natural property/predicate "belonging" to an exclusive group or if it is mobilized as a political category. In other words, we would like to know if symbolic identifications can have a *revolutionary usage*. To explain this, we need to only return to two exemplary quotes:

> When people ask, 'Where are you from?' If I say 'I am from Australia' they will say 'no, no, no,' then I say "Oh you mean I am Chinese 'coz I look different?

> You get more problems over there because obviously they look at your face. I remember when I studied French for a year there was an Italian student asking me where I came from and I said I'm from Australia. And she's like "You can't be from Australia, what's wrong with you?" and I said I was born in Australia. And I guess they can't understand why I would be calling myself Australian. This was about ten years ago. I have been back to Europe last year and things are not so bad now. And I had the same thing in England too with these white South Africans. They were just crazy. They would be surprised that I could use a knife and fork! And it's like, "what are you talking about!" So people in other parts of the world find it very difficult to understand me. So they sort of label you. Even in Sydney, they immediately make a judgment like that. Unless they hear me speak, they think I'm a recent migrant. But once they hear you talk, they just speak to you normally. So it's quite funny!

The jarring effect of these two quotes lies in their implications for political praxis. To put it simply, there *is* something subversive about insisting upon one's right to lay claim to a certain predicate, to affirm that it is not the exclusive property of some enclosed community, but a locus of conflict open to litigious contestation.

We can finally say that our reservations toward deconstructive exaltations of fluid, mobile identities are perfectly justified. As far as identity goes, some have the liberty to choose from a limitless smorgasbord of lifestyles and identifications, while others are bound to assigned predicates, or relegated to inexistence altogether (immigrant workers, refugees, the poor, the elderly). At the same time, can we not say that this restless metamorphosis from one "identity" to the other testifies to a deeper ontological fissure, which prevents one from ever closing the gap between the negativity of the subject and the positive identifications that are grafted upon it? It is this prepredicative dimension of the subject, this relentless negativity that Zizek can justifiably refer to as the Cartesian "subject before subjectivation"—an ontological insight that, having inaugurated modern philosophy as such, has been brought to its logical conclusion in our fully reflexivized societies, where concrete individuals are so many "floating signifiers" forming attachments that are ultimately soluble. Besides this, Laclau and Badiou have, in their own ways, highlighted the fact that the contemporary individual exists in a number of existential worlds simultaneously, that he or she is traversed by a number of subjectifying vectors that are not reducible to one another (One is a father, a factory worker, a Christian, Chinese, married to a white Australian woman, etc.). This is why, for these two thinkers, the theme of "class struggle" can no longer be considered *the* privileged operator of political subjectivation—*any* of these vectors can lead to political confrontations and it is impossible to determine beforehand *which* of these identifications will become politicized in a given circumstance. The positive condition for politics in postmodernity, then, is a double one: not only is the subject constitutively "unhinged," unbound from any fixed signification, the identifications that compose him or her are themselves "floating"—subject to political contestation and appropriation—yet, nonetheless, floating identifications still provide consistency and significance to everyday life. Or so it seems.

References

ABS (2001). Family-family formation: Cultural diversity in marriage. *Australian social trends 2000*. Australia Bureau of Statistics.
Abu-Lughod, L. (1991). Writing against culture. In R. G. Fox & S. Santa Fe (Eds.), *Recapturing anthropology* (pp. 137–162). New Mexico: School of American Research Press.
Alba, R., & Nee, V. (1999). Rethinking assimilation theory for a new era of immigration. In C. Hischman, P. Kasinitz, & J. DeWind (Eds.), *The handbook of international migration* (pp. 137–160). New York: Russell Sage Foundation.
Alcoff, L. M. (2006). *Visible identities: Race, gender and the self.* Oxford: Oxford University Press.
Alcoff, L. M., & Mohanty, S. P. (2006). Reconsidering identity politics: An introduction. In L. M. Alcoff, M. Hames-Garica, S. P. Mohanty, & P. Moya (Eds.), *Identity politics reconsidered* (pp. 1–9). New York: Palgrave.
Alwin, D. F., & McCammon, R. J. (2003). Generations, cohorts and social change. In A. T. Mortimer & M. J. Shanahan (Eds.), *Handbook of the life course* (pp. 23–50). New York: Springer.
Australian Heritage Commission. (2002). *Tracking the dragon.* Retrieved March 1, 2011, from http://www.environment.gov.au/heritage/ahc/publications/commission/books/pubs/tracking-thedragon.pdf.
Anderson, B. (1983). *Imagined communities: Reflections on the origin and spread of nationalism.* London: Verso.
Anderson, M. (1999). Children in-between: Constructing identities in the bicultural family. *Journal of the Anthropological Institute, 5*, 13–23.
Ang, I. (1998). Can one say no to Chineseness? Pushing the limits of the diasporic paradigm. *Boundary, 2*, 223–242.
Ang, I. (2001). *On not speaking Chinese: Living between Asia and the West.* London: Routledge.
Ang, I. (2004). Beyond transnational nationalism: Questioning the borders of the Chinese diaspora in the global city. In B. S. A. Yeoh & K. Willis (Eds.), *State/nation/transnation: Perspectives of transnationalism in the Asia-Pacific* (pp. 179–198). London: Routledge.
Anthias, F. (2001). New hybridities, old concepts: The limits of 'culture'. *Ethnic and Racial Studies, 24*, 619–641.
Appadurai, A. (1993). Number in the colonial imagination. In C. A. Breckenridge & P. V. D. Veers (Eds.), *Orientalism and the postcolonial predicament perspectives on South Asia* (pp. 314–340). Philadelphia: University of Pennsylvania Press.
Appadurai, A. (1997). *The production of locality. Modernity at large.* Minneapolis: University of Minnesota Press.
Australian Bureau of Statistics. (2000). Family–family formation: Cultural diversity in marriage. In *Australian social trends 2000.* Canberra: Australian Bureau of Statistics.
Balibar, E. (1991). Is there a 'neo-racism'? In E. B. A. I. Wallerstein (Ed.), *Race, nation, class: Ambiguous identities* (pp. 17–28). London: Verso.

Basch, L., Glick-Schiller, N., & Szanton-Blanc, C. (1994). *Nations unbound: Transnational projects, postcolonial predicaments, and deterritorialized nation-states*. Luxembourg: Gordon and Breach.

Bauman, Z. (1998). On glocalization: Or globalization for some, localization for some others. *Thesis Eleven, 57*(1), 37–49.

Bauman, Z. (2000). *Liquid modernity*. Cambridge: Polity Press.

Baurdillard, J. (2008). *Fatal strategies*. New York: Semiotext (e).

Berger, P. (1984). *And our faces, my heart, brief as photos*. London: Writers and Readers.

Bhabha, H. (1991). The third space: Interview with Homi K. Bhabha. In J. Rutherford (Ed.), *Identity: community, culture, difference* (pp. 207–221). London: Lawrence and Wishart.

Bhabha, H. (1994). *The location of culture*. London: Routledge.

Bohannan, P. (1979). The six stations of divorce. In P. I. Rose (Ed.), *Socalisation and the life cycle*. New York: St Martin Press.

Bois, Du. (1903). *The souls of black folk*. New York: New American Library.

Bond, M. H., & Hwang, K. K. (1986). The social psychology of Chinese people. In M. H. Bond (Ed.), *The psychology of the Chinese people* (pp. 213–266). Oxford: Oxford University Press.

Borrie, W. D. (1949). *Immigration: Australia's problems and prospects*. Sydney: Angus and Robertson.

Bourdieu, P. (1972). *Outline of a theory of practice*. Cambridge: Cambridge University Press.

Breton, R., Isajie, W. W., Kalbach, W. E., & Reitz, G. J. (1990). *Ethnic identity and equality: Varieties of experience in a Canadian city*. Toronto: University of Toronto Press.

Carter, N. A. (2004). Strategies of study: Approaching the analysis of identity. *International Politics, 41*, 430–439.

Castonguay, C. (1998). The fading Canadian duality. In J. Edwards (Ed.), *Language in Canada* (pp. 36–60). Cambridge: Cambridge University Press.

Chambers, I. (1994). *Migrancy, culture, identity*. London: Routledge.

Chan, H. (1999). The identity of the Chinese in Australian history. *Queensland Review, 6*, 1–10.

Chan, K. B. (1991). *Smoke and fire: The Chinese in Montreal*. Hong Kong: Chinese University Press.

Chan, K. B. (2005a). *Chinese identities, ethnicity and cosmopolitanism*. London: Routledge.

Chan, K. B. (2005b). The stranger's plight and delight. *Social Transformations in Chinese Societies, 1*, 191–219.

Chan, K. B. (2011). *Hybridity: Promises and limits*. Toronto: de Sitter Publications.

Chan, K. B., & Helly, D. (Eds). (1987). Coping with racism: The Chinese experience in Canada. *Canadian Ethnic Studies, 19*(Special Issue 3).

Charney, M. W., Yeoh, B. S. A., & Tong, C. K. (Eds.). (2003). *Chinese migrants abroad: Cultural educational and social dimensions of the Chinese diaspora*. Singapore: Singapore University Press.

Choi, C. Y. (1975). *Chinese migration and settlement in Australia*. Sydney: Sydney University Press.

Chow, R. (1991). *Woman and Chinese modernity: The politics of reading between West and East*. Minneapolis: University of Minnesota Press.

Chow, R. (1998). Introduction: On Chineseness as a theoretical problem. *Boundary, 2*, 1–24.

Chun, A. (1996). Fuck Chineseness: On the ambiguities of ethnicity as culture as identity. *Boundary, 2*(23), 111–138.

Clausen, J. A. (1986). *The life course: A sociological perspective*. New Jersey: Prentice-Hall.

Clifford, J. (1997). *Routes: Travel and translation in the late twentieth century*. Cambridge: Harvard University Press.

Clyne, M. (1991). *Community languages*. Melbourne: Cambridge University Press.

Cohen, M. L. (1994). Being Chinese: The peripheralization of traditional identity. In W. M. Tu (Ed.), *The living tree: The changing meaning of being Chinese today* (pp. 88–108). Stanford: Stanford University Press.

Cook, P. (2005). *Screening the past: Memory and nostalgia in cinema*. London: Routledge.

Cornell, S., & Hartmann, D. (1998). *Ethnicity and race: Making identities in a changing world*. Thousand Oaks: Pine Forge Press.

Davidson, A. (1991). Rethinking household and livelihood strategies. In D. Clay & H. K. Schwarzweller (Eds.), *Research in rural sociology and development: Household survival strategies* (pp. 11–28). London: JAI Press.

Davidson, A. (2004). Transnational spaces and sociocultural networks: Chinese women migrants in Sydney. In K. E. Kuah-Pearce (Ed.), *Chinese women and their cultural and network capitals* (pp. 21–43). Singapore: Marshall Cavendish.

Deleuze, G., & Guattari, F. (2004). *A thousand plateaus*. London: Continuum.

Dunn, R. G. (1998). *Identity crises: A social critique of postmodernity*. Minneapolis: University of Minnesota Press.

Elder, G. H., Jr., Johnson, M. K., & Crosnoe, R. (2003). The emergence and development of life course theory. In A. T. Mortimer & M. J. Shanahan (Eds.), *Handbook of the life course* (pp. 3–22). New York: Springer.

Elvin, M. (1994). The inner world of 1830. In W. M. Tu (Ed.), *The living tree: The changing meaning of being Chinese today* (pp. 35–63). Stanford: Stanford University Press.

Erikson, E. (1950). *Childhood and society*. New York: Norton.

Finocchiaro, C. (1995). Intergenerational language maintenance of minority groups in Australia in the 1990s: An Italian case study. *Journal of Intercultural Studies, 16*, 41–54.

Fitzgerald, S. (1997). *Red tape, gold scissors: The story of Sydney Chinese*. Sydney: State Library of New South Wales Press.

Fitzgerald, J. (2007). *Big White lie*. Sydney: University of New South Wales Press.

Foner, G. E., & Glick-Schiller, N. (2002). The generation of identity: Redefining the second generation within a transnational social field. In P. Levitt & M. Waters (Eds.), *The changing face of home: The transnational lives of the second generation* (pp. 168–210). New York: Russell Sage.

Foucault, M. (1977). *Discipline and punish: The birth of the prison* (Alan Sheridan, Trans.). London: Allen Lane, Penguin. (First published in French as *Surveiller et punir*. Paris: Gallimard, 1975).

Gans, H. (1979). Symbolic ethnicity: The future of ethnic groups and cultures in America. *Ethnic and Racial Studies, 2*, 1–20.

Giddens, A. (1990). *The consequences of modernity*. California: Stanford University Press.

Gilbert, H., Lo, J., & Khoo, T. (Eds.). (2000). *Diaspora: negotiating Asian-Australia*. Brisbane: University of Queensland Press.

Gilroy, P. (1987). *There ain't no Black in the Union Jack: The cultural politics of race and nation*. London: Hutchinson.

Gilroy, P. (1994). *The Black Atlantic: Modernity and double consciousness*. Cambridge: Harvard University Press.

Gilroy, P. (2000). *Against race: Imagining political culture beyond the color line*. Cambridge: Harvard University Press.

Gilroy, P. (2004). *Between camps: Nations, culture and the allure of race*. London: Routledge.

Glick-Schiller, N., Basch L., & Blanc-Szanton, C. (1991). Towards a transnationalization of migration: Race, class, ethnicity, and nationalism reconsidered. *The Annals of the New York Academy of Sciences 645*, New York: New York Academy of Sciences.

Goffman, E. (1959). *The presentation of self in everyday life*. New York: The Overlook Press.

Greif, S. W. (1974). *The overseas Chinese in New Zealand*. Singapore: Asia Pacific Press.

Hall, S. (1996). Introduction: Who needs identity? In S. Hall & P. D. Gay (Eds.), *Questions of cultural identity* (pp. 1–17). London: Sage.

Hames-Gracia, M. R. (2000). "Who are our own people?" Challenges for a theory of social identity. In P. M. L. Moya & M. R. Hames-Gracia (Eds.), *Reclaiming identity: Realist theory and the predicament of postmodernism* (pp. 102–132). Berkeley: University of California Press.

Hareven, T. K. (1996). Introduction: Aging and generational relations over the life course. In *Aging and generational relations over the life course*. Berlin: Walter de Gruyter.

Hawkes, T. (1992). *Structuralism and semiotics*. London: Routledge.

Hertz, R. (1960). *Death and the right hand*. New York: Free Press.

Hibbins, R. (2006). Sexuality and constructions of gender identity among Chinese male migrants in Australia. *Asian Studies Review, 30*, 289–303.

Ho, E., Ip, M., & Bedford, R. (2001). Transnational Hong Kong Chinese families in the 1990s. *New Zealand Journal of Geography, 111*(1), 24–30.

Hochschild, A. R. (1989). *The second shift*. New York: Avon Books.

Hockey, J., & James, A. (2003). *Social identities across the life course*. China: Palgrave Macmillan.

Hsu, C. Y. (1994). A reflection on marginality. In W. M. Tu (Ed.), *The living tree: The changing meaning of being Chinese today* (pp. 239–241). Stanford: Stanford University Press.

Hsu, D., Hui, M., & Waters, J. A. (2001). Filial piety and sexual prejudice in Chinese culture. Paper presented at the 109th annual conference of the American Psychological Association, San Francisco, CA.

Huddart, D. (2006). *Homi K. Bhabha*. London: Routledge.

Hutnyk, J. (1999). Hybridity saves? Authenticity and/or the critique of appropriation. *Amerasia Journal, 25*, 39–58.

Inglis, C. (1972). Chinese in Australia. *International Migration Review, 6*, 266–281.

Ip, M. (2002). Chinese female migration: From exclusion to transnationalism. In L. Fraser & K. Pickles (Eds.), *Shifting centres: Women and migration in New Zealand history* (pp. 149–166). Otago: Otago University Press.

Ip, M. (2003). *Unfolding history, evolving identity: The Chinese in New Zealand*. Auckland: Auckland University Press.

Khoo, S. E. (2004). Intermarriage in Australia: Patterns by ancestry, gender and generation. *People and Place, 12*, 35–44.

Khu, J. M. T. (2001). *Cultural curiosity: Thirteen stories about the search for Chinese roots*. California: University of California Press.

Kibria, N. (1998). The contested meaning of 'Asian American': Racial dilemmas in the contemporary US. *Ethnic and Racial Studies, 21*, 935–958.

Kuah-Pearce, K. E. (2006). Transnational self in the Chinese diaspora: A conceptual framework. *Asian Studies Review, 30*(3), 223–239.

Kuah-Pearce, K. E., & Davidson, A. (Eds.). (2008). *At home in the Chinese diaspora: Memories, identity and belonging*. Hampshire: Palgrave Macmillan.

Lee, R. G. (1999). *Orientals: Asian Americans in popular culture*. Philadelphia: Temple University Press.

Legge, V., & Westbrook, M. T. (1991). The frail aged living in the community and their carers: a survey of Chinese, Greek and Anglo Australians. *Australian Journal on ageing, 10*(3), 3–10.

Leung, M. W. H. (2004). *Chinese migration in Germany: Making home in transnational space*. Frankfurt: IKO.

Levinson, D. J. (1978). *Seasons of a man's life*. New York: Ballantine Books.

Levitt, P. (2002). The ties that change: Relations of the ancestral home over the life cycle. In P. Levitt & M. C. Waters (Eds.), *The changing face of home: The transnational lives of the second generation* (pp. 123–144). New York: Russell Sage.

Levitt, P., & Glick-Schiller, N. (2004). Conceptualizing simultaneity: A transnational social field perspective on society. *International Migration Review, 38*, 1002–1039.

Levitt, P., & Waters, M. C. (2002). Introduction. In P. Levitt & M. C. Waters (Eds.), *The changing face of home: The transnational lives of the second generation* (pp. 123–144). New York: Russell Sage Foundation.

Ma, L. J. C. (2003). Space, place and transnationalism in the Chinese diaspora. In L. J. C. Ma & C. Cartier (Eds.), *Chinese diaspora: Space, place, mobility* (pp. 1–50). Lanham: Rowman & Littlefield.

Macqueen, H. (1970). *A new Britannia*. Victoria: Penguin.

Man, G. C. (2004). Chinese immigrant women in Canada: Examining local and transnational networks. In K. E. Kuah-Pearce (Ed.), *Chinese women and their cultural and network capitals* (pp. 44–69). Singapore: Marshall Cavendish International.

Markus, A. (2001). *Race: John Howard and the remaking of Australia.* Sydney: Allen and Unwin.

Martin, J. (1978). *The migrant presence, Australian responses 1947–1977.* Sydney: Allen and Unwin.

Mathews, G. (2000). *Global culture/individual identity: Searching for home in the cultural supermarket.* London: Routledge.

Merton, R. (1988). Some thoughts on the concept of Sociological autobiography. In M. W. Riley (Ed.), *Sociological Lives.* Newburg Park: Sage.

Mohanty, S. P. (2000). The epistemic status of cultural identity: On beloved and the postcolonial condition. In P. M. L. Moya & M. R. Hames-Gracia (Eds.), *Reclaiming identity: Realist theory and the predicament of postmodernism* (pp. 29–66). Berkeley: University of California Press.

Moya, P. M. L. (2000a). Introduction: Reclaiming identity. In P. M. L. Moya & M. R. Hames-Gracia (Eds.), *Reclaiming identity: Realist theory and the predicament of postmodernism* (pp. 1–28). Berkeley: University of California Press.

Moya, P. M. L. (2000b). Postmodernism, "realism," and the politics of identity: Cherrie Moraga and Chicana feminism. In P. M. L. Moya & M. R. Hames-Gracia (Eds.), *Reclaiming identity: Realist theory and the predicament of postmodernism* (pp. 67–101). Berkeley: University of California Press.

Murry, D. J. N. (2005). Asian gay men's body. *Journal of Men's Studies, 13*(3), 291–300.

Nagata, J. (1979). *Malaysian mosaic.* Vancouver: University of British Columbia Press.

Nagel, J. (1994). Constructing ethnicity: Creating and recreating ethnic identity and culture. *Social Problems, 41,* 152–170.

Ngan, L. L. S. (2012). Identities and decentered transnational linkages: Returned migrants in Hong Kong. In C. Pluss & K. B. Chan (Eds.), *Living intersections: Transnational migrant identifications in Asia.* Dordrecht: Springer.

Nguyen, M. T. (2000). "It matters to get the facts straight": Joy Kogawa, realism and objectivity of values. In P. M. L. Moya & M. R. Hames-Gracia (Eds.), *Reclaiming identity: Realist theory and the predicament of postmodernism* (pp. 171–204). Berkeley: University of California Press.

Nonini, D. M., & Ong, A. (1997). Towards a cultural politics of diaspora and transnationalism. In A. Ong & D. M. Nonini (Eds.), *Ungrounded empires: The cultural politics of modern Chinese transnationalism* (pp. 323–332). New York: Routledge.

O'Bryan, K. G., Reitz, J. G., & Kuplowska, O. (1976). *Official languages: A study in Canadian multiculturalism.* Ottawa: Department of the Secretary of State.

Ong, A. (1999). *Flexible citizenship: The cultural logics of transnationality.* Durham: Duke University Press.

Papastergiadis, N. (2000). *The turbulence of migration: Globalization, deterritoralization and hybridity.* Cambridge: Polity Press.

Park, R. E. (1928). Human migration and the marginal man. *American Journal of Sociology, 33*(6), 881–893.

Pascal, B. (1996). *The essential Pascal.* New York: Mentor Books.

Pe-Pua, R., Mitchell, C., Iredale, R., & Castles, S. (1996). *Astronaut families and parachute children: The cycle of migration between Hong Kong and Australia.* Canberra: Australian Government Publishing Service.

Phizacklea, A. (2000). Introduction. In S. Westwood & A. Phizacklea (Eds.), *Transnationalism and the politics of belonging* (pp. 1–18). London: Routledge.

Pickering, M. (2001). *Stereotyping: The politics of representation.* New York: Palgrave.

Price, C. A. (1956). *Assimilation, citizenship digest.* Canberra: AGPS.

Riley, M. W., Abeles, R. R., & Teitelbaum, M. S. (1982). *Aging from birth to death: Volume II: Sociotemporal perspectives.* Colorado: Westview.

Rivas, E. E., & Torres-Gil, F. M. (1992). Politics, diversity, and minority ageing. In E. P. Stanford & F. M. Torres-Gil (Eds.), *Diversity: New approaches to ethnic minority aging* (pp. 91–111). Amityville: Baywood.

Robb, S. (2003). Myths, lies and invisible lives: European women and Chinese men in North Queensland 1870–1900. *Lilith, 12,* 95–109.

Ryan, J. (2003). Chinese women as transnational migrants: Gender and class in global migration narratives. *International Migration, 40,* 93–116.

Said, E. W. (1978). *Orientalism.* London: Penguin.

Sax, W. S. (1998). The hall of mirrors: Orientalism, anthropology and the other. *American Anthropologist, 100,* 292–301.

Simmel, G. (1950). *The sociology of Georg Simmel.* New York: Free Press.

Skeldon, R. (1995a). Australia, Hong Kong and 1997: The population connection. *People and Place, 3,* 9–15.

Skeldon, R. (1995b). The last half century of Chinese overseas (1945–1994): Comparative perspectives. *International Migration Review, 29,* 546–579.

Smith, R. C. (2002). Life course, generation and social location as factors shaping second-generation. In P. Levitt & M. Waters (Eds.), *The changing face of home: The transnational lives of the second generation* (pp. 145–168). New York: Russell Sage.

Tan, C. (2001). Chinese families down under: The role of the family in the construction of identity amongst Chinese Australians, 1920–1960. In International conference "Migrating identities: ethnic minorities in Chinese diaspora", ANU, Centre for the Study of Chinese Southern Diaspora.

Tan, C. (2004a). *Chinese inscriptions: Australian-born Chinese lives.* School of Languages and Comparative Cultural Studies, PhD thesis. Brisbane: University of Queensland.

Tan, C. B. (2004b). *Chinese overseas: Comparative cultural issues.* Hong Kong: Hong Kong University Press.

Tejapira, K. (2001). Pigtail: A prehistory of Chineseness in Siam. In C. K. Tong & K. B. Chan (Eds.), *Alternate identities: The Chinese of contemporary Thailand* (pp. 41–66). Singapore: Times Academic Press.

Tham, M. (2001). Travels afar. In J. M. T. Khu (Ed.), *Cultural curiosity* (pp. 39–57). Berkeley: University of California Press.

Thompson, P. (1995). Transmission between generations. In J. Brannen & M. O'Brien (Eds.), *Childhood and parenthood.* London: Institute of Education.

Tong, C. K., & Chan, K. B. (Eds.). (2001a). *Alternate identities: The Chinese of contemporary Thailand.* Singapore: Times Academic Press.

Tong, C. K., & Chan, K. B. (2001b). One face, many masks: The singularity and plurality of Chinese identity. *Diaspora: A Journal of Transnational Studies, 10*(3), 361–389.

Tong, C. K., & Chan, K. B. (2001c). Rethinking assimilation and ethnicity: The Chinese of Thailand. In C. K. Tong & K. B. Chan (Eds.), *Alternate identities: The Chinese of contemporary Thailand* (pp. 9–40). Singapore: Times Academic Press.

Trinh, M. (1991). *When the moon waxes red.* London: Routledge.

Tu, W. M. (1994a). Cultural China: The periphery as the center. In W. M. Tu (Ed.), *The living tree: The changing meaning of being Chinese today* (pp. 1–34). Stanford: Stanford University Press.

Tu, W. M. (Ed.). (1994b). *The living tree: The changing meaning of being Chinese today.* Stanford: Stanford University Press.

Uhlenberg, P., & Mueller, M. (2003). Family context and individual well-being: Patterns and mechanisms in life course perspectives. In A. T. Mortimer & M. J. Shanahan (Eds.), *Handbook of the life course* (pp. 123–148). New York: Springer.

Urry, J. (2000). *Sociology beyond societies: Mobilities for the twenty-first century.* London: Routledge.

Van-Gennep, A. (1960). *The rites of passage.* London: Routledge and Kegan Paul.

Vasta, E. (2005). Theoretical fashions in Australian Immigration Research (Working Paper No. 11). Oxford: Centre on Migration, Policy and Society, University of Oxford.

Wang, G. (1985). South China perspectives on overseas Chinese. *The Australian Journal of Chinese Affairs, 13*, 69–84.

Wang, G. (1991a). Among non-Chinese. In W. M. Tu (Ed.), *The living tree: The changing meaning of being Chinese today* (pp. 127–147). Stanford: Stanford University Press.

Wang, G. (1991b). Introduction. In G. Wang (Ed.), *The Chineseness of China* (pp. 1–10). Hong Kong: Oxford University Press.

Wang, G. (1991c). Power, rights and duties in Chinese history. In G. Wang (Ed.), *The Chineseness of China* (pp. 165–186). Hong Kong: Oxford University Press.

Wang, G. (2000). *The Chinese overseas: From earthbound China to the quest for autonomy.* Cambridge: Harvard University Press.

Wang, G. (2001). *Don't leave home: Migration and the Chinese.* Singapore: Times Academic Press.

Wang, F. T. Y., Bih, H. D., & Brennan, D. (2009). Have they really come out: gay men and their parents in Taiwan. *Culture, Health and Sexuality, 11*(3), 285–296.

Waters, J. L. (2002). Flexible families? 'Astronaut' households and the experiences of lone mothers in Vancouver, British Columbia. *Social and Cultural Geography, 3*, 117–133.

Weber, M. (1951). *The religion of China.* New York: The Free Press.

Werbner, P. (1997). Introduction: The dialectics of cultural hybridity. In P. Werbner & T. Modood (Eds.), *Debating cultural hybridity: Multi-cultural identities and the politics of anti-racism* (pp. 1–25). London: Zen Books.

Williams, M. (1999). *Chinese history in New South Wales: A thematic history.* Sydney: Heritage Office of New South Wales.

Wilton, J., & Bosworth, R. (1984). *Old worlds and New Australia: The post war migrant experience.* Victoria: Penguin Books Australia.

Winland, D. (1998). Our home and native land? Canadian ethnic scholarship and the challenge of transnationalism. *The Canadian Review of Sociology and Anthropology, 35*, 555–577.

Wolf, D. L. (1997). Family secrets: Transnational struggles among children of Filipino immigrants. *Sociological Perspectives, 40*, 457–483.

Wolf, D. L. (2002). There's no place like "home": Emotional transnationalism and the struggles of second generation Filipinos. In P. Levitt & M. C. Waters (Eds.), *The changing face of home* (pp. 255–294). New York: Russell Sage Foundation.

Work, N. (2001). Full circle. In J. M. T. Khu (Ed.), *Cultural curiosity* (pp. 1–19). Berkeley: University of California Press.

Young, R. (1995). *Colonial desire: Hybridity in theory, culture and practice.* London: Routledge.

Zizek, S. (2009a). *The sublime object of ideology.* London: Verso.

Zizek, S. (2009b). *The plague of fantasies.* London: Verso.

Index

A

Abeles, R.R., 45
Abu-Lughod, L., 21
Adaptation, 32, 33
Adoption, 68, 126, 155–156, 176
Age-based identities, 16, 141, 142, 144, 166, 193
Alba, R., 39, 145, 156
Alienation, 22, 187
Alternating identities, 169
Alwin, D.F., 46, 142, 145
Ambiguity, 23, 26, 28, 41, 150, 156
Ambivalence, 8, 41, 44, 139, 140, 150, 157–159, 167–190, 196
Ancestors, 31, 34, 43, 103, 112, 169, 174
Ancestral home, 114, 168, 184
Anderson, B., 11, 29, 128
Anderson, M., 9, 25, 127, 178
Ang, I., 9, 26, 28–30, 33, 35, 36, 38, 39, 41, 42, 44, 117, 119, 122–124, 135, 158, 176, 185, 188, 196
Anglo-Celtic culture, 3
Anglo-Celtic society, 3, 44, 119, 155
Anthias, F., 41
Appadurai, A., 22, 157, 168
Appearance, 4, 11, 26, 35, 36, 49, 82, 87, 88, 90, 104, 115, 119–123, 125, 136, 139, 158, 172
Asianess, 7, 26, 39
Asian men, 44, 65, 152, 157–159
Asian women, 44, 152, 157–159
Assimilation, 3, 8, 9, 16, 30, 38, 39, 42, 86, 87, 89, 115, 119, 130, 135, 167, 169, 170, 184, 188, 189
Astronaut families, 31, 36, 43, 45

Australian-born Chinese, 4, 5, 7, 9, 10, 12–17, 21, 24, 46, 52, 65, 69, 82, 102, 104, 105, 113, 115, 117, 118, 120–122, 124–128, 130, 132, 133, 136–140, 145, 147–153, 156, 158, 160, 161, 163–166, 170–180, 188–197
Australianess, 127, 178, 188, 189
Authenticity, Authenticating, 16, 23, 27, 29–30, 33, 34, 41, 117–140, 174, 181, 193, 196
Autobiographies, 16, 48–83, 86–115, 169, 171, 197

B

Balibar, E., 119
Basch, L., 167
Bauman, Z., 20, 22, 28, 185
Baurdillard, J., 201
Becoming, 1, 8, 38, 51, 61, 65, 67, 68, 71, 72, 78, 100, 133, 142, 143, 153, 166, 186
Bedford, R., 36
Beijing, 25, 33, 123, 193
Being Australian, 15, 104, 121, 146, 149, 150, 177
Being Chinese, 2, 4, 9, 11, 20, 27–29, 32–34, 42, 48, 87, 89, 90, 108, 113, 117, 123, 125, 126, 128, 130, 135–138, 140, 142, 145, 146, 148–150, 156, 158, 164–166, 182, 183, 185, 187, 188, 192, 193
Belongingness, 22, 46, 86, 126, 128, 139, 169, 170, 180, 195, 196
Berger, P., 22
Betrayal, 123, 158
Bhabha, H., 22, 40–41, 169, 176, 177

L.L.-S. Ngan and K.-b. Chan, *The Chinese Face in Australia: Multi-generational Ethnicity among Australian-born Chinese*, DOI 10.1007/978-1-4614-2131-3, © Springer Science+Business Media, LLC 2012

U
Uhlenberg, P., 45
Urry, J., 20

V
Vancouver, 88, 104, 107
Van-Gennep, A., 143
Vasta, E., 120, 133
Visual sociology. *See* Photographs

W
Wang, F.T.Y., 164
Wang, G., 2, 9, 28, 43, 130, 133
Waters, J.A., 164
Waters, J.L., 168, 171, 179
Waters, M.C., 171

Weber, M., 43
Werbner, P., 41
White Australian Community, 191
Williams, M., 130
Wilton, J., 38
Winland, D., 168
Wolf, D.L., 40, 184

Y
Yeoh, B.S.A., 9, 39
Young, R., 21
Yum Cha, 109

Z
Zhongshan, 92, 102, 113, 114, 137
Zizek, S., 200, 203, 204

CPSIA information can be obtained at www.ICGtesting.com
Printed in the USA
LVOW100218050712

288809LV00007B/8/P